3D Modeling & Animation: A Primer

3D Modeling & Animation: A Primer

Magesh Chandramouli

CRC Press
Taylor & Francis Group
Boca Raton London New York

CRC Press is an imprint of the
Taylor & Francis Group, an **informa** business

First Edition published 2022
by CRC Press
6000 Broken Sound Parkway NW, Suite 300, Boca Raton, FL 33487-2742

and by CRC Press
2 Park Square, Milton Park, Abingdon, Oxon, OX14 4RN

© 2022 Taylor & Francis Group, LLC

CRC Press is an imprint of Taylor & Francis Group, LLC

Library of Congress Cataloging-in-Publication Data
A catalog record has been requested for this book

ISBN: 978-1-032-13773-5 (hbk)
ISBN: 978-1-498-76491-9 (pbk)
ISBN: 978-0-429-18634-9 (ebk)

DOI: 10.1201/9780429186349

Typeset in Myriad Pro
by codeMantra

Access the Support Material: www.routledge.com/9781498764919

To Raju

Contents

Foreword

From the tranquil fluttering of a butterfly's wings to the mystifying motion of the celestial objects in the cosmos, countless animations transpire incessantly in God's creation. Animation symbolizes life. 3D digital animations can serve as powerful vehicles to communicate complex plots and concepts to broader audience. From conception to execution, the animation production pipeline includes processes such as sketching, drawing, lighting, texturing, rendering, and composition. Without overwhelming the reader, this book covers these disciplines as applicable to animation using a highly visual approach.

As Michelangelo said, "A man paints with his brains and not with his hands." Similarly, an engaging animation is not created by a computer, but by the human brain. One should not expect to create a good animation by relying only on digital tools. While the advances in modeling and animation software can enhance efficiency and save time, the "heart" of the animation rests solely on the animator's creativity. Throughout this book, the narrative focuses on the importance of creativity, and the chapter on ideation covers the artistic side of animation and its role in composition.

Animation is communication: It involves conceiving a plot and communicating it flawlessly through engaging characters. This involves an understanding and appreciation of the character's personality and emotions. Modeling the character using proper techniques and using it to effectively communicate the plot entails sound knowledge of the basics of 3D modeling and animation. By complementing the abstract theoretical concepts with engaging illustrations and practical examples, the book enables the reader to gain mastery over the basic concepts on which the advanced aspects of animation are built.

As an author of textbooks in computer graphics, I take a keen interest in books on the subject. This book is a great text for students or anyone interested in learning the fundamentals of computer graphics and animation. The computer science underlying graphics and animation can be intimidating to anyone interested in the application of animation. This book does a great job of introducing complex topics in a very straightforward and easy-to-understand method. The book is well-written with many illustrations to help the learner to understand the topics being presented. Although the word "animation" tends to be associated with the game and motion-picture industries, animation has numerous applications in education, creative arts, visualization, medicine, engineering, and many other disciplines. While learning modeling and animation, it is important to develop an understanding and appreciation for visual ideation and the underlying communication process.

If I were still teaching introductory computer graphics, I would not hesitate to use this textbook as it has just the right amount of coverage of the topic for a semester course and is presented in a highly appealing manner to engage the reader.

Magesh has written an excellent textbook not just for university students, but for anyone with an interest in learning the basics of computer graphics and animation. If you have an interest in computer graphics and animation, you will find this book to be interesting.

Gary R. Bertoline, Ph.D.

Senior Vice President Purdue Online & Learning Innovation

Distinguished Professor of Computer Graphics Technology

Purdue University, West Lafayette, IN, USA

Preface

Already, so many books are available on modeling and animation. **Why one more?**

Explaining my own experience when learning 3D modeling and animation may help you understand this. Originally, I had a background in engineering before I moved to Computer Graphics. While building "cool" 3D models and animating them was my ultimate objective, I also really wanted to understand what is going on in the background. To understand the basic concepts, I had to refer many sources and read many books. Unfortunately, I could not find a book that covered the basic concepts in a simple and straightforward manner. While some books employed a sophisticated writing style, some others provided a lot of unnecessary information, both of which were quite difficult to comprehend for a beginner-level user.

Computer graphics, modeling, and animation are truly exhilarating disciplines which can be better learned with an easier and engaging approach. I wanted to author a book that can present the fundamental concepts behind modeling and animation in a simple and straightforward manner using a *highly visual approach*. This book includes numerous pictures that are intended to help you easily understand abstract concepts and strengthen your basics. Using a meticulous method of selection (of what should be covered in the book) and even more meticulous process of elimination, this book provides you the relevant information without overloading you, while also being careful not to leave out any foundational information. Animation and modeling are highly stimulating subject areas, and hence should not be watered down by pure theory and erudite equations. Using both conventional and unconventional methods, this book endeavors to enable a beginner-level student to learn modeling and animation.

This book is intended to be a stepping stone not just for a beginner-level graphics student, but also for anybody interested in learning 3D modeling and animation. This book employs a balanced approach, whereby it is neither too technical nor too artistic. Without being too generic and too detailed, the book aims to present to you the right amount of material to provide a firm grasp of the underlying principles.

This book is NOT intended to be a complete reference for 3D modeling and animation; it is practically impossible for any single book to serve as one. Computer graphics is an extremely large discipline with numerous sub-disciplines. Volumes have been written on any one chapter that you can randomly pick from the table of contents of this book. Each topic, for example lighting and composition, is so vast that a full book can be written on every one of them.

Keeping it fully technical can make the reading process monotonous. There is an artist in each one of us. To appeal to our artistic side and to keep the journey interesting, here and there you will find some artistic quotes, anecdotes, personal experiences, or a funny phrase. I do not remember reading anywhere that technical reading MUST be boring. This book has simplified the concepts and presented them in an appealing manner.

Software tools keep changing and new techniques are emerging at a rapid rate. However, the concepts of modeling and the basic principles behind animation are followed by professionals all over irrespective of the tools they are using. This book uses a **Software Agnostic** *approach as it does not focus on the software itself, but on the concepts themselves*. An engineer who knows the concepts of construction can choose to use automatic tools or purely mechanical tools or a combination of both to build a house. But, without knowing the concepts, having the tools will not be of use. Similarly, once you understand the basic concepts, you can choose to use any software tool or programming tool that you choose to.

You, the reader, are the best judge of whether I succeeded or not. I will be very happy to hear back from you. Wish you all the best in your learning. Please email me your comments and feedback at magesh@purdue.edu or magesh.purdue@gmail.com.

Acknowledgments

If the only prayer you ever say in your entire life is **thank you**, it will be enough.

– Meister Eckhart

I thank my father and mother for their motivation and support and for always encouraging to explore and learn. Through all the ups and downs, my parents supported us uncompromisingly in all our educational pursuits and led by example. Anything accomplished was only because of their perseverance and guidance.

I thank my brother and sister for their everlasting love and support always. I have been blessed to have such great siblings. I thank my wife for the numerous hours of meticulous editing, and persistent input through the various stages of the book. I am grateful to my wife and kids for their patient support, feedback, and putting up with me during prolonged periods of writing.

I thank Sean Connelly and Jessica Vega for their editorial support. I thank all staff members at CRC Press/Taylor & Francis Group and all others who contributed to the publishing process.

I am immensely grateful to the following people for providing their work for use in the book:

Bitzivis Theodoros, Chandramouli Nagarajasastri, Dhruva M., Justin H., Mike Y., George H., Nachiket M., Lakshmi C., Pavithra A., Stephanie A., Tom B., and Vaishali M.

I thank Dr. Gary R. Bertoline (Senior Vice President Purdue Online & Learning Innovation) and Dr. Tien Yin Chou (Jimmy), Director of the GIS Research Center, Taiwan for their amazing mentorship throughout my career.

I am grateful to the following people and organizations for allowing me to use few parts from my earlier books: Purdue University Press/Skyepack and FCU Press/GIS Research Center (ISBN: 9781626710245 and ISBN 9789867621603).

I would like to thank all my friends, family, colleagues, teachers, advisors, collaborators, and students.

Author

Magesh Chandramouli is a Professor of Computer Graphics Technology at Purdue University Northwest. He is currently serving as the Director of Programs of the Engineering Design Graphics Division of the American Society of Engineering Education. He was a Frederick Andrews Fellow at Purdue University, West Lafayette, where he completed his doctoral studies in the Department of Computer Graphics Technology. He received his Master of Science degree from the University of Calgary, Master of Engineering degree from the National University of Singapore, and Bachelor of Engineering degree from the College of Engineering, Guindy, India. He has received several national and international awards for his scholarly accomplishments, and his work has been published and presented in reputed journals and conferences.

CHAPTER 1: Production Pipeline and Pre-Production

Give me six hours to chop down a tree and I will spend the first four sharpening the axe.

– Abraham Lincoln

CHAPTER LEARNING OBJECTIVES

After carefully studying this chapter, you will be able to answer the following:

- What is a production pipeline?
- What is pre-production and why is pre-production important?
- What is storyboarding?
- Where is storyboarding used?
- What are the elements of storyboarding?
- What are the functions of the different elements of storyboarding?
- What are the various other important elements of the production pipeline and how does storyboarding fit into the picture with them?

DOI: 10.1201/9780429186349-1

What Will You Learn in This Chapter?

With modern digital animation, truly "the sky is your limit." This is a creative field with practically unlimited freedom for you to dream, envision, and give form to your idea, concept, or story. You have the chance to awe and spellbind your audience. So, it goes without saying that you will be thrilled (or animated) when you are about to work on an animation. You have a computer with all the required software right in front of you. So, what is stopping you? You should start working on your computer to jump right into the project, right? *Wrong*. A word of caution about the animation process and the production pipeline: The foolproof way to ensure the absolute failure of your animation project is to start working on the computer first. *Never* do that, ever. You need to do meticulous planning before you turn on your computer, and for this, all you need are paper and pencil (and of course, your creativity).

Just as a classic symphony results from the synchronized efforts of an orchestra beautifully conducted by a maestro, a great animation can result from a well-planned and executed production pipeline. You should start working on the computer only when you have completed the steps involved in pre-production, especially storyboarding. Even extremely talented people may end up making poor-quality animation due to their disregard for the pre-production process. In a typical feature film, the 1.5 or 2 hours of movies we watch have actually been edited from a hundred thousand feet of film. You would be surprised to find that some blockbuster movies originally involved several hundred thousand feet of filming, corresponding to numerous viewing hours. So, if the actual movie we see is only 2 hours long, what happened to the rest of the film? All of that has been edited, despite the time and effort that went into filming those innumerable hours. This applies to 3D animation as well. Ultimately, what matters is only what the audience sees in the final version. If there are scenes or scene elements that are never going to be included in your final animation or rendered, then the time and man-hours invested in creating them are wasted resources. All this can be avoided by careful pre-production exercises such as storyboarding and animatic (story reel). To succeed in animation, you need to make a strong resolution that you will respect the pre-production exercises and will pursue all components therein with determination and perseverance.

Animation is both an art and a science. Mother Nature is the best modeler and animator; throughout the book, we will look at modeling and animation lessons from nature to keep the learning process lively. Learning the techniques and science of animation need not be boring, not if we are willing to look and learn from the beautiful lessons from nature. This chapter will provide an overview of the production pipeline and the fundamental steps in a production pipeline.

The Production Pipeline: Yes, It Does Take a Village...

All the great computer graphics (CG) animations or games or movies or any other CG masterpiece that you have seen are the result of colossal amount of well-coordinated work by numerous teams. In this chapter, we will primarily focus on the pre-production stage, especially on storyboarding, and we will take a quick look at the other aspects of production. We will delve into the individual production elements in the subsequent chapters individually. A brief look into the few important art forms and their development will go a long way in understanding the production pipeline and in gaining true appreciation for pre-production.

What Is a Production Pipeline?

The production pipeline represents the basic framework used to develop the animation. It is at the heart of the digital creation process, whether the product is an animated movie or a game animation or anything involving an animation. Think of your favorite TV ad. A simple 30-second commercial could require weeks or months of work. Creating 3D models and animating them can take a long time indeed. The entire process of production from start to finish involves a lot of personnel including storyboard artists, modelers, animators, technical directors, character animators, effects animators, production coordinators, directors, and many more. The efforts of such a variegated mix of personnel must culminate seamlessly into the final result – the animated game or movie. This is easier said than done and impossible without a coordinated and concerted effort on the part of all those involved. The production pipeline provides the reference framework to design and develop the overall animation. Milestones are identified and serve as a benchmark for the entire crew (Figures 1.1 and 1.2).

The three main stages in a production pipeline are:

1. Pre-production
2. Production
3. Post-production

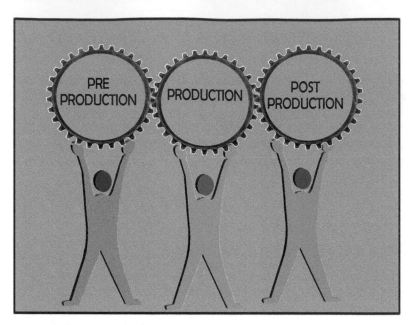

FIG 1.1 Production pipeline.

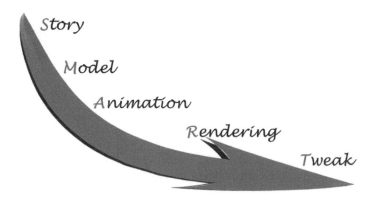

FIG 1.2 Simple animation breakdown: "SMART."

We will look at the various processes involved in the production pipeline. But, as you are getting started, let us think of a simple mnemonic to help you remember the basic steps involved. At the very simplest form, an animation would typically require a **S**tory, **M**odel(s), **A**nimation, **R**endering, and **T**weaking. Consider the mnemonic **SMART** (Figure 1.2) to help you remind of these steps. Animation essentially involves an artistic element that goes hand in hand with the technical element. Complex, large-scale projects will require a more elaborate breakdown of each of these steps into more constituent parts and processes.

Generally, 3D animation production pipelines follow a typical path with common elements of pre-production, production, and post-production. However, the detailed specifics vary from industry to industry and from application to application. For instance, let us compare and contrast movies with games. There is one very basic difference between a movie and a video game. While the final content of a movie is essentially the same for all users (audience), with a video game, each user chooses the content (and its flow) based on the decisions they make while playing a game. Typically, a movie's ending remains the same wherever it is screened; however, a video game's ending depends on how the game is played. This is because games typically require input from the user and the output is driven by this input. In summary, one of the key aspects that distinguishes a game from a movie is the "interactive nature." Hence, the production pipeline of a video game must accommodate this interactivity. Even if a game is based on the same plot or story as a movie, the production pipeline for a game will have differences to include the interactive component. *The bottom line is that there is no single format of a production pipeline that can be applied to all games, movies, or animation projects.* So, when you are learning the basics of a production pipeline, keep in mind that each one of them needs to be customized for your specific project.

Pre-Production: Laying the Foundation

Pre-production serves as the foundation for the success of an animation. Animation is not only a labor- and resource-intensive process, but it also involves considerable amount of money. It can take several months, and at times even a couple of years, to make an animated movie that lasts 90 minutes. Being a labor-intensive process, the overall effort involves multiple teams entailing numerous personnel. Tools such as storyboards, animatics, and previsualization facilitate the planning process so that time and money can be saved. These pre-production tools and techniques help foresee and avoid potential items that can cause disruptions and delays.

Essentially, pre-production involves planning and resource management. Irrespective of the nature of the animation project, the critical resources that require planning and management are time, budget, equipment (hardware/software), and people (human resources). Previsualization techniques such as storyboarding are used in a wide range of industries and applications, including gaming (video games), movie making, web page design, promotional videos, television, and mobile app development. The pre-production phase involves all the required planning to ensure a coherent and smooth execution during the production phase. Irrespective of whether the animation is intended for a movie or a game or a commercial, there will (and must) always be a purpose for your animation.

The *purpose* and the *target audience* should be key considerations when creating an animation. In addition, two key aspects that will dictate the planning and hence, the subsequent execution of an animation project are *time* and *money*. Typically, studios that create animations for movies and games face strict deadlines and operate within limited budget. Coordinating such projects involves managing not only the budget and time, but also the other resources such as the personnel and computational resources.

Pre-production and the planning therein serve as excellent means of estimating what is to be expected and plan accordingly.

An important step in any production pipeline and the quality of the previsualization and *storyboarding* (part of pre-production) greatly influence the ultimate success of the animation project. Undoubtedly, the most important part of any animation is the story, also referred to as the "plot." The animation is the vehicle or the medium used to convey this story in a captivating manner to the audience. If you consider the process of constructing a building, one of the most important prerequisites before the actual construction can take place is the blueprint. All things related to the final product, such as its usability, value, and even the ease of the construction process, depend on the quality and accuracy/precision of the blueprint. Without a proper set of blueprints and careful initial planning, a construction project will experience inordinate delays and result in unnecessary additional costs.

The same holds true for graphics animation projects and pipelines. As in the construction analogy, there are three stages in the animation production pipeline: pre-production, production, and post-production. Pre-production involves preparing and laying the foundation for the upcoming production process, the second stage is the actual production process itself, and the final stage involves cleaning up and adding enhancements. Modeling and animation are the key processes that we will be covering in detail in this book. However, these processes cannot begin until an essential step of the pre-production stage is completed. This step is known as "storyboarding," and we will delve into this in the following section. At this point, it is important to understand that you need to be flexible and willing to explore different ways of telling your story and make modifications as you progress.

Story: Essence of Animation

You are telling a story. Period.

Your success depends on whether your intended audience understands your story. Whether for film, television, or a video game, animation is about stories, period. Behind every great animation is a great story. State-of-the-art advances in graphics, a brilliant background musical score, top-notch voice cast, and the best of everything else can *never* make up for a poor story. Of course, if you have a good story, then all the other things mentioned above can greatly aid the storytelling process. But never be misguided into thinking that you can make up for a poor story using advanced CG tools and techniques. It does not work that way. Stories are the primary elements; the other elements are auxiliary in that they play a crucial role in assisting the narration but cannot supplant the story.

The journey from the script to a finished storyboard involves considerable work regarding the story, drawing thumbnail sketches, and refining them into roughs. Good storyboarding entails thorough reading of the script, even multiple times if required. It is important to visualize the script through the storyboard and clearly specify the beginning and ending of the scenes or shots in the animation. There may be several rounds of iterations involved in the overall process, and a good storyboard research involves asking many relevant questions, which reduces ambiguity and increases clarity. Various elements that need to be clarified include:

- Who are the intended audience? (An animation or movie targeted primarily at kids needs to be storyboarded differently from one that is aimed at adults.)
- What is the conflict?
- Who is/are the protagonist(s)?
- What is the overall setting of the story?
- What action is involved?

Navigating through thumbnails and roughs helps refine the final storyboard. **Thumbnails** (Figure 1.3) are time-tested tools for efficient ideation and brainstorming.

The basic idea behind thumbnails is to bring out ideas and explore. You should not be very critical at this stage. You are in the exploratory and discovery phase when you are fishing for ideas, and you can easily achieve that with quick doodles that are nothing more than simple stick figures. Thumbnails can be used for models or for environments (Figures 1.4 and 1.5).

It is important to understand that when you start working on building your animation skills, you must start simple. School students learn alphabets before they learn words, and words before sentences, and so on. Similarly, in your animation learning path, you need to start at a smaller scale before you can move over to larger animation projects. Initially, you should ideally be aiming for animation clips that last a few minutes at the most. Even large-scale projects involving huge budgets and numerous personnel have their limitations.

FIG 1.3 Thumbnails. (Image courtesy: Bitzivis, T.)

FIG 1.4 Concept thumbnail — model. (Image courtesy: George, H.)

FIG 1.5 Concept thumbnail — environment. (Image courtesy: George, H.)

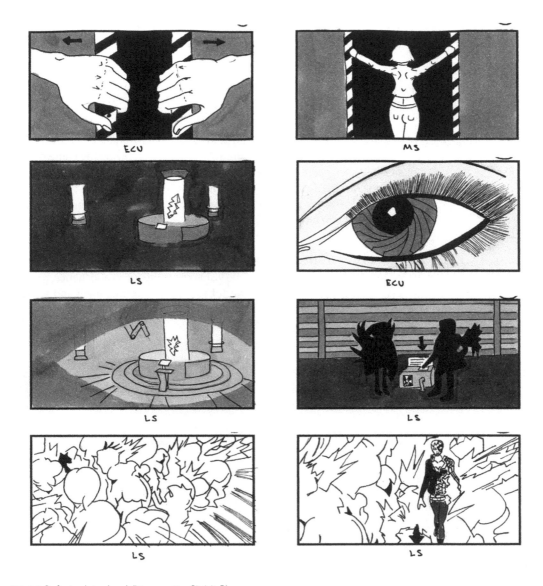

FIG 1.6 Professional story board. (Image courtesy: Bitzivis, T.)

Animations involving detailed storyboards (Figure 1.6) that are developed with due consideration of the practical time constraints have a greater chance of success than overambitious projects involving unreasonable expectations and poor time considerations.This applies for medium- and small-scale projects as well. You will always be working under limited time and resources. You will be producing your animation over a specific period of time, and the computational resources accessible to you will also have limitations.

Storytelling and Visual Storytelling

How is visual storytelling different? People dwelling in one country with an official language may not be able to read and understand the newspapers printed in another country. However, anybody from anywhere in the world can view and understand a photograph printed in the same newspaper. That is the power of visual communication.

Try this simple exercise. Below are pictures of eight common objects we come across in our daily life (Figure 1.7). Now without saying the name of the object such as "bulb" or "watch" or without telling what it does (shows time, emits light, etc.), try to communicate in verbal or written form to a friend about the geometric or appearance properties of the object. Even after a lengthy writing or verbal description, you might not have captured all that the image shows.

You can see how it is easier and quicker with the photograph; *a picture is indeed worth a thousand words*. The visual communication and, hence, the associated language is quite powerful. However, there are pitfalls and several other factors you should be aware of. Many cinematic adaptations of novels have been poorly received by audience, especially by those who have already read the novel. There are numerous reasons why this happens. With respect to our current discussion, it is important to note which version (written or visual) came first (e.g. whether the novel was written first, which is typically the case). Once you have a plot or a story, you need to come up with a way to communicate this story in an attention-grabbing manner.

Expressing the story in the most captivating manner is the cornerstone of any successful animation. This is what you do in storyboarding. Due to the nature of the topics we will be covering in this book under 3D animation, we are focusing on animation that is more oriented to films and games. To broaden our horizon and to understand the pre-production aspects in the greater context, we need to look at films and games from an entertainment perspective. You can learn a lot about storyboarding by looking back and comparing with one of your most favorite childhood hobbies: *comics*.

You can do a "compare and contrast" approach of storyboards with comics to learn more about the art of narration. While comics (such as Archie© and Batman©) represent the final outcome or a completed product, storyboards are only a part of the production pipeline. They are tools to help in the pre-production to plan the actual production. From an animation perspective, storyboarding involves contemplating deeply and in a focused manner about the various components of the actual animation and visualizing those using graphical depictions. Storyboards help the director and the crew to envision the story as seen through the camera. Typically, movies and animation have a specific time duration and play at a specific frames per second (fps) at which the audience watch the movie; on the other hand, comic book readers can take however long they want to read through the comic strips and gaze at the images. Storyboarding for a movie or animated video may be considered as a huge comic book (of the entire animation). In a comic book,

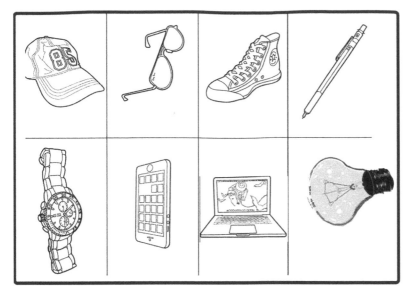

FIG 1.7 Common object. (Image courtesy: Bitzivis, T.)

even though the story is conveyed through "still" panels, the readers tend to fill the action through their mind's eye. The artist employs ingenious drawing techniques to establish the setting of the story and convey dynamic actions in a creative manner, albeit using still images. Be it a comic strip or a storyboard, composition is extremely important and they both communicate stories using a series of illustrations. In a comic book, this involves how the information is presented to the reader. Note how the sketch may not be "below" in the book presents the information to the reader in an engaging manner (Figure 1.8).

Let us consider an example of novel to movie. Let us say that the author is describing a scene in the story, such as a living room or an office or a church. The author can choose to be as detailed or as sketchy as he wants to be. The author can painstakingly portray the setting (say a room) in several sentences or even paragraphs describing its beauty or neatness or even disorderliness. On the other hand, the author can merely state, "…He ambled up to the doorway and beheld probably what he thought was the most beautiful home he had ever seen." The author can stop right there about the room and leave it to the reader to envision what "beautiful" means in their own mind. Now, this creates both challenges and opportunities issue in the cinematic adaptations. Readers create their mental pictures when reading a novel; about the milieu, about the things in a room, about the colors of the things, how they are arranged, and so on. Even when the author describes an action such as a ball being hit by a player and caught by another, there are numerous ways in which the readers can imagine this in their mind. The director of a movie tries to capture the written version according to his or her own perception. This may or may not go well with the readers depending on how well this aligns with their mental picture.

FIG 1.8 Narrative in comics. (Image courtesy: Mike, Y.)

FIG 1.9 Abstraction to visualization. (Image courtesy: George, H.)

The bottom line is that in the written version, the author can choose to be extremely detailed and describe everything or be sketchy and leave room for imagination. On the other hand, when it comes to showing the final *animated* work to the audience, there is no room for imagination, but the movie director is actually showing specific occurrences and examples. For instance, in a book, the author can write words like "stairs," "girl," "room," or "mountain." When reading a book, the readers can think of their own versions of "a room" or "a girl," but the visual depiction in case of a CG movie or animation is detailed (Figure 1.9). The abstraction (or vagueness or imagination) allowable in the written part does not exist here. While this indeed is a huge power of visualization, it is also a huge responsibility.

While the ability of visualization in reducing abstraction is powerful in revealing and narrating, it can also play spoilsport when not executed properly. This is the reason that storyboards and previsualization techniques are imperative in 3D movies and game animations. There are many other applications that use the visual storytelling technique of the storyboard. Even though storyboarding had its beginnings in the Disney Studios© and is typically associated with movie making, today it is being successfully used in diverse areas such as advertising, web design, project management and many other digital applications. The visual method of storytelling used by storyboards is effective because:

- Visual storytelling is capable of reducing cognitive overload
- Storyboards facilitate brainstorming and help in the early ideation
- Storyboards minimize abstraction by reducing ambiguity/uncertainty
- Storyboards facilitate moving from abstract notions to concrete details
- Visual storytelling can enhance the clarity of communication

- Visual storytelling stimulates the audience and aids collaboration
- Storyboards allow the evaluation of alternative scenarios
- Storyboards aid in identifying potential challenges/issues

Storyboards: Role in the Production Pipeline

Let us briefly look into what a story is before we dwell into storyboards.

In a dictionary, the word "story" has numerous definitions. One of the entries found on the Oxford English Dictionary (http://www.oed.com) defines a story as a "series of events that are narrated." A story, surprisingly enough, can be told in a single line. The following are sample one-liners:

- A spy rescues a scientist from enemy forces
- Three friends get lost in a jungle and survive ordeals before returning safely
- A disaster brings two fighting nations together
- A naïve rural kid fights his way up to become a champion sportsman
- A marine biologist struggles to save a species from extinction

Any of these very brief story descriptions could be the basis of a novel or a movie. In case of a novel, a lot is left to the reader's imagination. On the other hand, in a movie, you actually show how something is done precisely. One common category in any movie search index is *heist* (robbery/holdup). A brief description for this category could be "a thief or a gang of thieves hatch a plan to steal something from somewhere." Hundreds of movies have been made on this theme. What distinguishes one movie from another is the way the director goes about narrating the story (Figure 1.10).

Initially, a story just begins as a simple notion or concept or idea. Let us pick one from the earlier list, "A spy rescues a scientist from enemy forces." This would fall under the theme of "thriller" or "spy-thriller," to be more specific. There are numerous ways in which the events can unfold in a story like that. Let us consider a scene from the movie. Before the scene can be shot, the script and detailed storyboards should be carefully created. An actual sequence in the movie can be as follows: *The spy, while seemingly conversing to a bartender in a bistro, is actually shadowing a tall woman standing in a newsstand across the street. She is trying to stay out-of-sight and seems as if she is expecting somebody to arrive. A blue Chevy slowly pulls over near the newsstand and the woman gets in the car, which heads down the street. The spy gets into his Mustang and pursues the Chevy at a safe distance. Suddenly, the Chevy accelerates and swerves left into a narrow lane bringing a bus to a screeching halt. Not wanting to lose sight of the vehicle, the spy races behind while calling his sidekick on his cellphone.* Now, let us consider another different plot under the same category involving a secret agent. In this case, observe the storyboard in Figure 1.11 and see if you can get an idea of the scene being described. As you are trying to get the gist of the plot, you will see that the storyboard makes the idea clearer as it provides more concrete details.

FIG 1.10 Storyboard. (Image courtesy: Bitzivis, T.)

So many things need to be decided about filming an animated sequence such as decisions related to the kind of shot, camera position, orientation, and movement. Especially, as these shots are outdoors and involve a lot of other people and vehicles, filming such real-life sequences can be quite complicated. With a CG movie, things tend to become less complicated as much of the elements encountered in real-life outdoor shots can be minimized, if not eliminated completely. However, action sequences in CG films also need to be described clearly like in the example above. The scene layout needs to be done properly and shots need to be filmed to fit properly into the sequence. Various units including the layout department, animation department, rotoscoping department, and lighting department need to work in a coordinated manner to get a unified, coherent, and successful final outcome. Let us see how we can effectively employ pre-production tools and techniques to ensure a smooth production.

Every minute detail about the scenes and the shots composing the scene including the camera angle, perspective, camera movements, and framing height are explained clearly in storyboards. First and foremost, it is important that the crew members are clear and in agreement with what is to be shot and how? Storyboards help in the planning process and serve as a reference

FIG 1.11 Storyboard for a plot involving a secret agent. (Image courtesy: George, H.)

during the actual execution. In fact, storyboarding is an iterative process that involves several rounds of refinement whereby details are added and vague elements are eliminated.

Let us take a very brief look at the development of storyboarding as a craft. The Disney Studios© can aptly be called the "cradle of animation" as the crucial phase(s) in the development of the craft of storyboarding occurred in the Walt Disney Studios© in the 1930s and 1940s. Some of the most popular directors including Alfred Hitchcock, Ridley Scott, Terry Gilliam, Martin Scorsese, Christopher Nolan, and many others have employed meticulously sketched storyboards to draw even on a frame-by-frame basis to turn abstract ideas into concrete shots. Noted storyboard artist J. Todd Anderson stated, "…It's my job to get what's inside a director's head on the paper. It's my job to interpret their language into a visual language." The basic pre-production elements in a movie, whether a regular movie or a CG movie, still involve many similar steps. A director of a regular (non-CG) movie will not start filming until proper pre-production has been complete; similarly, production exercises such as 3D modeling will not start until and after proper pro-production has been completed. Acclaimed Japanese director Akira Kurosawa is known to have used storyboards and paintings to bring out the intricate details of every shot before actually filming them.

How a story is told to the audience is what distinguishes a successful movie from a flop. Narration can make a story engaging or not. The following is an example of what an author may write: "The hotel room window offered a beautiful view of the shops along the street below. The calmness was abruptly broken when a car swerved across the street and came to a halt in front of the bank. The front bumper crashed into the parked van, creating a huge dent." The above sentences describe the action; however, there are many details left to imagination, such as: What is the type of car? What is the type of van? Is it a narrow street or a wide one? Where is the hotel room located? (Is it on the third floor or the thirtieth floor?) All these questions need to be considered when depicting the scene visually. The bottom line is that the storyboard is not only used to visualize the ideas, but is also used to plan how a scene will be shot.

The most commonly used medium for storyboarding is simply paper and pencil. Even though several software tools are available for storyboarding these days, it is always a good idea to use paper and pencil for storyboarding. Some of the most acclaimed works in the movie industry started initially as sketches on a paper. Classics from Disney Studios such as *Bambi*© or *Dumbo*© were sketched down on storyboards before the actual animation could be created. Storyboard artists are the personnel involved in this phase of the production pipeline. They come up with the ideas to present the story in the form of graphical illustrations (sketches). Typically, storyboards undergo several rounds of revisions. The process involves taking an abstract idea and making it detailed. The initial Idea of the story is an abstract concept or a vague notion.

Let us consider a (seemingly) simple action, such as a ball bouncing and knocking a lamp off the table. However, from an animation perspective, this is still vague, meaning that several details are missing. See how the following cases explain the aforementioned action:

Case 1:	Case 2:
Ball enters through the open door	The door is partially open
Bounces off the floor onto the wall	Ball hits the door with huge speed
Hits the arm of the chair	Door is thrown open
Bounces back to the table	Ball hits recycle bin and changes direction
Rolls over and knocks the table lamp	Ball bounces off the floor onto the table

Case 3:	Case 4:
Ball drops from the ceiling	Ball is thrown through the window
Bounces off the floor and lands on chair	Bounces off the wall onto the floor
Ball rebounds and lands on the lamp	Ball rebounds and lands on the table
Lamp rolls over and lands on the floor	Balls rolls and slowly comes to a stop

There are innumerable ways in which a ball can bounce and knock a lamp. Writing down the cases as above is obviously neither very practical nor time-efficient. It is impractical because it is quite laborious to put into words every tiny bit of action, and the reason it is not time-efficient is quite evident if you read the cases stated above once again. If describing a simple action that is going to take such a lengthy, cumbersome description, then imagine writing down an entire movie in such a manner. Even writing a simple ten- or twenty-minute animation in the above manner will be laborious and time-consuming.

The storyboard artist plays a pivotal role in visualizing abstract notions by creating the pictorial representations. Typically, many ideas are explored and evaluated before one can be chosen for implementation. For these reasons, a pictorial representation with graphical illustrations is chosen to present the story (Figure 1.12).

After several revisions and after adding a whole lot of details, the storyboard artist or the team (if it is a large-scale work) "pitches" the idea to the director. So, what exactly are these details? The following sections cover the elements and functions of a storyboard.

The Breakdown: Story, Segment, Sequence, Scene, and Shot

Often times, the words "sequences," "scenes," and "shots" are used in an interspersing manner. Let us take a closer look and understand the entire hierarchy clearly. Each element plays a role in ensuring the coherent flow of the entire animation and to keep up the momentum. It is important to understand and distinguish between these terms: story, segment, sequence, scene, and shot.

Story is the essence of animation. An animated movie is your medium to tell (narrate) a story. Creating segments is the process of making an exhaustive story outline. A segment is divided in accordance with the sequential order. Those involved in the segmentation process can also opt to break down the segments as scenes, shots, or sequences. Breaking into smaller, manageable segments helps organizing and accessing huge volumes of video by facilitating indexing. In an animated movie, typically, a sequence is composed of "scenes", while a scene is considered as an action that occurs at a specific location (typically at a specific point in time). You may understand sequences better if you can imagine examples such as a fight sequence or a dance sequence. Within this sequence, the action continues to progress along the scenes.

Let us consider a movie beginning with characters chatting in a library and then cutting to the coffee shop across the street. Talking in terms of scenes, the library is considered one scene and the coffee shop is a new (or next) scene. Shots are the basic building blocks or the fundamental units of an animation video.

CU

MS

MS

LS

MS

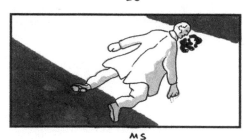
MS

LS

MS

FIG 1.12 Storyboard. (Image courtesy: Bitzivis, T.)

Storyboards: Elements and Functions

This section covers elements and functions as they both go hand in hand. Every element in a storyboard has a function, just as the storyboard itself has. One of the primary functions of a storyboard is to facilitate a successful animation project. While that is a very general description of the comprehensive and ultimate function of a storyboard, the various elements clarify the crucial subfunctions of a storyboard that contribute to the overall goal. Storyboard can be viewed as a tool for the brainstorming exercise. The purpose of this exercise is to add concrete details to the actual execution of your plot. Whether it is an animation for a game or for a movie, planning an animated project involves several departments. From the earlier discussions, you might have figured that the "story" department is essentially one of them. The storyboard personnel play a critical role in managing the rest of the project, as they lay the foundation work in deciding "how the story will be told."

Let us look more closely at some of the most common elements of a storyboard and how they facilitate the visual storytelling process.

Camera

We will look at camera in greater detail later when we cover rendering. For now, let us look at some common aspects pertaining to the camera from a storyboard perspective:

- Camera location (placement)
- Camera orientation
- Field of view (FOV)
- Type of shot

The camera location refers to the placement of the camera used to render or capture the scene, and orientation refers to the angle or the direction in which the camera is facing. The FOV refers to the degree or the amount of the scene (the environment) that can be viewed at a particular instance. While some sources tend to use FOV synonymously with orientation, there is a difference. At any particular location, a camera can face in any direction or angle (0°–360°).

Based on their FOV, lens types are categorized as follows:

- Wide-angle lens
- Normal lens
- Telephoto lens

Type of Shot

Good storyboards typically include clear details about the shot such as camera angles, movement, and framing. Shots are classified into many types based on the framing height. Framing height (or camera framing) is the distance between the camera and the character, and is actually more about how much of the character is viewed by or shown to the audience. There are different ways in which the shot types can be classified. Based on the shot size, the shots can be classified into various types ranging from long shots (LSs) to extreme close-ups (CUs; Figure 1.13).

Now, let us take a look at the most common types of shots.

FIG 1.13 Visual concepts. (Image courtesy: George, H.)

Long Shot (LS)/Extreme Long Shot (ELS)

Also called as full shot (FS) or wide shot (WS), these are used for staging or establishing the scene (Figure 1.14). As they show the entire character or the scene environment, they help define the overall ambience. Long shots reveal the whereabouts of the character and the surrounding scene elements. In this shot, the subject has been framed on the right one-third of the canvas. (*This will be covered in detail in Chapter 10 on Composition.*)

Medium Shot (MS)

Medium shots (MSs) portray a character from the thigh or the waist and above. As they occur between LSs and CUs, MSs are the more frequently used framing in movies for giving a customary feel to the audience. As these shots also show a good amount of the scene, they provide context to the audience and facilitate understanding the surroundings.

Medium Close-Up Shot (MCU)

Medium close-up (MCU) shots offer a close but not too near of a view of the subject. An MCU shot could be approximately from mid-torso to slightly above the head of the subject as shown in the figure. The notion of an MCU shot is to be able to show the background partially while also making it easy to recognize the subject's facial gesticulations and emotions.

Close-Up (CU) Shot

Normally, a CU shot shows the face or the head of the character in clear view. However, a CU shot can actually be used to show any part of the subject and can indeed be used to emphasize specific detail(s).

In addition to the above, there are several sub-classifications such as MCU, medium FS, and wide close-up (Figure 1.15).

FIG 1.14 Different types of shots.

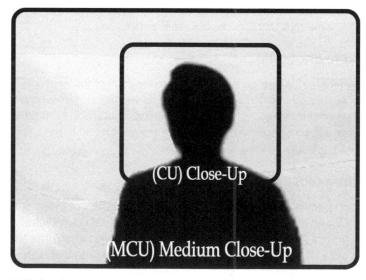

FIG 1.15 Medium close-up and close-up.

Extreme Close-Up (ECU) Shot

Extreme close-up (ECU) shots can be thought of as constricted CU shots. These can be used to capture emotions or even exaggerate them. However, these need not be necessarily only on facial details. ECUs can be used even on inanimate objects to intensify specific features. For instance, if during a movie climax, when

FIG 1.16 Character – extreme close-up. (Image courtesy: Mike, Y.)

a remote device is about to control an explosive, an ECU can be used to highlight the remote control trigger. Look at the ECU of the character shown below (Figure 1.16). Based on this ECU shot of the character, write the following:

- What is your perception of the character?
- What aspects of the drawing you think gave you the above perception of the character?

The angle of the shot can be varied for a low-angle shot or a high-angle shot. In a low-angle shot, the camera is situated at a low angle to the scene or the character and is aimed to look up at the scene. On the other hand, in a high-angle shot, the camera is positioned above and is aimed down upon the scene. We will discuss more about shots and angles in the chapter on composition and rendering (Figure 1.16).

Annotations

Storyboard annotations refer to descriptive comments or explanations added to the storyboard. Some storyboard artists use callouts to describe aspects which they are comfortable with explaining graphically or where they are not able to explain things using their drawing skills. Arrows are used to explain scene motion in detail and also to make camera movements clear. Zoom lines are used to explain the zoom in or zoom out process.

Number of Sketches

Now that we have looked at the various elements of storyboard, how many drawings are needed for an effective storyboard? Well, that varies. This is determined by the nature of your animation, the number of models involved in your animation, the complexity of the scene, the complexity of the models, the kind of motion required from these models, and so on. Remember, the more detail-oriented your storyboard, the greater the ease of animation and the success of your outcome. Do not skip any detail; it may prove to be a costly mistake at a later stage. Your storyboard should help you plan your animation as accurately as possible, and with a good storyboard, there will be no (or minimal) surprises or hiccups during the actual execution. On occasions, one may add too many details on the storyboard. Ask yourself: are the details relevant to the scene?

Captivating Your Audience: How to Create Better Story (Board)

Considering the two rough plots explained below, which one sounds more interesting? Idea A is insipid, dull, and uninteresting. There are no surprises or twists. On the other hand, Idea B shows something unusual and it triggers the reader's curiosity. This allures the reader and makes the reader wonder "what next?"

Idea A	Idea B
A tourist enters a museum.	A tourist enters a museum.
He buys tickets and picks up the brochure.	He buys tickets and picks up the brochure.
First, he sees the Stone Age collections.	First, he sees the Stone Age collections.
Next, he visits the Bronze Age section.	A strange artifact grabs his attention.
Then, he sees the Iron Age collections.	He grabs it in spite of the warning sign.
Finally, he goes to the cafeteria and exits.	The alarm gets triggered and….

When you read the descriptive text above, you created the scenes in your mind's eye. Let us try an alternative approach. Below you will find a storyboard for a plot titled "Voyage to the Bottom of the Sea". Try to write a descriptive narrative explaining your idea of the plot as seen from the storyboards in Figure 1.17

Characters

After the story is made, the characters need to be developed. The one-lined stories discussed earlier are basically the premise of your plot. Once you

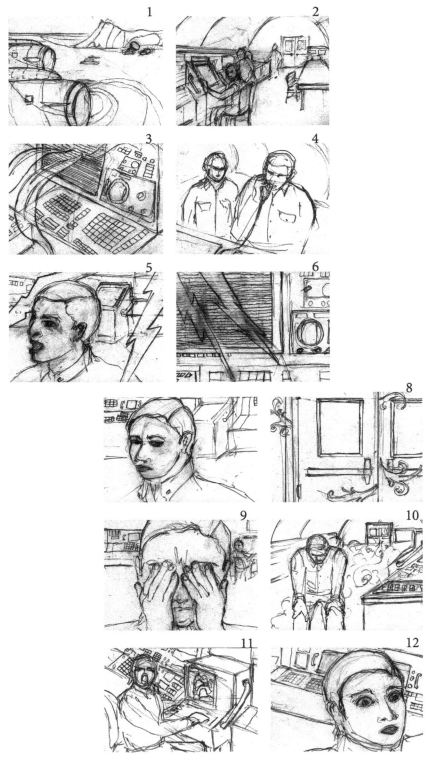

FIG 1.17 Storyboard – "Voyage to the bottom of the sea." (Image courtesy: George, H.)

decide the plot of your animation, you need to start thinking of the actual characters in your plot. It is through these characters that you actually execute the story (plot) of your animation.

See the images below and carefully study the characters portrayed (Figure 1.18).

What are your first thoughts when you see the images? Do you notice the panicky expression on the image on the right? Write these down so that you can use it as a reference when you are working on your own characters.

When you hear the word *characters*, characters like Woody©, Buzz Lightyear©, or Alex© (Madagascar©) may pop into your mind. All these characters have a body and limbs (hands/legs), but your animation need not always include characters like them. These need not be characters like human beings or animals or birds or insects. Your animation can include objects like cars or mechanical objects in a machine shop, or they can be anything else you want them to be or that your story demands. From a modeling perspective, your characters can be organic or hard-surfaced. We will look into these in greater detail in Chapters 4 and 5 on modeling. The words "organic" and "hard-surfaced" refer to the actual type of models. Organic characters or models typically refer to typically natural objects, while hard surface objects typically include objects such as machinery, automobiles, or buildings.

Animatic

After storyboarding, animators use an *animatic*, which can be considered as a demo or a test run. An animatic consists of a sequence of static images displayed with a simultaneous musical score or sound track.

FIG 1.18 Character expressions. (Image courtesy: Mike, Y.)

This helps to test the timing and the audio/video synchronization. Thus, by incorporating motion, an animatic takes storyboarding a step further and hence offers a better impression of the final scene. In fact, an animatic may lead to a revised storyboard and vice versa. This is an iterative chain involving revisions of animatic and storyboard until the team is completely satisfied. Such painstaking efforts minimize wasted efforts because elements of a scene that will never be captured by the camera or rendered need not be created in the first place. An animatic, also known as a *story reel*, is also used to pitch an idea to a client. The producer uses this to review and assess the potential of this idea being developed into a successful final animation. This is not final and is subject to several revisions.

In summary, let us do a comparison to understand modern animation vis-à-vis one of the ancient techniques. Let us consider the field of puppetry to associate with and understand modeling and animation. Typically, various forms of puppetry include the following elements:

- Story (the puppet show is normally about a play)
    - Includes script, scenario, performance description, and dialogue
- Proscenium booth
    - Scenery/background
    - Two- or three-dimensional
- Puppet construction
    Actual components depend on plot requirements and material availability
    - Puppet head (rubber, cardboard, plastic, fiberglass, cloth, carved)
    - Mouth (can be movable for dialogues)
    - Eyes (can be made to allow movement)
    - Body (a glove/carved body/rod hand)
    - Hands (with/without wrist/elbow joints; rope arms)
    - Legs (with/without knee and ankle joints)
- Puppet control
    - Control from above/below the booth
    - Rod control
    - Lever control
    - One-handed/two-handed
    - Hand control
    - Leg control
    - Joint control (leather/cord/screw-eye)
- Lighting
    - Spotlights
    - Sidelights
    - Footlights
    - Daylight
- Sound/music

As animation is a labor-intensive and time-consuming process, the overall effort involves multiple teams and personnel whose work needs to be coordinated. The next major step is production, which requires the actual steps involved in creating an animation.

Production Process

Having seen the pivotal role played by the storyboard in the preceding sections and its practical functions in the overall planning of the animation ahead, let us now look into the production process. In 3D digital animation, the layout process is a critical component wherein many details including the following are clearly specified before actual creation of models and execution of other related processes:

- A layout representation of the models
- Position and orientation of the models
- Position and orientation of the scene lights and the type of lights
- Position and orientation of the scene cameras and the type of cameras
- Details of the images and/or textures as applicable to the rendering process.

When carefully planned this way, this saves a lot of time as well as effort. This is because some objects like specific lights and other scene models may have to be used multiple times, and hence by planning in this manner, they can be created only once. Sometimes only minor features such as the color and intensity of the light may have to be changed or some minor attributes of models may have to be changed before replicating and reusing them.

Figure 1.19 shows the general tasks involved in the production pipeline; however, the specific processes and sub-processes for each animation project will be dictated by the actual project requirements and limitations.

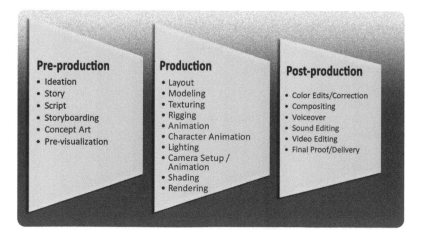

FIG 1.19 Major tasks in the production pipeline.

We will just take a brief look into these production processes here and leave the in-depth discussion to the actual chapters. You can consider this section as a brief description of the "road ahead". The rest of the chapters focus in detail on the various aspects of production including modeling, materials, textures, lighting, animation, and rendering.

Modeling is the process of creating or recreating the physical form of an object. Modeling involves building 3D objects, and then positioning, transforming, and modifying them in various ways until the final shape required is obtained. Modeling entails a strong understanding of the mathematical aspects underlying the creation, transformation, and modification of 3D objects. When we see a finished model, we are actually seeing the surface, which is a polygon or a collection of polygons.

Building 3D models involves creating and assembling (or organizing) the polygons (or faces) to resemble the object being represented. Figure 1.20 illustrates a mesh made of polygons representing a face.

But, before learning modeling, you will need to know the other basics to understand and create 3D models. The chapters on basic concepts and modeling will introduce you to the fundamental aspects of geometry, trigonometry, transformations, and projections, which will be extended in subsequent chapters. You will need to understand coordinates, measurements, and dimensions that will be covered in the following chapters to be able to model 3D objects and animate them as well. You will learn about the different methods of representing locations using different coordinate systems such as Cartesian, polar, cylindrical, and spherical. Afterward, you will learn about points, lines, and polygons, which form the foundation of creating your own custom-built 3D objects. Then, we will move on to polygonal meshes, which are used to create surfaces, and hence, models are made using points, lines, and polygons. The chapter will also cover tris or

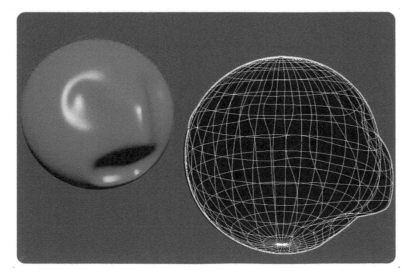

FIG 1.20 3D models and polygonal meshes.

quads, also known as triangles or quadrilaterals, which are used in graphics modeling. The notion of planarity will be used to help you understand the rationale behind the use of triangles by 3D rendering engines during the rendering process. Once the basics of modeling are covered, subsequently, we will move on to advanced modeling tools and techniques that build on the earlier knowledge. This chapter discusses polygonal and spline modeling, and introduces different types of modifiers and deformers that can be used to quickly model complex shapes from simpler ones such as primitives.

Animation as we know it today resulted from the conglomeration of several interesting inventions and scientific developments around the world over a long period of time. If we analogize digital animation to a puzzle, the various pieces of this puzzle were crafted by the works of many innovators over the past several centuries. Different aspects of graphics and animation have also been influenced by various major art forms, including those in the iron and bronze ages, medieval art, renaissance art, and modern art. Understanding these will help better understand and appreciate the current techniques of animation. In the initial parts of the animation chapters, we will look at many valuable inventions and contraptions that were made throughout the 19th and 20th centuries that contributed to the development of animation. Subsequently, we will cover the basic principles that allow us human beings to perceive animation and the foundational aspects including the physics of animation.

To create appealing animations, one should have an understanding of the underlying concepts of physics that govern motion in real life and need to properly be employed to recreate a good simulation. The principles of animation such as squash and stretch, overlapping action, follow-through, timing, slow in and slow out, and secondary action have a significant physics component. Hence, the basic elements of motion including gravity, speed, and balance are covered as required from the point of view of creating an engaging animation. Any appealing animation should be based on these foundational notions and should be used consistently across the board. Movement and timing are of tantamount importance as the spacing of the actions in the scene needs to be planned and executed accordingly. Attributes such as mass/weight, overall size of the character or a scene object, and the sizes and proportions of other body parts or components need to be considered when planning and spacing an animation sequence. Typically, the primary or the main action is accompanied by secondary action(s). In the real world, these automatically happen. For instance, when a stone is thrown in a lake, ripples are automatically created, when blowing wind moves a sailboat, the surrounding leaves and trees automatically move. However, in digital animation, it is important that the animator(s) make(s) sure that such secondary actions are properly modeled as required. The chapters on animation cover the basic concepts of physics such as motion, friction, acceleration, velocity, momentum, and force as applicable to animation. Next, we will cover the basic principles that allow us human beings to perceive animation and the foundational aspects including the physics of animation.

There are many basic forms of animation such as hand-drawn animation, stop-motion animation, or stop-motion photography before discussing key frame animation. We will also cover kinematics and its two major categories, namely, forward kinematics and inverse kinematics. To understand keyframing, it is important to understand interpolation, which is key to the process of filling the frames between the key frames to ensure a smooth transition. Subsequently, the chapter will discuss kinematics, which is a branch of mechanics that deals with object motion. We will discuss the variables involved therein such as position, orientation, time, distance, and speed. We will see the use of a hierarchical chain of bones and joints that are involved in the kinematic calculations for obtaining a desired position. This discussion will be continued by rigging, wherein the bones and joints are used to create the many different poses that the model will be eventually animated into. Subsequently, rigging and posing are covered in detail with examples (Figure 1.21).

A well-designed character is a great tool to narrate the story. The design of the character must show a good understanding of the plot and the script to align the character's traits and the overall personality accordingly. Design is a creative process, and there is no single correct approach to design. We will look at some of the common procedures employed in the design process. A good character design stems from a proper understanding of the character's true nature and the role of the character in the plot. Characters with distinctive traits and visually engaging personalities tend to resonate well with the audience. All decisions about character design should always consider the overall role of the character in the story and should result after careful deliberation of the range of actions (motions) that the character will be required to perform as the plot evolves.

Character design is an essential process in many fields including:

- Video games
- Animated movies
- Illustrated books
- Cartoons
- Mobile/computer games

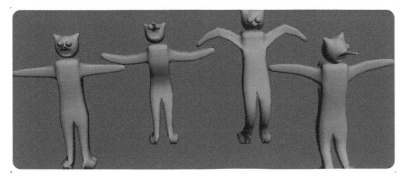

FIG 1.21 Posing and rigging.

The chapter on lighting explains the importance of lighting in digital CG scenes and how lights enable the audience to appreciate models in animation. This chapter explores the art and science of color, which is inherently interrelated to lighting and commonly used lighting scheme for organizing lights in a scene, namely, three-point lighting. Subsequently, we move on to some of the most common CG lights. Then, we will cover the elements of scene lighting and the relation between color and emotion. Lighting helps you get this message across and enables the audience to better appreciate your creation (Figure 1.22).

Good lighting can make or break your carefully created 3D model scene and animation. Lighting plays a critical role in presenting the overall plot of the animation in an engaging manner to the audience. An appreciation of art and studying the world around can help in creating better lighting in your scene. As we will see later in the chapter on composition, lighting significantly influences what parts of your scene are highlighted and what is not. Before we get into the aspects of lighting a 3D CG scene, we will take a brief look at the basic theory of lighting.

The final chapter will discuss the essential elements of composition that enable audience to grasp the message being conveyed. The chapter then discusses the appearance of the subject from an LS and a CU shot and from the point of view of positive and negative space. The significance of lines

FIG 1.22 Lighting in a scene. (Image courtesy: Stephanie, A.)

as elements of composition is covered as they tend to lead and direct the attention of the audience. Finally, the digital rendering process and the various file formats are discussed.

In this book, we will be predominantly focusing our discussion on modeling and animation from the perspective of movie animation and game industry. However, let us take a quick look at few other applications where you can use 3D modeling and animation skills.

Where Are Some Other Areas Where Models Are Used?

The earlier sections covered in detail the "what" and "why" of modeling. The future chapters will delve into the details of the how of modeling. In this section, let us spend some time on the "where". Likewise, other forms of visual representations including models condense a whole lot of information and convey them in a lucid manner. 3D models inherently have a visual appeal and hence can serve to reduce the cognitive load involved in comprehending complex information and relationships. In this section, let us look at a few areas where modeling is used with immense success.

The following are some of the key categories and subcategories where modeling has been and is being used:

- Automobile design
- Product design
- Clothing design
- Ergonomic furniture design
- Interior design
- Urban infrastructure planning and design
- Landscape design
- Architectural modeling
- Motion/game industry
  - Video game design
  - Motion picture industry
- Education/research/instruction
  - Biology (3D anatomical models)
  - Physics and chemistry (3D atomic and molecular models)
  - CADAM (computer-aided design and manufacturing)
  - Statistical modeling
  - Geographical modeling
- Training
  - Military and flight simulation applications
  - Driver training
  - Simulated training for risky environments (such as mining)

The above list of applications of 3D models is by no means exhaustive. Innumerable disciplines and subdisciplines continue to use 3D models for academic, research, and commercial purposes.

Architectural Modeling and Construction Graphics

Modeling is an indispensable tool in architecture and construction. Not only do the models help the stakeholders, administrators, and decision-makers view the finished product beforehand, but they also help the architects and the engineers plan the construction process. Models can be built with extreme precision to incorporate all the measurement details and the geometric relationships. The subsequent chapters will cover in extreme detail the complete set of steps involved in the modeling process. The following sections will provide a brief overview of the basic steps involved in the use of modeling for a sample application. A blueprint is an important pre-production exercise, which consists of line drawings, buildings or architectural works, or mechanical drawings. Blueprints serve as the planning tools and designs for the construction project and include essential information pertaining to the numerical details, size, shape, and several other data pertaining to the construction to be made. Conventional practices require the blueprint to be revised after several rounds of inspection, and it needs to be finalized before the actual planning is carried out. The purpose of a blueprint is to avoid mistakes during the actual construction process and to ensure the optimal results for the project. However, in reality, people do not dwell in 2D but 3D spaces. We live, sit, stand, walk, sleep, and cook in places that are characterized by length, width, and height (the three dimensions). Hence, a 3D model can better serve the actual purpose of delivering optimal results. By using modeling to visualize for applications such as architectural modeling, more details are added. There is less abstraction and more refinement. 3D modeling (Figure 1.23) enables an efficient planning procedure and hence contributes to increasing productivity.

Modeling enables envisioning the completed outcome/product (the present construction project) beforehand. When the planners and designers view the finished building instead of a proposed layout, it facilitates nondestructive

FIG 1.23 Finished 3D model of a building.

testing. If, after construction, the decision-makers are not satisfied with the orientation of structural and/or architectural elements for aesthetic and/or other reasons, this would amount to a tremendous amount of wasted time and resources.

Models for Simulation/Training

When simulations are used for instructional training purposes, the users or participants get a feel of the real-world situations and undergo the practical constraints minus the risks involved. A blunder on the actual work scenario, a wrong maneuver while piloting a flight or driving a train, or a careless step during the assembly-line process can lead to catastrophic results and even be fatal at times. However, simulation-based training minimizes or eliminates the hazards inherent in such processes and thus aids a harmless training milieu. Furthermore, training encompasses both aspects that are explicit and some features that are ambiguous and are relatively challenging to comprehend. The comprehension of such problematic and indirect aspects is vital for a thorough knowledge of everyday situations and systems that intrinsically pose risks to lives and property. After being modeled or generated, the simulation models (Figure 1.24) could be run as many times as necessary to acquaint the apprentices/interns/trainees comprehensively with the system. Instructors do not necessarily have to be hired repeatedly to conduct the training, and no extra money is needed to redevelop or reperform the training scenario.

Figure 1.24 demonstrates the use of immersive virtual worlds to facilitate training for train drivers. Also, modeling using computer-generated simulated environments assists in picturing the completed product (built rail station) in advance. The planners and decision-makers can view and navigate through the model at the convenience of an office desktop, and changes can be made without wasting any money.

FIG 1.24 Simulation/training for train drivers.

Other Types of Models

Before concluding this chapter, let us take a quick look at some other classifications of models. Based on time, models can be classified as follows:

- Models of objects from the past
- Models of the present
- Futuristic models

3D reconstruction has been used to recreate objects from the past such as reconstructing past monuments from ancient civilizations and reconstructing extinct creatures such as dinosaurs. Models of the present include a broad range of models such as modeling 3D cities, interior design, and architecture. Futuristic models are used for forecasting future developments, such as urban growth, and creating models for a construction yet to be done.

From the animation perspective, models can be divided into two broad categories, namely, static and dynamic models. Static models, as the name describes, are motionless, that is, devoid of animation. The dynamic models, on the other hand, are capable of animation or movement. The static 3D models are typically used for design and planning purposes. The dynamic models are used for animation, simulation, and training purposes.

A Sample Checklist

You can use the following as a checklist to help you in the process of creating a good storyboard. Try to answer these questions. Remember that not all these questions may apply to your actual animation and you use them based on your situation.

- What is the story of your animation?
- What/who are the characters in your animation?
- Who is the protagonist? Who is the antagonist?
- What is the conflict?
- Action definition
  - What kind of model movements are involved?
  - What is the primary motion?
  - What are the secondary motions involved?
  - What kind of camera motions are involved?
  - Are there overlapping motions or motion holds?
  - (Arrows, annotations, or both can be used to clarify)
- Scene lighting
  - Is this an indoor scene or an outdoor scene?
  - What are the locations of the key lights, fill lights, and/or rim lights?
  - How many lights are there?
  - What kind of lights are they (point/spot/directional or a combination)?
  - What are their colors?

- What are their intensities?
- Where are they positioned?
- How are they oriented?
- Scene cameras
  - How many cameras are there in the scene?
  - What types of cameras are used (target or free)?
  - What is their field of view (FOV)?
  - What shots are involved (close-up shots, long shots, medium, etc.) and when?
- Materials
  - What kind of materials (or textures) are used for characters?
  - What kind of materials are used for the background?
  - What are the predominant (primary) colors in the scene?
  - What is the mood of the scene?

The above does not cover all the elements that should go in a storyboard. There is no general rule of thumb that defines what must be included in a storyboard. But, the list does state some of the common elements that good storyboards should consider.

In a Nutshell

Just as someone will have trouble understanding gibberish or poor verbal communication, poorly created visuals or pictures are hard to understand. One of the key elements of communication is clarity. The visual elements of a storyboard need to be clear – whether it is a scene layout, a character, or an action. The more detailed a storyboard, the clearer the communication. A well-planned story board not only saves lot of time but also helps with the budget by saving production costs. Storyboarding is part of pre-production. There are no rules of thumb in storyboarding. This is a creative exercise, and you as the creator have the freedom to create a storyboard as your animation demands. However, there are guidelines to help you in the process, because storyboarding is done for a purpose: to make an animation. Unless the storyboard helps you in realizing your ultimate goal of creating a good animation, the storyboarding exercise is futile. However, this chapter discussed various important aspects and functions of storyboarding, which will help you in creating an effective storyboard. As animation is a creative exercise, the elements that must go in a storyboard are dictated by the needs of the kind of animation. The process of storyboarding also exposes the challenges, limitations, or constraints in a project, and the iterative workflow facilitates modifying the narrative accordingly. This ensures that obstacles that may otherwise be encountered during the production process can be safely eliminated or at least minimized. When learning about the production pipeline, you need to remember one very important notion. It is not strictly sequential or linear. The processes need not occur in the exact same order or not all the processes need to occur. This step in the production pipeline and the sequence in which they occur is determined by the needs of the animation process and the constraints/limitations in place.

In this chapter, we mainly discussed the pre-production aspects of the production pipeline, explaining storyboarding in detail with many examples. I will repeat this again and again. You are telling a story, which starts with an idea. This idea that originates as a small seed needs to be nurtured well enough to sprout and grow into a healthy plant before it can yield the fruit (the final product). What we saw earlier in this chapter is how you can streamline the processes of imagination and innovation during the ideation process to give shape to an abstract idea.

Digital animation and modeling today have borrowed immensely from the various art forms such as opera, play, theater, puppetry, and comic arts. All those people who contributed to these art forms are truly pioneers as they did not have much to rely on.

You can create a perfectly functional storyboard by paying attention to the details required for your animation and attending to them in the storyboard. Remember, the keyword is *functional*, not *fancy*. It is the attention to detail that makes a storyboard effective. A good storyboard, while trying to be as informative and detail-oriented as possible, will still need to be flexible by being amenable to alterations as the plot evolves.

Finally, remember these important points when storyboarding:

- Be practical; do not be overambitious.
- Be mindful of your time and resource constraints.
- Keep your eyes and ears open – that great idea can be from anywhere.
- Solicit feedback and reflect actively on comments/criticisms.
- Be willing to modify your storyboard as the plot evolves.

Chapter 1 Quiz

PART I

True/False (Circle the Correct Choice)

1. The first step in pre-production involves working on the computer to create your model.
True False

2. A rendering can be thought of as a visually narrated script.
True False

3. In a typical feature film, the 1.5 or 2 hours of movie that you see in a theater has actually been edited from a hundred thousand feet of film.
True False

4. Digital animation and modeling today have borrowed immensely from the traditional crafts such as opera, play, theater, and puppetry.
True False

5. The more detailed a storyboard, the clearer the communication.
True False

6. You do not need to be an artist to be good at storyboarding.
True False

7. A storyboard consists of a sequence of static images displayed with a simultaneous musical score or sound track.
True False

8. An animatic, also known as a story reel, is also used to pitch an idea to a client.
True False

9. The production pipeline represents the basic framework used to develop the animation.
True False

10. According to the acronym SMART, at the very simplest form, an animation would typically require a style, monitor, animation, rendering, and test reel.
True False

11. Normally, a long shot shows the face or the head of the character in clear view.
True False

12. Camera location refers to the angle or the direction in which the camera is facing.
True False

13. To create appealing animations, one should have an understanding of the underlying concepts of physics that govern motion in real life.
True False

14. Framing height (or camera framing) is the distance between the camera and the character, and is actually more about how much of the character is viewed by or shown to the audience.
True False

15. The basic idea behind thumbnails is to bring out ideas and explore.
True False

16. Modeling is the process of creating or recreating the physical form of an object.
True False

17. A full shot (FS) or wide shot (WS) is used for staging or establishing the scene.
True False

18. Long shots portray a character from the thigh or the waist and above.
True False

19. Extreme close-ups can be used even on inanimate objects to intensify specific features.
True False

20. Zoom lines are used to explain the zoom in or zoom out process.
True False

PART II

Multiple Choice Questions (Choose the Most Appropriate Answer)

1. _____represents the acronym discussed in this chapter that stands for the processes that typically constitute the making of an animation.
   a. SMART
   b. MARS
   c. SORT
   d. STAR
   e. None of the above

2. Behind every great animation is a great
   a. Rendering engine
   b. Computer
   c. Display
   d. Story
   e. None of the above

3. The _____ refers to the degree or the amount of the scene (the environment) that can be viewed at a particular instance.
   a. Camera location
   b. Orientation
   c. Field of view
   d. Spectrum
   e. None of the above

4. _____ is the distance between the camera and the character, and is actually more about how much of the character is viewed by or shown to the audience.
   a. Framing height
   b. Frame width
   c. Lens height
   d. Angle of view
   e. None of the above

5. _____ shots portray a character from the waist and above.
   a. Long
   b. Wide
   c. Close
   d. Medium
   e. None of the above

6. Normally, a _____ shot shows the face or the head of the character in clear view.
   a. Long
   b. Wide
   c. Close-up
   d. Medium
   e. None of the above

7. _____close-up shots can be thought of as constricted close-up shots.
   a. Long
   b. Wide
   c. Extreme
   d. Medium
   e. None of the above

8. Storyboard _____refer to descriptive comments or explanations added to the storyboard.
   a. Plots
   b. Annotations
   c. Arrows
   d. Boxes
   e. None of the above

9. An animatic is also known as a_____.
   a. Model sketch
   b. Story reel
   c. Rendering
   d. Anime
   e. None of the above

10. _____ are the basic building blocks of an animation video.
    a. Sequences
    b. Shots
    c. Segments
    d. Streams
    e. None of the above

11. Typically, the primary or the main action is accompanied by _____ action.
    a. Typical
    b. Secondary
    c. Trigger
    d. Reasonable
    e. None of the above

12. Long shots are also referred to as
    a. Extreme close-up shots
    b. Medium shots
    c. Medium close-up shots
    d. Full shots
    e. None of the above

13. Which of the following offers a close, but not that close of a view of the subject?
    a. Extreme close-up shots
    b. Medium shots
    c. Medium close-up shots
    d. Full shots
    e. None of the above

14. Two major types of kinematics are forward kinematics and _____ kinematics.
    a. Initial
    b. Inverse
    c. Return
    d. Reasonable
    e. None of the above

15. To understand keyframing, it is important to understand _____, which is key to the process of filling the frames between the key frames to ensure a smooth transition.
    a. Interaction
    a. Interpolation
    b. Concurrence
    c. Segmentation
    d. None of the above

16. Modeling can be used in which of the following areas?
    a. Architecture
    b. Video games
    c. Motion picture
    d. Education
    e. All the above

17. Long shots are also referred to as
    a. Extreme close-up shots
    b. Medium shots
    c. Medium close-up shots
    d. Wide shots
    e. None of the above

18. _____ is the distance between the camera and the character, and is actually more about how much of the character is viewed by or shown to the audience.
    a. Extreme height
    b. Framing height
    c. Camera height
    d. Full height
    e. None of the above

19. FOV stands for
    a. Film view
    b. Field of view
    c. Full view
    d. Frontal view
    e. All the above

20. The S in the SMART mnemonic stands for
    a. Shot
    b. Segment
    c. Segment
    d. Story
    e. None of the above

CHAPTER 2: Conceptual Foundations: *Basic Building Blocks*

Before anything else, preparation is the key to success.

– Alexander Graham Bell

CHAPTER LEARNING OBJECTIVES

After carefully studying this chapter, you will be able to answer the following:

- What are coordinates, dimensions, and coordinate systems?
- What is Cartesian coordinate system?
- What is polar coordinate system?
- How can a modeler build shapes using points, lines, and polygons?
- What are the basic mathematical/geometric concepts of modeling?
- What are left- and right-handed systems?
- What are Euclidean and projective geometry?

DOI: 10.1201/9780429186349-2

- What are transformations?
- What are global and local transformations?
- What are absolute and relative values?
- What are points, lines, and polygons?
- How are polylines different from polygons?

What Will You Learn in This Chapter?

First, the chapter will cover the fundamentals of geometric coordinates and coordinate systems. You need to understand coordinates, measurements, and dimensions to be able to model objects and animate them as well. You will learn about the different methods of representing locations using different coordinate systems such as Cartesian, polar, cylindrical, and spherical. Subsequently, you will learn about points, lines, and polygons, which form the foundation of creating your own custom-built 3D objects. Then, we will move on to polygonal meshes, which are used to create surfaces, and hence, models are made using points, lines, and polygons. The chapter will also cover tris or quads, also known as triangles or quadrilaterals, which are used in graphics modeling. The notion of planarity will be used to help you understand the rationale behind the use of triangles by 3D engines during the rendering process.

First and foremost, you need to understand a very important aspect of axes conventions. There are different programming languages and modeling platforms that are available and used for modeling 3D objects and scenes. Remember that despite the variations in the conventions employed by different systems, the coordinate systems are a reference system for the user to model the 3D objects in a scene; *they are not part of the objects*. Consider measurement, for example. The property of the object remains the same whether you measure it in metric system or the US standard system of measurement. The numbers used to express the height of the Empire State building in meters and feet may be different. Nevertheless, the property (height) being measured and expressed is the same. Similarly, the notations used by different modeling platforms depend on several factors including convenience, background, and familiarity of the developers of such platforms. What you are about to learn in this chapter is the foundation to your journey ahead and will form the cornerstone to what you will learn in the future chapters.

Basic Building Blocks

Coordinates, Measurements, and Dimensions

We do live in a 3D world, which for geometric purposes, we refer using x-, y-, and z-axes (Figure 2.1). As a matter of fact, all things big or small, that we come across in our day-to-day life are within this 3D world, either directly or indirectly. The positions and geometric relations of these are quite important and in a great way determine the usability and functionality of these things.

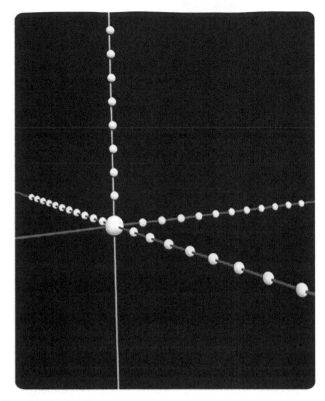

FIG 2.1 Three-dimensional world.

With digital modeling, directly and indirectly we are dealing with data. This data involves measurements, coordinates, and dimensions. Whether your model is factual or fictional is a critical factor in determining the proportions. Just as in the process of building a house, when building 3D objects we need to know where to position things and how long or wide they should be and how much space they should occupy. Modeling systems use a reference system to help in this process.

There is a reason why the distinction between factual and fictional was mentioned in the earlier paragraph. Realistic (factual) objects need to maintain scale and proportions as audience know approximately how big a soccer ball or how large a car is when compared to a truck. However, fictional objects are allowed the creative latitude or freedom. In movies with alien creatures or monsters, the characters do not always maintain 'proper' proportions. As long as the plot requires that and the characters are relevant to the plot engaging, you can have a human-like (anthropomorphic) character with three legs of unusual size or an animal with arms like tree branches at disproportionate sizes.

Any and every modeling program or platform uses some kind of coordinate system. A coordinate or coordinates is/are the numerical representation(s) of the location or position of something. Be it a house or a car or an aircraft or a printed poster, the final finished product is made by careful spatial arrangement of constituent parts. In the real world, we construct things within the 3D space.

For building anything, we need a reference system to position and orient the objects. This reference system is known as the coordinate system.

Cartesian Coordinate System

One commonly used coordinate system is the Cartesian coordinate system. The Cartesian system was invented by Rene Descartes, a French mathematician who was a pioneer of analytical geometry. Figure 2.1 shows a 3D coordinate system and Figure 2.2 shows a 2D coordinate system. Let us initially consider the 2D system for simplicity. You can see that two straight lines run across horizontally and vertically. The horizontal line is known as the *x*-axis, which divides the space into two equal vertical parts to the left and right. The vertical line is known as the *y*-axis, which divides the space into two equal horizontal parts (above and below). The central point of reference in this coordinate system is known as the origin, represented by (0, 0). The values on the horizontal *x*-axis to the right-hand side of the origin are positive values (+1,+2,+3…), and those on the left are negative values (−1,−2,−3…). Similarly, the values on the vertical *x*-axis above the origin are positive values (+1,+2,+3…), and those below the origin are negative values (−1,−2,−3…). The three axes *x*, *y*, and *z* are perpendicular to each other.

The two intersecting axes, *x* and *y*, also divide the space into four components, each one of which is called a quadrant. These are numbered Quadrants I, II, III, and IV in an anticlockwise direction starting with the upper-right quadrant. As you can see, the upper-right quadrant (Quadrant I) is made of completely positive values of *x* and *y*, and the lower-left quadrant

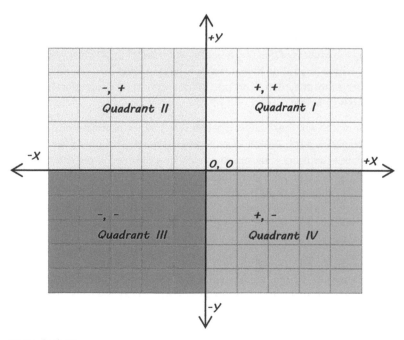

FIG 2.2 Quadrants.

(Quadrant III) is made of negative *x* and *y* values. The upper-left quadrant (Quadrant II) has negative *x* and positive *y* values, while the lower right has negative *y* and positive *x* values.

As can be seen from Figure 2.2, the *x* and *y* coordinates are used to define the position of a point within the coordinate space divided into the quadrants. Figure 2.2 shows the divisions along the axes of the coordinate systems, and each one of these is called a quadrant. These are numbered I, II, III, and IV in an anticlockwise direction starting with the upper-right quadrant. As you can see, the upper-right quadrant (Quadrant I) is made of completely positive values of *x* and *y*, and the lower-left quadrant (Quadrant III) is made of negative *x* and *y* values. The upper-left quadrant (Quadrant II) has negative *x* and positive *y* values, while the lower right has negative *y* and positive *x* values. The *z*-axis is used to represent the third dimension (depth) to this representation.

We will primarily refer to the Cartesian coordinate in this book. Also, in this book, we will use the commonly used practice referred in Figure 2.2, where *x* values to the right side of *y*-axis are considered positive and *y* values above *x*-axis are considered positive. With respect to the third dimension represented by the *z*-axis, there are two common conventions referred to as the right- and left-handed systems. Figure 2.3 shows a right-handed system, and Figure 2.4 shows a left-handed system. Consider the *x*- and *y*-axes are along the plane of the computer monitor. For convenience, *x*-axis is represented with red and *y* with green. In a right-handed system, the positive *z* direction will be facing towards you, the user. In the left-handed system, the positive *z* direction will be pointing away from the user (into the monitor). Why are these systems called right- and left-handed?

Imagine sitting (or actually sit) on a chair resting your hands on a table and staring at a PC monitor. First, let us understand the right-handed system. Resting your right elbow on the table, open the palm of your right hand in such a way that your thumb is pointing to the right and your index finger straight up (perpendicular or at 90° to your thumb). Your thumb and the index finger now represent the *xy* plane (plane of the monitor). Straighten out your middle finger (actually, now it will be pointing at you) so that it is perpendicular to the index finger. In Figure 2.4, this is represented by the blue

FIG 2.3 Right-handed system.

FIG 2.4 Left-handed system.

fingertip (of the middle finger). The directions of the thumb, index finger, and middle finger show the positive x-, y-, and z-axes. Now that you know the directions of the positive x-, y-, and z-axes, you can also use the right-hand thumb to find out the direction of positive rotation for each axes. Visualize grabbing each axis with your right hand (while making a fist) such that your thumb is pointing to the positive direction; then, the direction in which your fingers bend shows the direction of positive rotation.

Similarly, to understand the left-handed system, resting your left elbow on the table, open the palm of your left hand in such a way that the thumb is pointing to the right and your index finger straight up (perpendicular or at 90° to your thumb). Your thumb and the index finger now represent the xy plane (plane of the monitor). Straighten out your middle finger (actually, now it will be pointing away from you), and this represents the positive z direction (Figure 2.4). To find the direction of positive rotation in a left-handed system, visualize grabbing each axis with your left hand (while making a fist) such that your thumb is pointing to the positive direction; then, the direction in which your fingers bend shows the direction of positive rotation.

We earlier looked at Cartesian coordinate system, which is what we will be referring to in this book. However, we will take a quick look at another coordinate system known as the polar coordinate system.

Polar Coordinate System

The Cartesian coordinate system is just one way to represent locations in space. There are different kinds of coordinate systems. One primary objective of a coordinate system is to precisely define an object's position within space. This can be accomplished in many possible ways based on the specific application for which the location is required. Some other popular kinds of coordinates include polar coordinates, cylindrical coordinates, and spherical coordinates.

In the polar coordinate system, a point is represented as a function of angle and distance. The distance (r) is referred to as the radial coordinate, and the angle (θ) is referred to as the angular coordinate (Figure 2.5).

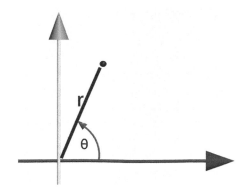

In terms of Cartesian coordinates (x and y), these can be defined as follows:

$$x = r\,Cos\theta$$

$$y = r\,Sin\theta$$

where,

Cos (cosine) is the trigonometric function corresponding to the ratio of the adjacent side to the hypotenuse (Figure 2.6).

Sin (sine) is the trigonometric function corresponding to the ratio of the opposite side to the hypotenuse (Figure 2.6).

$$Cos\theta = \frac{Adjacent\ Side}{Hypotenuse}$$

$$Sin\theta = \frac{Opposite\ Side}{Hypotenuse}$$

The radial distance (r) can be expressed in terms of x and y Sine as follows (Figure 2.5):

$$r = \sqrt{\left(x^2 + y^2\right)}$$

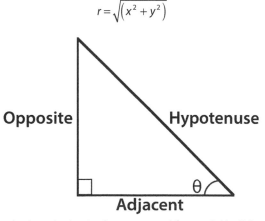

Now, let us look at the basic elements used for model building namely points, lines, and polygons.

FIG 2.6 Hypotenuse, adjacent, and opposite sides.

Points, Lines, and Polygons

A point, also known as the vertex, is the very basic element used to build the other elements that make up a polygonal model. As we will see in this section, points are connected together to form edges (lines) that in turn are used to make a polygon. A point actually specifies only the position and, in fact, has no dimensions. Hence, a point is also known as a *zero-dimensional object*. A point, also known as vertex in computer graphics (CG) terminology, cannot be rendered. Just as (x, y) is used to represent a point in a 2D coordinate system, (x, y, z) is used to represent a point in a 3D coordinate system. The point is only used to represent a location, and it is not an actual physical entity. This means that a point cannot be captured in an image rendering of the 3D model because a point has none of the three dimensions, namely, length, width, and height (or width, depth, and height as some modelers may choose to represent it).

In the Cartesian system, a point's location is specified on a plane using numerical values, x and y coordinates, corresponding to the horizontal x-axis and the vertical y-axis. Ordered pair refers to two numbers, (x, y) for representing the location of a point with respect to a reference point (origin). Consider the origin as the starting point. The x value denotes the distance along the x- and y-axes denotes the distance along the y-axis. Figure 2.7 shows a vertex (in red color) whose location is (4, 3).

Different authors, books, and tools that discuss x-, y-, and z-axes may refer to them using different conventions. For the purposes of this book, we will use the following convention. Typically, the x-axis is horizontal and the y-axis is vertical. That gives us two dimensions (2D) as in a plane or a graph. So, let us continue to use x to represent horizontal and y for vertical axis. The z-axis can be considered the depth axis.

As you may note in Figure 2.8 (3D world), the axes are colored using red, green, and blue (RGB). As we quite frequently use the RGB notation, this can help you to associate them with the three axes, namely, x, y, and z. Figure 2.8 shows a point being represented in a coordinate system. This point is located

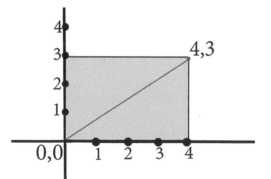

FIG 2.7 Point in 2D coordinate system.

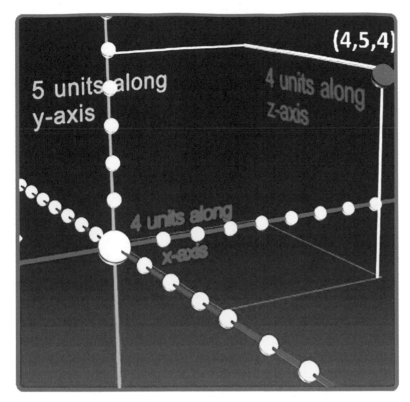

FIG 2.8 Vertex in 3D Cartesian system.

(starting from the origin) 4 units along the x-axis, 5 units along the y-axis, and 4 units along the z-axis. Hence, the notation used to represent this point is (4, 5, 4) corresponding to (x, y, z). We saw earlier that a point is zero-dimensional (no dimensions).

In the real world, typically, we refer to measurements only in positive numbers. For instance, we say that the pillar should be located at least 8 feet from the entrance. On the roads, specific amounts of vertical clearances must be employed, ranging somewhere between 14 and 16 feet approximately based on whether it is a freeway in rural or urban setting and other conditions. The measurement values we are used to (as above) are positive. Even when we are referring to digging a hole or a pit, we still use positive values, but we refer to how deep it is, instead of how tall it is? If we were to erect a pole on the ground, we refer to it as standing 18 feet tall above the ground, but for a tube inserted into the ground, we call it 18 feet deep into the ground (Figure 2.9).

However, in computer systems, it is much convenient to use positive and negative numbers. Instead of mentioning, up and down, positive and negative y-axes are used; similarly, for locating to the right or left, we use positive and negative x-axis, instead of, and similarly, for front or behind, we use z-axis.

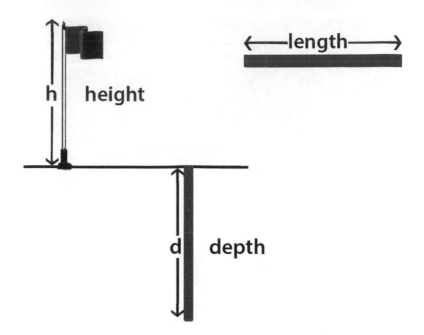

FIG 2.9 Length depicted as height (or) depth.

In the Cartesian coordinate system, the length of a line between two points x_1, y_1 and x_2, y_2 is given by

$$\sqrt{(x_2 - x_1)^2 + (y_2 - y_1)^2}$$

The distance between two points (0, 0) and (4, 3), represented by the red line, is obtained as follows:

$$\text{Distance between}(4,3)\text{ and }(0,0) = \sqrt{(4-0)^2 + (3-0)^2}$$

$$= \sqrt{16+9} = \sqrt{25} = 5\,\text{units}$$

In Figure 2.7, you can see that there is a rectangle (green color) shown with one the vertices being (4, 3). The following are the vertices (anticlockwise starting from origin) of the rectangles: (0, 0), (0, 3), (4, 3), (4, 0). The area of a rectangle is obtained by multiplying the length and the width.

$$\text{Area} = \text{length} * \text{width}$$

For the green rectangle shown in the figure,

$$\text{length} = 4\,\text{units \& width} = 3\,\text{units}$$

So, area of the rectangle = length * width = 4 * 3 = 12 square units.

Lines can be straight or curved. A straight line represents the shortest distance between two points. Geometrically, a straight line can be considered as a point traveling in a constant direction. In the words of the Swiss-German painter Paul Klee "A line is a dot that went for a walk". In case of a straight line, the direction remains constant, whereas for a curved line, the direction changes. From a CG point of view, lines are important, starting from modeling all the way to rendering. Lines are an important compositional element that we will discuss later in the chapter on rendering.

As we will see later in Chapter 10 on composition, lines are actually a phenomenon in themselves. They are among those uniquely beautiful objects that are all around us but seldom noticed. Experienced artists and painters can talk volumes about the beauty of "lines." Lines are important elements of painting, any various other art forms, and of course, 3D modeling. We just call them lines, but there are many categories of lines: broken, solid, curved, straight, single-curved, double-curved, dotted, dashed, thin, thick, regular, irregular, gray, colored, parallel, perpendicular, intersecting, and tangential, and there are many other subtle classifications.

A *line* is one-dimensional and can be defined by two points. From a CG perspective, a line is a geometric primitive that plays an extremely crucial role in modeling. A line can be characterized by length and direction. In the Cartesian coordinate system, the length of a line between two points x_1, y_1 and x_2, y_2 is given by

$$\sqrt{(x_2 - x_1)^2 + (y_2 - y_1)^2}$$

Figure 2.10 demonstrates a straight line connecting two points: (0,0,0) and (8,7,0). The distance between two points in 3D can be calculated using the following formula: $\sqrt{(x_2 - x_1)^2 + (y_2 - y_1)^2 + (z_2 - z_1)^2}$

In graphics terminology, the line is also referred to as edge defined by two vertices. The edges of a single polygon are pictured in red in the image below.

Figure 2.11 illustrates a planar surface. A planar surface represents a flat surface completely lying on one plane. Just as a line is created by a point moving in a particular direction, a line moving in a specific direction in a specific manner creates a surface. This can be a flat surface lying on a single plane or a curved surface (Figure 2.11).

Consider the rectangular area shown below in the 2D Cartesian coordinate system. The coordinates are (1,2), (6,2), (6,5), and (1,5) (Figure 2.12).

Let us apply the above formula to calculate the length and the height.

For length, let us consider the two points (1,2) and (6,2) as (x_1, y_1) and (x_2, y_2), respectively.

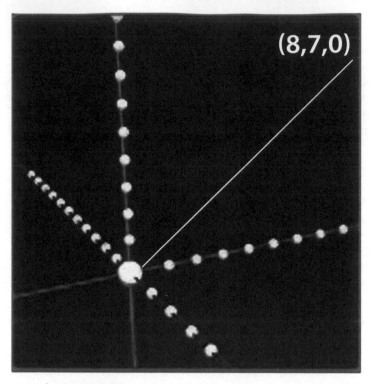

FIG 2.10 Line from (0, 0, 0) to (8, 7, 0).

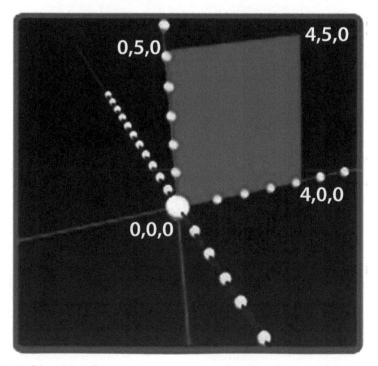

FIG 2.11 Polygon in a coordinate system.

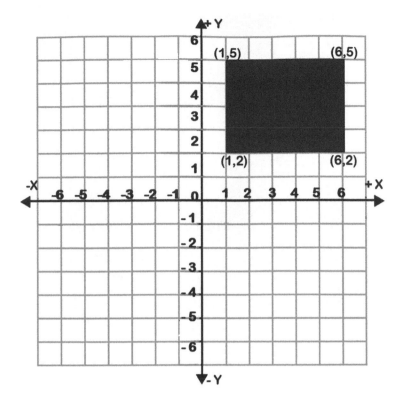

FIG 2.12 Area calculation.

$$\sqrt{(x_2 - x_1)^2 + (y_2 - y_1)^2}$$

$$= \sqrt{(6-1)^2 + (2-2)^2} = \sqrt{5^2 + 0^2}$$

$$= \sqrt{25}$$

$$= 5$$

For height, let us consider the two points (6,2) and (6,5) as (x_1, y_1) and (x_2, y_2), respectively.

$$\sqrt{(x_2 - x_1)^2 + (y_2 - y_1)^2}$$

$$= \sqrt{(6-6)^2 + (5-2)^2} = \sqrt{0^2 + 3^2}$$

$$= \sqrt{9}$$

$$= 3$$

The number of units it spans across on the x-axis is 5 (from 1 to 6) and 3 units along the y-axis (from 2 to 5). So, the area of this rectangle is 5 times 3, which is 15 square units.

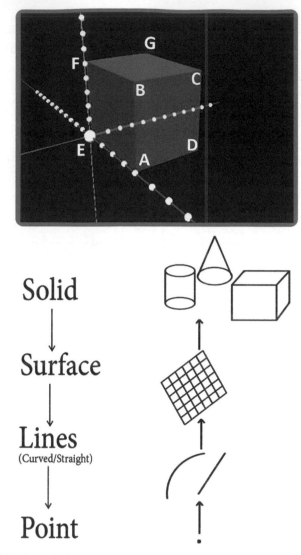

FIG 2.13 Points, lines, and polygons.

In graphics modeling, solid objects can be decomposed into surfaces (polygons) which can be divided into lines (Figure 2.13). In other words, the basic entities of point, lines, and polygons are used to construct the three-dimensional solid forms.

Polygons and Polylines

Theoretically, a line can continue to extend infinitely in both directions. For this reason, the term line segment is used to distinguish lines that have distinct end points. When line segments connect a series of points (vertices), we get what are known as polylines. The difference between a polyline and polygon is that a polygon is a closed figure (Figure 2.14).

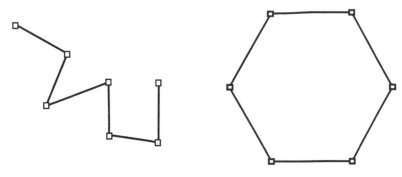

As you can note in Figure 2.14, the first vertex and the last vertex in case of a polyline are distinct. In case of a polygon, the first vertex and the last vertex are the same. In other words, this results in the shape being closed. A polygon is a closed 2D shape or figure made by connecting line segments, typically a minimum of three, endwise. There are many different types of polygons. Common polygonal objects that we know of include triangle, rectangle, quadrilateral, pentagon, and hexagon.

Tris, Quads, and *n*-Gons

Given that a polygon is a closed figure, the minimum number of sides with which a polygon can be made is three. As we know, a three-sided polygon is a triangle, a polygon with the least number of sides. In CG modeling, the models are typically built using triangles or quadrilaterals, which are referred to as *tris* or *quads*, respectively. Typically, 3D graphics engines employ triangles during the rendering process (rendering is the process of creating a 2D image from a 3D model). Rendering is the process by which an image is created from a model. Why do graphics engines prefer triangles? For the simple fact that a triangle is made of three vertices and these are always *planar* or *co-planar* (lying on the same plane).

Triangles are closed polygons, with three vertices that are located on the same plane. The planarity of polygons is another important aspect for consideration. When all vertices are on the same plane, it is considered to be planar. For any three points, we can always find a plane passing through them. This is the reason that a triangular face is always planar, since there is always a plane containing the three vertices of a triangle. However, a polygon may not only have three vertices, but it can also have four or more vertices. In the case of a polygon with four vertices, if one of the vertices is in the same plane as the other three vertices, then the polygon is considered nonplanar. Quads refer to polygons with four vertices, and polygons with more than four vertices are known as *n*-gons. In terms of rendering, planar polygons (triangles) are typically preferred as they produce better results.

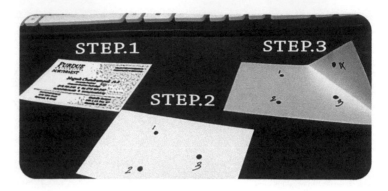

FIG 2.15 Planarity.

You can try this yourself. Take a business card (or any blank card), and place it on the table (Step 1). Turn over to the blank side, and mark three points (Step 2). Now these three points are planar as they all are on the same plane (points 1, 2, and 3). Now bend the card near one edge (Step 3), and mark a new point. The four points are not planar as one of them (4) is on a different plane (Figure 2.15).

Thus, now you know that a triangle can always be a planar object, as for each triangle there is always a single plane passing through the three vertices. In other words, a triangle can never be nonplanar. Other polygons may or may not be planar. Instead of points 1,2,3 in Figure 2.15, if you were to consider 2,3,4 you can still find a single plane that passes through them. You can fold the paper in such a way to have points 2,3, and 4 on the same plane.

Polygonal models are quite common in the game industry as well as the movie industry. A polygon with more than four sides is called an *n-gon* in CG. *n*-gons are normally not preferred for graphics work as they are easy to use for building models, and from a computational perspective, they are complex to store and manipulate.

Mesh

The geometric entities that we saw earlier including vertices, edges, and faces form the constituents of what is known as a *mesh*, which in turn is used to approximate a 3D surface. A mesh used in CG is not very different from the wire meshes with small openings that we have seen in our day-to-day life. A mesh is a collection of polygons that are connected together, which is how a polyhedron is defined in 3D geometry (Figure 2.16).

Convex and Concave Polygons

In order to be used for modeling 3D objects and surfaces, polygons must satisfy the convexity property. Conventionally, meshes employ polygons that are convex and tend to avoid non-convex polygons because non-convex polygons may not always render properly. A simple way to determine if a polygon is convex is to check the internal angles. If all the internal angles are less than 180 degrees, then the polygon is known as a convex polygon.

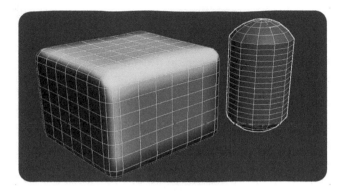

FIG 2.16 Meshes.

In Figure 2.17, you can see non-convex polygons on the right-hand side, wherein all the angles more than 180 degrees have been indicated. When a shape is convex, as can be seen from Figure 2.17, a line segment connecting any two points inside the shape will never go out of the shape, while there are line segments that go out of the actual polygon even when connecting points within the non-convex polygon. This also applies to diagonals, which are lines connecting two nonadjacent vertices of a polygon. Also, in a convex polygon, basically any line that is drawn across the polygon will intersect the polygon boundary only two times, unless it is tangential to an edge or a corner (Figure 2.17).

Another easy way to distinguish between convex and non-convex (concave) polygons is to extend the sides or the line segments of the polygon. If the extended line segments intersect one of the actual sides of the polygon, then it is a non-convex polygon. In a convex polygon, the extended line segments will not cut across any of the sides of the polygon.

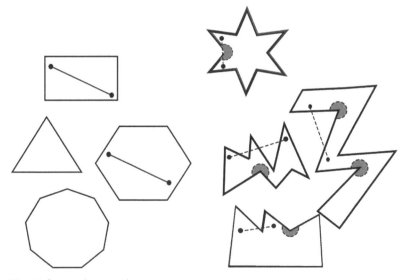

FIG 2.17 Convex and concave polygons.

Two important characteristics of a mesh are connectivity and geometry. Mesh connectivity is also referred to as topology. Connectivity defines the spatial relationship among the mesh components (edges, vertices, etc.) and that of the edges and faces between the mesh vertices. The mesh geometry indicates the positional values of the vertices. Using these vertices, how the connections are made determines the topology. So, it is possible that using the same geometry (set of vertices), different topological representations can be made. As we saw in the earlier discussions, polygons are used to make meshes, and these can be closed polygon meshes or open polygon meshes. As you can imagine, meshes obviously have directions, similar to the axes we saw earlier in the chapter. In a closed mesh, in a specific direction, the starting and the ending edges intersect and thus there will be no unshared edges.

In a closed mesh, such as a mesh representing a box object, the edges are generally shared by faces. On the other hand, in an open mesh, the starting and ending edges do not intersect. In open meshes, there will be some edges that are not shared among faces. The number of mesh elements (points, lines, polygons) per unit area of a mesh is referred to as *mesh density*. When representing intricate, curved surfaces, higher mesh density creates more accurate results; however, greater number of polygons also increases the rendering time.

Normal Vector

Modeling software need to determine the orientation of a polygon's face to estimate how the surface will appear or will be viewed by the user. This is an important consideration since polygons are made visible from the front only. Remember that each polygon has two sides – front and back. So, how do the modeling platforms determine the front and back of a polygon. If polygons are used to construct 3D objects, then how do the rendering engines determine which the inward-facing polygon is and which is the outward-facing polygon? For instance, if the sphere model above is used to represent a soccer ball and you are viewing it from outside (which is most commonly the case), you are seeing the polygons facing outward. However, there are also polygons that face towards the center of the sphere. This is referred to in Chapter 4 in terms of internal and external navigation. If an object is being modeled to be viewed from both inside and outside, then the polygons on either side should be made visible (or rendered). However, at times, some models may be required to be viewed only from outside or inside. This is done using the concept of a normal. A normal is a hypothetical line, which is at right angles (perpendicular) to the surface of a polygon (Figure 2.18). So, when a polygonal mesh is used to approximate (represent) an organic or curved surface, in addition to the information about the points, lines, and polygons (constituting the mesh), information about the normal vectors is also stored in the modeling database. This information is important for accurately calculating aspects such as scene illumination and shading, which are in turn based on how the light rays are reflected, refracted, absorbed, and/or transmitted within the 3D scene.

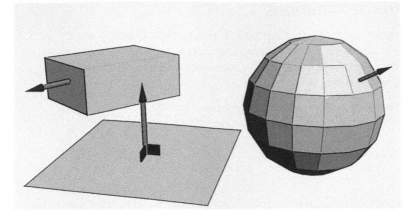

FIG 2.18 Normal vector.

Typically, vertices and edges in polygonal meshes that are common to more than one face (polygon) are known as shared vertices or shared edges. However, several software allow enabling or disabling double-sided display to reduce the number of polygons. For instance, we know that a box is made of six polygons – top, bottom, left, right, front, and back. Each polygon also has two sides – front and back. So, actually there are 12 polygons to be considered. However, when the box is viewed from the outside, then only the front of the polygons needs to be displayed (Figure 2.19).

The structure or the order in which the vertices are organized around a polygon helps estimate the direction the polygon faces. In other words, which side of a polygon is the front and which side is the back is determined by the order of arrangement of the vertices. Generally, a face is considered to be downward facing if the vertices are arranged in a clockwise direction. Likewise, a face is considered to be facing upward if the vertices are arranged in an anticlockwise direction. However, different modeling platforms may employ different conventions. Normal vectors are also important during the shading and lighting stages. The direction of the normal determines light behavior (reflection, refraction, etc.) by the surface.

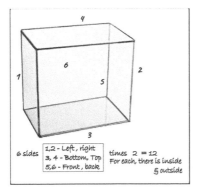

FIG 2.19 Inside and outside faces of objects.

Transformations

Transforming objects within a 3D CG scene refers to moving objects or groups of objects and altering their shapes, proportions, and sizes. These operations are referred to as geometric transformations or simply transformations.

Three broad categories of transformations include:

- Translation
- Rotation
- Scaling

Translation refers to moving an object from one position to another, either in 2D or in 3D. Figure 2.20 shows a box primitive object that has been moved (translated) within the 3D coordinate system.

- When done in 2D, this involves moving the object along either the x-axis, the y-axis, or both. In 3D, this involves any combination of x-axis, y-axis, and z-axis. For instance, if the translation occurs only on the xy plane, there is no change in the z value. Rotation refers to orienting (moving) an object about an axis and center. Scaling refers to modifying the size and proportion of an object in a 3D scene. Figures 2.20, 2.21, and 2.22 illustrate the operations of translation, rotation, and scaling, respectively. When transforming objects within digital modeling environments, numerical values need to be used in the software program to specify coordinates and angles.

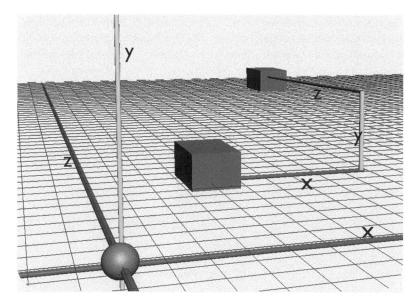

FIG 2.20 Translation.

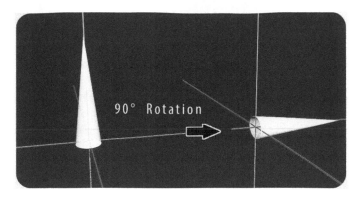

FIG 2.21 Rotation.

FIG 2.22 Scaling.

Figure 2.21 shows a conical object that has been rotated 90 degrees about the z-axis. Based on whether the direction of rotation is clockwise or counterclockwise, a sign is assigned. Commonly, a ccw (counterclockwise or anticlockwise) rotation is considered positive, while a clockwise rotation is denoted by a negative value. Program codes can use either radians or degrees to specify rotational values.

$$\pi \text{ radians} = 180°$$

For instance, in VRML (Virtual Reality Modeling Language), the code "rotation 0 1 0 1.57" produces a clockwise rotation of 90 about the y-axis. To rotate about the x-axis, 0 1 0 must be changed to 1 0 0, and similarly 0 0 1 indicates rotation about the z-axis. (1.57 refers to the number of radians through which rotation is done.)

Another transformational operation is known as scaling, which means to increase/decrease the dimensions of an object proportionally. In other words, scaling refers to enlarging or reducing the size of an object. Let us say that an unscaled object's size is represented using the default value 1. If the size of this object needs to be doubled, then the object is said to have been scaled by two. Figure 2.22 shows an unscaled object on the left most side. The object in the center has been scaled proportionately (scaled 1.5 times along each axis). This is known as uniform scaling. The rightmost object has been scaled down (from 100% to 60%) along the x-axis, but the height has been increased twice that of the original object, and the third dimension has not been changed. This is an example of nonuniform scaling wherein the proportions of axes have not been maintained. Scaling can be employed when you have already built a model of an object and need to use an enlarged or reduced version of the same object at another instance.

Scaling can be classified into two types:

1. Uniform scaling
2. Nonuniform scaling

Scaling is said to be uniform if the amount of scaling is equal along all three axes. In uniform scaling, an object is scaled equally along x-, y-, and z-axes. If the size of an object before scaling is represented x units along each axis, then after uniformly scaling it twice, the size of the object along each axis will be 2x units. However, if the same objects are scaled two times along the x- and y-axes and three times along the z-axis, then it is known as nonuniform scaling.

Global and Local Transformations

In order to understand global and local transformations, we need to understand world and local coordinate systems. A world coordinate system refers to the coordinate system of the whole environment or scene you are modeling. In other words, the global coordinate system can be thought of as a method of absolute referencing. The local coordinate system refers to the local reference framework that applies to a restricted or smaller region. In other words, the reference frame applies to a local region. These local reference systems are especially employed by modelers for modeling convenience.

An absolute value refers to the precise location (of an object). A relative value refers to the location of something with respect to another position or location. For instance, the following sentence defines the location of one place relative to another.

Milwaukee is about 92 miles north of Chicago.

Here, we are defining Milwaukee's location with respect to or in relationship to Chicago. However, if you define the position with respect to latitude and longitude as 43° 2′ 20″ N/87° 54′ 23″ W (Figure 2.23), then you are using the absolute values and referring to an exact point in space.

FIG 2.23 Absolute value.

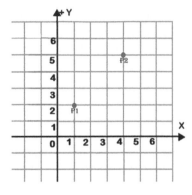

FIG 2.24 Relative value.

To understand how relative values work, consider these two points (P1 and P2). Let P1 be denoted by (1, 2) (this means that P1 is located 3 units from the origin along the x-axis and 4 units from the origin along the y-axis). Let us say that P2 is denoted relative to P1 (Figure 2.24). So, if the relative value of P2 with respect to P1 is (3, 3), that means that the absolute value of P2 is (4, 5).

Depending on the reference system to which transformations are applied, they are classified as either global or local. When you are performing a global transformation, you are moving objects about the scene's center (center of the world/global coordinate system). Any translation or rotation you perform when doing a global transformation is done with respect to the scene's reference system. However, when you are performing a local transformation on an object, the transformation is done with respect to the object itself. Just for the purpose of understanding, let us consider an analogy of one day and one year. One day is the Earth's rotation about itself on its axis (local transformation), and the planet's rotation around the Sun (assuming that to be the center of the environment) is an example of global transformation.

Closely related to global and local transformations is the notion of object and world spaces. The coordinate systems which are used to create the digital 3D worlds are also referred to as *spaces*. Object space refers to the coordinate system from a specific object's viewpoint, and it is local to the specific object. There are many software applications that use the object's pivot point as the origin of its object space. So, when you select and rotate an object in object space, it would rotate about its own default center or pivot point. After their creation, the objects can be moved or rotated with respect to the coordinate space of the entire scene or environment that is known as the world space. One of the important purposes of world space is to provide a reference to establish spatial relationships among the different objects within the scene.

Euclidean and Projective Geometry

Euclidean geometry, also popularly known as high-school geometry, deals with the flat space. Euclidean geometry, also referred to as traditional or conventional geometry, studies objects with dimensions such as length and breadth and polygons with sides that intersect at angles. Here, we learn that if a line stands upright on another line, then it is perpendicular, and if two lines are parallel, then they never intersect (Figure 2.25).

A point represented by (x, y) in Euclidean geometry (flat space or geometry of plane figures) is represented as $(x, y, 1)$ in projective geometry. Projective geometry is concerned with how something seems or appears, while Euclidean geometry is all about what things actually are. The study of graphics, modeling, animation, and other related disciplines requires at least a basic understanding of the relationship between Euclidean and projective geometries. The computational algorithms employed to render 3D models involve a notion of projective geometry that is based on the notion that infinity can be represented as we saw earlier in this section. While according to Euclidean geometry, two parallel lines never intersect, according to projective geometry, two lines always intersect.

A point in 3D in projective geometry is denoted as (x, y, z, w). Graphics modeling environments control transformations using what are known as transformation matrices.

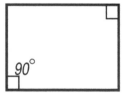

What it is actually?

Euclidean

How it seems?

Projective

FIG 2.25 Euclidean geometry and projective geometry.

When represented as a *matrix*, a rectangular array of numbers that are organized in rows and columns, this is shown as a column:

$$X$$
$$Y$$
$$Z$$
$$W$$

Let us say that the point P (X, Y, Z, W) is to be transformed. Point P is to be translated by a distance T (T_x, T_y, T_z, T_w). So, the point new position (transformed position) can be obtained as follows:

$$X' = X + T_x$$
$$Y' = Y + T_y$$
$$Z' = Z + T_z$$
$$W' = W + T_w$$

This is represented as follows in matrix transformation:

$$\begin{bmatrix} X' \\ Y' \\ Z' \\ W' \end{bmatrix} = \begin{bmatrix} 1 & 0 & 0 & T_x \\ 0 & 1 & 0 & T_y \\ 0 & 0 & 1 & T_z \\ 0 & 0 & 0 & 1 \end{bmatrix} \begin{bmatrix} X \\ Y \\ Z \\ W \end{bmatrix}$$

Geometry inherently involves studying the relationships including angles among the fundamental entities mentioned above. This will be discussed in detail subsequently under trigonometry. Geometry has two broad classifications, namely, plane geometry (Figure 2.26).

Plane geometry deals with flat shapes such as circles, squares, and triangles. In other words, flat geometry deals up to a maximum of two *dimensions*. Point or vertex represents only a position and has no dimensions. A line, connecting points, is an example of 1D (one-dimensional) object. A plane (flat surface) that can be made from lines is an example of 2D object. Solid geometry involves 3D objects such as the ones we come across most frequently in our day-to-day

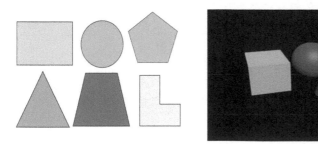

FIG 2.26 Plane geometry and solid geometry.

lives (Figure 2.26). The objects we come across daily such as pizza, ice cubes, eggs, and cookies are all examples of 3D objects.

Polyhedron

A polyhedron is a geometric entity that is made of plane faces, as is seen from the meaning of the word *hedron* (face). For instance, a tetrahedron is a solid composed of four triangular faces. In Figure 2.27, if you consider any set of three points (ABC, BCD, ACD, DAB), they are planar. But, if all four points are considered, then they are nonplanar, as they do not lie on the same plane.

Typically, Euler's formula is used to capture the relationship between the number of vertices, edges, and faces of a *polyhedron*.

$$\text{Num}_{\text{Vertices}} - \text{Num}_{\text{Edges}} + \text{Num}_{\text{Faces}} = 2$$

Consider Euler's formula above in the context of a tetrahedron.

For a tetrahedron,

Number of vertices $= 4$
Number of edges $= 6$
Number of faces $= 4$
$\text{Num}_{\text{Vertices}} - \text{Num}_{\text{Edges}} + \text{Num}_{\text{Faces}} = 2$
$4 - 6 + 4 = 2$

There are a whole lot of polyhedral shapes that are available (Figure 2.27).

The ability to create a variety of polyhedrons and modify them appropriately to create the model (character or background scenery) is very handy in modeling. Polyhedral 3D models are commonly used in Computer-Aided Design and Computer-Aided Manufacturing (CAD/CAM) applications. The 3D polyhedrons are normally made from an interconnected mesh of polygons, whose information is stored in the form of a list, table, or other database structures.

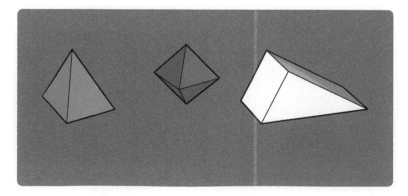

FIG 2.27 Planar and nonplanar points

In a Nutshell

This chapter covered the fundamental aspects of modeling and the basic aspects of creating a model. The chapter provided a detailed description of the uses on models in multifarious disciplines and their diverse applications. There are numerous other applications where models can be put to effective use including scientific visualization, simulation, training, and medicine. The chapter emphasized the need to have a strong grasp of the foundational theoretical elements behind the software tools of modeling. After reading this chapter, you must understand that tools may vary, but the principles are the same. The chapter emphasized the need to know fundamental aspects of geometry, trigonometry, transformations, and projections. The chapter also discussed about modeling categories and approaches to modeling. The various basic skill sets such as spatial ability, mathematical skills, geometry, artistic skills, and digital skills were outlined. The chapter highlighted some of the key categories and subcategories where modeling has been and is being used. Modeling enables envisioning the completed outcome/product (the present construction project) beforehand. When the planners and designers view the finished building instead of a proposed layout, it facilitates nondestructive testing.

In this chapter, we discussed about coordinates and coordinate systems, which serve as a reference for building the 3D models and help position and orient the models with respect to each other. Another important set of data that are important for 3D modeling are the attributes that describe the objects, which are also known as parameters. These parameters are used in a category of modeling known as parametric modeling. A principal characteristic of parametric modeling is that the parameters (attributes) describing the 3D object are spontaneously interconnected among each other. Hence, with parametric modeling, the 3D modeler has the option to modify one parameter (for instance, length) in order to adjust the other related parameters (width and depth) get adjusted automatically. Different software platforms exploit this parametric modeling in different ways and provide multiple options to control the final 3D object.

This chapter covered the basics of 3D modeling such as building your 3D objects and transforming them. The chapter discussed coordinate systems in detail and covered the dimensionality of objects. Subsequently, the chapter covered the basic building blocks such as points, lines, and polygons. The following are some important takeaways from this chapter:

- A coordinate or coordinates is/are the numerical representation(s) of the location or position of an object.
- The origin is typically at the center of the reference coordinate system. However, the origin need not necessarily be at the center of the modeling space.
- Different conventions are used by programming language and modeling platforms that are available and used for modeling 3D objects and scenes.
- Graphics modeling environments control transformations using what are known as transformation matrices.

- The basic building blocks used in modeling are points, lines, and polygons.
- In CG modeling, the models are typically built using triangles or quadrilaterals, which are referred to as *tris* or *quads*, respectively.
- Triangles are closed polygons, with three vertices that are located on the same plane. This is the reason that triangles are used by 3D engines for rendering.
- The number of polygons in your model or your whole scene is an important consideration when it comes to rendering your scene.

Chapter 2 Quiz

PART I

True/False (Circle the Correct Choice)

1. In Quadrant III, both x and y values are positive.
True False

2. The Cartesian coordinate system is the only way to represent locations in space.
True False

3. In the Cartesian system, a point's location is specified on a plane using numerical values, x and y coordinates, corresponding to the horizontal x-axis and the vertical y-axis.
True False

4. In the right-handed system, the middle finger showing the z-axis will be pointing towards you.
True False

5. In the Cartesian coordinate system, a point is represented as a function of angle and distance.
True False

6. In 3D graphics, a point cannot be rendered.
True False

7. Different conventions are used by programming language and modeling platforms that are available and used for modeling 3D objects and scenes.
True False

8. A rectangle or a triangle is an example of solid geometry.
True False

9. Triangles are closed polygons, with three vertices that are located on the same plane.
True False

10. A view is a collection of polygons that are connected together, which is how a polyhedron is defined in 3D geometry.
True False

11. Polygons such as squares and rectangles are two-dimensional.
True False

12. Euclidean geometry is concerned with how something seems or appears.
True False

13. Euclidean geometry is about what things are actually.
True False

14. According to Euclidean geometry, two parallel lines never intersect.
True False

15. World space refers to the coordinate system that is local to the object or that applies to that object.
True False

16. Any translation or rotation you perform when doing a global transformation is done with respect to the scene's reference system.
True False

17. If an object is scaled two times along the x-axis, three times along the y-axis, and four times along the z-axis, the transformation is known as uniform scaling.
True False

18. Ordered pair refers to two numbers (x, y) for representing the location of a point with respect to a reference point (origin).
True False

19. The number of polygons in your model or your whole scene is an important consideration when it comes to rendering your scene.
True False

20. Geometrically, a straight line can be considered as a point traveling in a constant direction.
True False

PART II

Multiple Choice Questions (Choose the Most Appropriate Answer)

1. _____ is composed of positive values.
   a. Quadrant I
   b. Quadrant II
   c. Quadrant III
   d. Quadrant IV
   e. None of the above

2. What is the area of a rectangle in a Cartesian system with the following vertices: (3, 2), (–3, 2), (–3, –2), (–3, 2)?
   a.   12 sq. units
   b.   15 sq. units
   c.   24 sq. units
   d.   48 sq. units
   e.   None of the above

3. The reference point within a coordinate system is known as _____.
   a.   Point
   b.   Vertex
   c.   Dot
   d.   Origin
   e.   None of the above

4. A point has _____ dimensions.
   a.   One
   b.   Two
   c.   Three
   d.   Zero
   e.   None of the above

5. A line is _____ -dimensional and can be defined by two points.
   a.   One
   b.   Two
   c.   Three
   d.   Zero
   e.   None of the above

6. A _____ line represents the shortest distance between two points.
   a.   Curved
   b.   Straight
   c.   Poly
   d.   Mini
   e.   None of the above

7. _____ is the process of creating an image from a model.
   a.   Modeling
   b.   Compositioning
   c.   Rendering
   d.   Culling
   e.   None of the above

8. In the polar coordinate system, a point is represented as a function of
   _____ .
   a. Position
   b. Angle
   c. Distance
   d. Location
   e. Both b and c above

9. _____ is the trigonometric function corresponding to the ratio of
   the opposite side to the hypotenuse?
   a. Alpha
   b. Sin
   c. Cos
   d. Tan
   e. None of the above

10. _____ is the trigonometric function corresponding to the ratio of
    the adjacent side to the hypotenuse?
    a. Alpha
    b. Sin
    c. Cos
    d. Tan
    e. None of the above

11. In the polar coordinate system, which of the following is referred to as the
    radial coordinate?
    a. Position
    b. Angle
    c. Distance
    d. Location
    e. Both b and c above

12. Real-world objects such as cups, pens, and tables are _____-dimensional.
    a. One
    b. Two
    c. Three
    d. Zero
    e. None of the above

13. A point within a coordinate system is also known as _____ .
    a. Point
    b. Vertex
    c. Dot
    d. Line
    e. None of the above

14. An edge is also represented as _____ .
    a. Point
    b. Vertex
    c. Dot
    d. Line
    e. None of the above

15. _____ geometry deals with how something seems or appears.
    a. Euclidean
    b. Solid
    c. Plane
    d. Projective
    e. None of the above

16. _____ geometry is known as traditional geometry.
    a. Euclidean
    b. Solid
    c. Plane
    d. Projective
    e. None of the above

17. Moving an object from one position to another is known as _____.
    a. Translation
    b. Rotation
    c. Scaling
    d. Rendering
    e. None of the above

18. _____ refers to modifying the size and proportion of an object in a 3D scene.
    a. Translation
    b. Rotation
    c. Scaling
    d. Rendering
    e. None of the above

19. _____ refers to orienting (moving) an object about an axis and center.
    a. Translation
    b. Rotation
    c. Scaling
    d. Rendering
    e. None of the above

20. π radians = how many degrees?
    a. 90
    b. 180
    c. 270
    d. 360
    e. None of the above

CHAPTER 3: Ideation, Visual Expression, and Elements of Art

Above and beyond the abundance of electronic marvels, the human vision and imagination remains the most important element and that its nurture should not be replaced by excessive reliance on devices.

– Erwin Hauer

Of all of our inventions for mass communication, pictures still speak the most universally understood language.

– Walt Disney

CHAPTER LEARNING OBJECTIVES

After carefully studying this chapter, you will be able to answer the following:

- What is ideation?
- What is the role of "purpose"?
- What are the important steps in ideation?
- Where is storyboarding used?

DOI: 10.1201/9780429186349-3

- What is the role of mind maps in ideation?
- What are lines, shapes, and forms?
- What are value and space?
- How to use depth cues to create the illusion of space?
- What are convergence, overlap, atmospheric perspective, and foreshortening?
- What are the relevant principles of design?
- How can you observe and learn from "Mother Nature"?

Animation and 3D modeling are interdisciplinary areas symbolizing the union of art, science, mathematics, and technology, among many others. As modeling and animation are visual art forms, they are inherently related to many basic aspects of design, drawing, color, layout, and composition. While learning modeling and animation, it is important to develop an understanding and appreciation for visual ideation and the underlying communication process. Be it an image or an animation, we are essentially dealing with pictures (static). In case of a photograph or a picture, it is a single image, while it is a sequence of images in an animation.

While, undoubtedly, digital tools and technology have simplified complex tasks, creativity and originality take precedence in modeling and animation. Architectural marvels such as the Eiffel Tower, Egyptian pyramids, and Taj Mahal were constructed when the digital computer modeling software were still not invented. William Shakespeare, Charles Dickens, Lewis Carroll, and Victor Hugo produced works without the support of any digital tools, including the plethora of text editing software that are available today. These authors and architects had their own creativity, which is what has rendered their works timeless and remarkable. Even today, we have brilliant literary works and architectural splendors that are being accomplished by creative people. However, the essence of the work is based on the creativity of the people involved and the digital tools are a means to shape this creativity. Originality and creativity form the basis of good craftsmanship, just as they were centuries earlier.

Today, we are using digital tools, and hence, we are "digital craftsmen." Still our digital craftsmanship is founded upon originality and creativity. As Michelangelo aptly said, *"A man paints with his brains and not with his hands"*. Similarly, be it your hands or be it digital tools, be it a clay pot or a 3D model, have NO doubt that you are ultimately creating it with your brain.

In other words, the digital tools and software are facilitators. Any architect and civil engineer must know the fundamentals of building construction and architecture. An author must know the rules of the language. A musician must be knowledgeable in basic elements such as timbre, beat, tempo, pitch, melody, and harmony. Similarly, if you want to succeed as a modeler or an animator, you MUST know the fundamentals of modeling and animation. Knowing to use a modeling software tool is not the same as having a strong grasp of the foundational elements of modeling. Even though software tools and the vendors of such software may change over time, the basic concepts involving coordinate systems, transformations, curvature, polygonal modeling, and so on remain the same. Once your become knowledgeable and experienced in the fundamental aspects of modeling, switching between various modes of modeling will not be a problem at all.

What do the following have in common?

A cartoon character, a computer graphics (CG) model, an electric bulb, an armchair, a yoga mat, a shirt, a bicycle, an egg slicer, a pizza cutter, a selfie stick, a shaving razor, a battery charger, and a stress ball: There may be several commonalities that can possibly be identified among these items. But, one common aspect of all these items that is pertinent to this book and this chapter is that "all the above items" are based on an idea or ideas.

The word "idea" seems to have originated in Greece. Idea refers to a form or a pattern, which was derived from the root idein, which means "to see."

If tools and techniques were sufficient to build a house, state-of-the-art hardware tools can be bought instead of hiring architects and engineers to build multimillion dollar structures. But, ideas and the method of their execution are more important than the tools or equipment. Even with the very best hardware (tools) and materials, one cannot construct a bridge or a shopping complex. That is because, a clear "IDEA" and a clearer plan of execution are needed. At the heart of any creation is the idea.

Ideation

However, mere idea(s) will not suffice. This idea which originates as a small seed needs to be nurtured well enough to sprout and grow into a healthy plant before it can yield the fruit (the final product). An idea needs to be evaluated and refined through many rounds of iterations (among teams in case of larger projects) before it can be finalized for execution. Renowned sculptor Erwin Hauer stated, "It is an important token reminder for the younger generation and their tutors, that above and beyond the abundance of electronic marvels, the *human vision and imagination* remains the most important element and that its nurture should not be replaced by excessive reliance on devices." This is similar to the notion of tooling mentioned by Von Glitschka in his interview. This book has simplified the concepts and presented them in an appealing manner. Let us first look at the process of ideation before we further dwell into the refinement and implementation.

Truly, the sky is your limit when you are doing modeling and animation. In the real world, our elbows cannot make a 360 degrees rotation; in the real world, we do not walk on our heads; in the real world, animals do not type; but, with digital tools, you can create anything that you can think of and make what you create do whatever it is that you want it do. But, remember that you will not be doing something just because you can. You will be creating something because it has a "purpose."

Purpose (or) Function

Always remember the bottom line. You are telling a story. Do not make an animation for the sake of making it. Have a purpose. Your purpose and motivation should be the propelling force in shaping the decisions regarding your modeling and all related aspects such as effects, lighting, shadows, rendering, and composition. If you, the creator of the animation, do not have a purpose or a story that you want to communicate, then there is no way that your audience will relate to it.

Try to picture the cartoons or CG movies that you like the most, and ask yourself, *"what made them so appealing?"* The plot might involve the hero trying to rescue the princess from the monster or two kids trying to reunite a lost bear cub with its family. As a viewer, you want them to succeed in their quest and you root for that to happen. This is the key to any successful animation (be it a movie or a video game). It is about a quest or a mission or a search or a hunt or anything else that engages the audience. The story you are narrating (what you want to communicate) and the manner you narrate it (how) should drive all the choices starting with the ideation stage. *This will ensure that your final composition is united, and not untied.* We will delve into the details of composition in later chapters. Remember that "what" (the plot or the story) and "how" are both important. You can even transform seemingly mundane and normal daily occurrences into exciting high-octane sequences. The way you narrate can make or break the success of your animation.

Let us go back to the basic aspect, which is your idea about the story or the plot. Just as anything else worth accomplishing, ideas are the result of thought process. So, how come sometimes people get a brilliant idea suddenly. That is because of the preparation that has been going on for considerable time in the background. As Alexander Fleming said, "Chance favors the prepared mind", you must allocate time to explore and examine the various potential options available. The process of ideation helps in the resourceful thinking process to ultimately yield innovative and appealing ideas. There are no shortcuts to landing on that brilliant idea. You need to respect the "ideation" process.

The AHA Moment

The discovery of penicillin was a critical accomplishment in the field of medicine. During World War I, many soldiers died from sepsis (infection) brought about from the wounds. Time and again, antiseptics used to disinfect the wounds aggravated the injuries. Alexander Fleming was performing rigorous research in this area to find a remedy. When he returned from a holiday, he observed something unusual on a petri dish left in his laboratory; something that curbed bacterial growth. He had discovered penicillin. Alexander said, "When I woke up just after dawn on September 28, 1928, I certainly didn't plan to revolutionize all medicine by discovering the world's first antibiotic, or bacteria killer. But I suppose that was exactly what I did". Not everybody could have made that observation. Those who had not done the prior hard work might have dismissed what they saw as a contamination. But, what might have been an abomination or a curse appeared as a blessing in Alexander's eyes because his mind was "prepared." That is why he rightly quoted, "Chance favors the prepared mind". So, in order for you to get your "Aha" moment, you must prepare yourself.

Ideation is inherently tied to the storyboarding process. The process of the initial stages of modeling and character modeling, especially the conceptual stages, can be quite abstract, and idea generation can be quite challenging during such times. In this chapter, we will look at some techniques that can be used to effectively generate ideas that can be successfully transformed into 3D models that are not just well aligned with the plot but will contribute more to the plot's appeal and help engage the audience.

I5 Technique: The Five I's of Ideation

There are five essential pillars of ideation: imagination, innovation, iteration, inspection, and interpretation. As one of the key aspects of ideation is to promote exploration, it is important that you think in a diverging manner (Figure 3.1).

Imagination and innovation go hand in hand, especially during the ideation process. What authors and writers may call as the "fear of the blank page" can also be experienced when you initially do not know where or how to start. There are several simple tools and techniques that you can use as part of the ideation process to overcome the mental block. Unfortunately, you may be your worst enemy when you are trying to imagine and innovate,

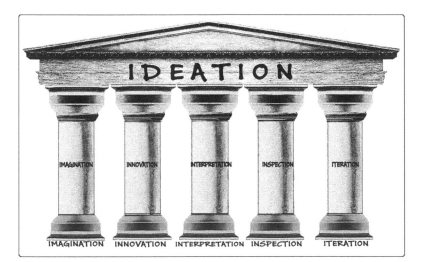

FIG 3.1 Ideation I5 technique.

and it happens more frequently than you may think. Tending to be overly self-critical and insecure can ruin your creativity. At least in the initial stages, you must truly go ahead and let the ideas flow freely. This is a critical step in turning those vague or amorphous thoughts and perceptions into something concrete. When trying to write down or draw things on a sheet of paper, you are literally transforming those things from "gray to black and white."

Dare to Imagine

During the stages of imagination and innovation, *do not perform any kind of judgment or evaluation*. Here the goal is to "proliferate" and generate as many ideas as possible without being prejudiced. Remember, *prejudice inhibits creativity* (Chandramouli, 2011) (Figure 3.2).

This is especially true in the initial stages of conceptualization and more the reason why you must respect the five I's explained here. If you think of some idea and are enamored with it so much that you directly take the plunge, you are running into a great risk because you have not actually explored other

FIG 3.2 Imagine.

options, which may be more optimal for your current project. Also, remember that your four great friends in this process are your eyes and ears, implying that you must truly learn to observe and listen. Sometimes, that brilliant idea is right in front of you, just like the petri dish in front of Alexander Fleming. You may fail to spot it because your eyes and ears are not trained to recognize them. *Keep your eyes and ears open*. There are no rules of thumb here. You can use some techniques we discuss here or any of your own. You can use post-it notes, a white sketch board, flash cards, photographs (Image?), or anything else that you can think of. Some of the most successful products or movie ideas actually originated as a doodle on a paper napkin. In many disciplines, especially the creative fields, *mind maps* are proven tools to generate ideas.

In animation and 3D modeling, you can indeed turn to nature for inspiration as Mother Nature is the best modeler and animator. The intricate shapes found in nature and the mind-boggling animations in the animal kingdom are indeed matchless and can serve as abundant sources of inspiration.

Mind maps are excellent tools for brainstorming that can be extremely fun to use. Mind maps can help you explore unexplored areas, recognize and categorize related areas, identify specific interests, and eventually narrow down. This kind of exercise provides more meaning and direction to the brainstorming process, and also eventually shows the way to unearth creative and original ideas. There are no hard-and-fast rules with mind maps. You can use whichever format (Figure 3.3 – text or graphic or both) that suits your need and more importantly with which you are comfortable.

Typically, with mind maps, you write down the primary challenge or subject matter in the center of the paper (Figure 3.3). Starting from the center, write ideas in a branching manner as shown. Try to add new branches (connections) from each thing that you write down. If you see that one of these new ideas is beginning to cluster, then use some kind of symbol (encircling or anything else) to show that a nucleus (or hub) is getting formed. Keep on doing this

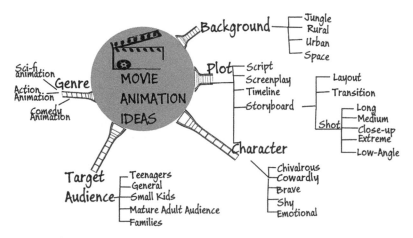

FIG 3.3 Mind mapping.

till the white board or the white page is almost full with writing. By now, you should have a whole lot of ideas to open up your imagination and to facilitate innovation. If you still think there is more, see if you can reconfigure the ideas, look again at the nuclei, and start the process again. Finally, you can see that at the end of the "Imagination and Innovation." After you feel satisfied with this brainstorming, you can select the ones you want to proceed with further. Essentially at this point, you may be doing selection by elimination, wherein you have to discard many ideas and perform careful selection. Remember that during "Imagination and Innovation," you tend to go broad, before you go deep with interpretation and inspection.

Remember that the rule for ideation is *"there are no rules."* Initially, it is whatever that works for you. After you are done with the preliminary stages of imagination and innovation, you proceed to interpretation, which is the stage of clarification. With interpretation or clarification, you start refining your ideas, while taking a closer look at them to inspect them (inspection). You are digging deeper now. Finally, depending on how satisfied you are with the overall process, you can choose to iterate. The goal of iteration is to help you exploit the earlier processes and narrow down further if you feel there is a need.

Enemies of Ideation: Impulsiveness and Imitation

Impulsiveness

This is actually a tricky area. Earlier we saw that ideation helps generate potential ideas within a short period of time. However, you should be able to draw a line between accelerated and hotheaded. You want to be rapid but not reckless. While swiftly flushing out ideas can help, working too hurriedly can be damaging and disadvantageous. So, remember to respect the ideation process, and over time and with experience, you will be able to discern between being fast and being foolhardy.

Imitation

Beware of imitation. You must read, observe, and listen a lot to understand the earlier works done. But do not be a "copy-cat." It is good to be inspired, but do not be an imitator. You are unique, and you have your own strengths. Work on recognizing your own strengths and mold them effectively to create your own style. When you look at others' work, try to follow their thought process and understand the rationale behind their decisions to use or not use something. Think of your favorite animated movie and ask yourself why the director (or the modeler or animator) chose that particular character or environment for that scene? If it were you, how would you have handled that? What kind of character would you have created? What kind of background would you have created?

FIG 3.4 Ideation practices.

In trying to understand the rationale behind the choices made by other directors, modelers, and animators, you will better convey the various aspects of visual narration, flow, and engaging the audience with your style. This will help you better inspect your own model choice and animation choices and hence help you create your own style to better engage the audience (Figure 3.4).

Collaborative Ideation

You can resort to collaborative I5 process when two or more members of your team work on the brainstorming processes (imagination and innovation) and perform the interpretation and inspection (and iteration, if needed) in a collective manner involving all team members. Collaborative drawing can be done by a team with the members gathered around a table and doing mind maps or brainstorming in an absolutely unrestricted manner. Initially, this process may seem to be extremely disorganized or unstructured. However, when you use the I5 technique and for the two I's of imagination and innovation with interpretation and inspection, things will slowly start falling in place. The steps in the I5 technique will help channelize and filter the ideas. The final iteration step will help further narrow down, thereby reducing the abstraction and facilitating coordination that can ultimately result in unison and harmony.

For optimal results, the communication (visual expression) of your story should make a seamless transition from the ideation step.

Elements of Art: From a "Visual Expression" Perspective

A background knowledge of the "elements of art" could go a long way when you are trying to visually express your idea. It can be a book or even few volumes to cover the various elements of art themselves; however, we will take a brief look into the elements of art, especially from the perspective of visual composition for modeling and animation.

An understanding of the "elements of art" will help you better "compose" your work. Later, in the rendering and composition chapters, we will take a detailed look at the various aspects of composition.

When you are watching an animated CG movie or a regular movie, the director is NOT standing next to you telling where to pay attention to. Nobody moves our head pointing us to look at a specific thing in the movie. However, that is what clever directors do. By creating a compelling visual composition, the creators of various forms of art (photographs, paintings, movies, etc.) "direct" the audience to see exactly what they want to see in their work. To be able to create a work that can compel and engage the audience, you need to have a grasp of the various visual "elements of art" and also the "principles of art." The elements are more like the constituents, while the principles are similar to the actual way in which they (the constituent elements) are used. For example, consider four circular shapes (elements) and see how the way in which they are arranged can lead to different visual expressions (Figure 3.5).

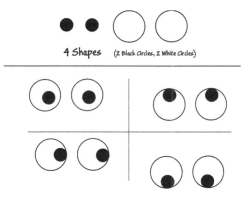

FIG 3.5 Elements and principles.

Typically, in modern times, most authors and works refer to the seven elements that we will discuss subsequently.

- Line
- Shape
- Form
- Value
- Texture
- Space
- Color

Effective communication and visual expression entail the astute use these elements of art. We will once again revisit several of these later in the chapter on composition. For now, let us take a quick and simple look at them so that you are well aware of them as you are working your way up the modeling and animation ladder.

Line

Earlier, we looked at the line as one of the fundamental geometric entities of modeling. In the artistic sense also, lines are the foundational elements of most drawing. We see lines all around us, even though not as lines exactly. The edges of buildings, horizon, river edges, and the outlines of various other objects also appear as lines in drawings and photographs. Lines are inherently related to various other elements of art and the principles of art. Lines can be used to depict distance, form (3D), shape (2D), depth, and are used to communicate a wide range of emotions as well.

While mechanical and man-made objects such as boxes and buildings typically have straight edges, most of the natural objects including our eyes, body organs, and leaves have curvilinear lines.

The written scripts of the world's languages and religious symbols are composed of straight and curved lines (Figure 3.6). Lines are extremely powerful in depicting emotions. We come across straight and curved lines frequently in our daily lives (Figure 3.7). All other features remaining the same, see how a horizontal line or a curved line affects the visual expression. Lines can be used to express motion or movements. Such drawings that can be done extemporaneously to indicate gestures are known as, of course, *gesture drawings*.

FIG 3.6 Straight and curved lines in languages and symbols.

FIG 3.7 Straight and curved lines.

Shape

A shape is a two-dimensional (2D) entity that represents a closed line or path. There are many different classifications of shapes. One important type of classification is *geometric* or *organic*. Polygons such as squares, rectangles, and circles represent geometric shapes. Geometric shapes are made of mathematically precise edges. Typically, shapes are flat and have length and width as their two dimensions. Natural or free-form shapes are considered organic shapes.

Shapes can also be classified as regular or irregular. Regular shapes are composed of sides that are equal in length, and in a regular polygon, the inside angles (on the interior of the sides) are all equal. On the other hand, irregular shapes are composed of unequal sides and angles (Figure 3.8).

Using simple shapes, you can actually draw any bigger or complex shape you want to draw. Using simple primitive shapes such as squares, circles, ellipses, and triangles, you can draw much bigger compound shapes. In other words, you can break down any shape into these primitives. The ability to be able to observe and disintegrate a bigger shape into smaller constituent shapes is an excellent skill both in 2D (shapes) and in 3D (forms). This is not only useful in ideation and visual expression but also in the actual execution and modeling steps (Figure 3.9).

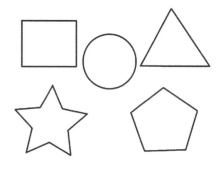
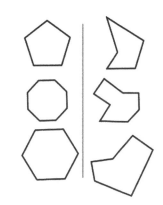

FIG 3.8 Simple 2D regular and irregular shapes.

FIG 3.9 Drawing complex shapes.

Form

Form denotes 3D objects and 3D composition. Form includes depth besides the length and width (Figure 3.10). Some prefer to think of a form as a 3D shape. We are surrounded by "forms" in the 3D real world we inhabit. As 3D modelers, you must have a good knowledge of the 3D form of objects, as you will be creating the stereoscopic depth perception in your renderings. Rendering in digital terminology refers to the creation of a 2D image from a 3D model (Figure 3.11).

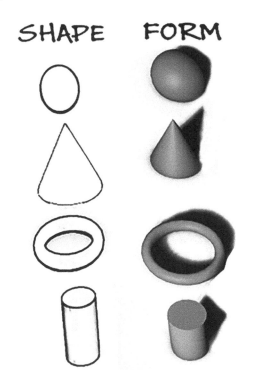

FIG 3.10 Shape and form.

FIG 3.11 3D designs.

By creating the perception of depth on a 2D canvas, artists depict even large-scale scenes with mountains and rivers with tremendous realism. A good grasp of the concept of geometric shapes and forms and the ability to observe and isolate constituent form elements (or shapes) in 3D objects (or 2D shapes) make the modeling (or drawing) process much easier and efficient. When we are talking about shapes, we are talking about areas. For 3D objects, volume refers to the space occupied by an object in the real world. Just as the medium and tools may differ and artists may employ oil painting or acrylic or watercolor to create this "illusion" of form on a flat 2D medium, in the process of 3D modeling, you are digital sculptors who use computers and digital tools to create the illusion of 3D scenes and objects.

The ability to deduce basic forms from complex real-world objects helps with modeling ideation. When you are creating forms in 3D modeling, you may be using various methods; for instance, a spline-based cross section may be used to create the basic form for an electronic appliance or a gadget you are trying to model. Your knowledge and skills of shapes and forms will contribute to your ability to brainstorm and perform the ideation process for innovative design solutions.

Value

Value refers to the lightness or darkness of an object or its surface. In the real world, typically, objects are seldom perfectly black or perfectly white, and artists use the degrees of variation in light and shade to create the illusion of depth. In digital terms, this darkness or lightness of a color is expressed through a value scale to describe the overall strength or intensity of a CG light. Your knowledge and experience with color values will help you to master the use of appropriate combinations in your digital creations including models and the final renderings. As you can see from this illustration (Figure 3.12), value ranges from black (shown at the bottom) to white. In real-world drawing/painting, artists mix white with colors to lighten the value and use black with colors to darken the value. In digital graphics and digital color models, proper use and adjustments of "value" can be used to define the spatial form (3D) of object(s).

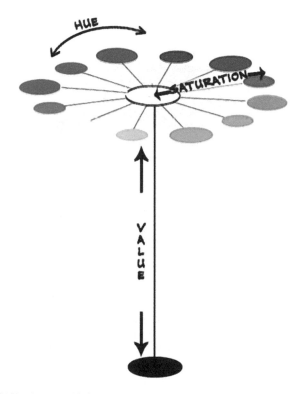

FIG 3.12 HSV (Hue, Saturation, Value).

Light also plays a crucial role in establishing the mood of a scene. The overall ambience and the visual charisma of your digital rendering are greatly influenced by the choice and intensity (value) of light. From the point of realism, as we will see in later chapters, there are two types of renderings known as photorealistic renderings (PR) and non-photorealistic renderings (NPR) (Figure 3.13).

PR, as their name suggests, are so real-looking that the audience are generally not able to distinguish between the rendering and reality. On the other hand, NPR are, once again as their name suggests, not exactly realistic. These are commonly used in cartoons and have a general style as seen in drawings, sketches, and paintings. Among other things, one important element that determines the degree of photorealism in a rendering is the appropriate use of illumination. Even though illumination might immediately make one think of lights only, illumination from the point of view of graphics renderings and CG lighting essentially involves both light and shadows. In Figure 3.14, you will see that the one above is an example of NPR and the one on the right is an example of PR. The PR illustrates proper use of light, values, and shadows which create the impression of photorealism. Hence, a good understanding of light and light values, and especially shadows, is important in graphics modeling and especially in order to be able to create PR. Furthermore, from the perspective of forms and shapes, you can see that the image in the upper part of Figure 3.13 shows shapes (and not forms), while in

FIG 3.13 Non-photorealistic rendering (above) and photorealistic rendering (below).

FIG 3.14 Non-photorealistic pencil/water color sketch (L) and photorealistic rendering (R).

the image in the lower part of Figure 3.13, the form is visible due to the use of lights and shadows that create the illusion of depth.

We will continue our discussion on light and how it influences the mood or ambience in Chapter 10 on Composition. As you can see from the above example, the proper use of light, highlight, shadows, etc. enhances the appeal and the overall quality of the digital rendering.

Space

The term space refers to the region or area above, below, around, and even within an object. Right now, as you are reading this book, you are in some kind of space – a library, your bedroom, a university classroom, or any other kind of space. Every space or place has its own characteristic features

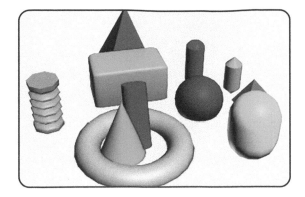

FIG 3.15 Object volumes.

that make it unique. Just as different light colors can be associated with different moods and emotions, spaces can also create and be associated with different emotions. Think of some of your favorite places and also, in general, some spaces that you have been to in your life. Some of these places can make you nostalgic, some may make you cheerful, you may think of some as scary, some as boring, and so on. On the other hand, when we are talking about the space inside objects, we are referring to the volume. For instance, when you are talking about a water bottle, a milk container, or a juice carton, you refer to its capacity, which is the volume that it can hold. Similarly, when you are creating 3D models in your modeling space, you are creating the spheres, boxes, cones, etc. within, say for example, the coordinate space.

Continuing in the context of our earlier discussion of shapes and forms, creating the illusion of space is important to create the illusion of form. This knowledge and understanding will help you to create the 3D illusion within your digitally created virtual environments (Figure 3.15) so that they are capable of simulating realistic spaces.

Illusion of Space: Depth Cues

In real-world drawings or paintings, different methods have been used to create the illusion of space. In sketches, paintings, and drawings, artists create an illusion of depth (3D), even though their work is on a 2D surface with no actual depth. Similarly, digital artists and modelers must intuitively understand the proper use of depth cues, also known as distance cues, to be able to simulate that illusion of space. Let us look at some of these depth cues below.

Depth Cue: Convergence

We see this quite frequently in the real world when edges of roads or sidewalks, which actually run parallel, seem to approach each other (converge) as they move away from us. Even though such lines are parallel, they appear to taper or merge as they recede from the point of observation (Figure 3.16).

FIG 3.16 Convergence.

Depth Cue: Overlap

Overlapping refers to the blocking of distant objects by those objects closer to us. In a 2D drawing or a 3D digital scene, when one object blocks or conceals another object in part, then the viewer gets the idea that partly hidden object must be farther (than the object that blocks) from the observer. Viewers tend to perceive the obstructed or blocked object as being afar or behind the object that blocks it. This allows the viewer to judge how the objects in your scene are situated with respect to each other and creates an excellent stereoscope of depth perception. For example, let us look at the two images below. In the real-world image on the left, we can clearly see that the light green-colored leaves (blocking the view behind) are closer than the dense vegetation (afar). Similarly, in the other figure with primitive objects, you can see that the sphere object is in front of cylinder because part of the cylinder is obscured by the sphere (Figure 3.17).

FIG 3.17 Overlap.

Depth Cue: Atmospheric Perspective

Atmospheric perspective is the result of distant objects taking on the colors of atmospheric haze. Atmospheric perspective is also referred to as aerial perspective. The colors of far-off objects merge or blend with and take on some of the atmosphere's colors. When creating your scenes, you can use varying effects (weak or strong or in between) to create different kinds of effects (Figure 3.18).

Depth Cue: Foreshortening

Foreshortening refers to the creation of depth by the use of shortened forms. When we see objects at a distance or from a specific angle, there is usually a distortion, and this effect can be applied to create the illusion of space and depth. Artists, when making a perspective drawing, suppose that the viewer is looking at the painting from a specific angle and a particular distance.

In day-to-day life, objects seem to be different from their original forms and shapes, when we look at them from different angles. A cube-shaped box object does not always seem to be made up of equal sides (Figure 3.19). The objects look quite different when seen from different points of view. Accordingly, artists scale their objects relative to that viewer (where they assume where the drawing is being viewed from) and draw accordingly to

FIG 3.18 Varying atmospheric perspectives.

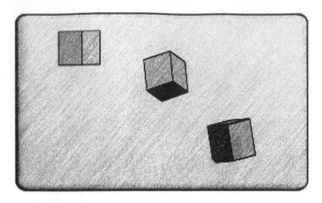

FIG 3.19 Varying points of view.

FIG 3.20 Foreshortening.

create that impression. Similarly, a circle can look like an ellipse or a rectangle like a trapezium. This distortion, foreshortening, is also shown in photos (Figure 3.20).

Texture

Texture refers to the quality of an object's surface, both tangibly and visually. The former aspect (tangible) indicates how things actually feel when you touch them or pick them up, and the latter (visual) refers to how things seem they feel. In other words, in the real world (3D), things have a specific perceptible feeling when they are touched. Rocks are among such natural

FIG 3.21 Textures.

things that exhibit a wide range of textures (Figure 3.21). The different types of textures such as igneous, sedimentary, and metamorphic rocks have many different types of textures such as coarse-grained, glassy, granular, fine-grained, and sandy.

Most objects that we come across in the real world have a wide range of textures ranging from chocolate-smooth to rock-hard with many different types in between (Figure 3.21). Creating such a range of complicated textures both digitally and in the physical world poses a big challenge to artists and digital craftsmen. A sketch artist or a painter tries to recreate or simulate the illusion of the real world in their creations and the objects therein. The illusion of texture created in artworks is highly dependent on the "value" (element of art we discussed earlier; Figure 3.22).

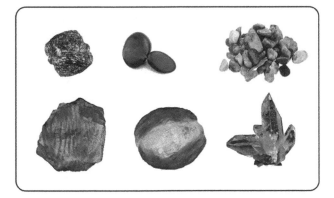

FIG 3.22 Rock textures.

Interview with an Industry Expert

Von is creative director of Glitschka Studios, a small boutique design firm located in the Pacific Northwest. His diverse range of illustrative designs have been used by some of the most respected brands in the world. He creatively collaborates with ad agencies, design firms, in-house corporate art departments, and small businesses to produce compelling visual narratives.

http://www.glitschkastudios.com

1. **Why and how are "analog tools and techniques" relevant in today's modern industry?**

   The creative process for a vast majority of creatives completely avoids drawing, even thumbnail sketching. Instead, their process immediately goes to digital, and they noodle away hours playing around with software trying to create something they haven't fully thought through. It's like an atomic scientist not knowing the absolutes of nuclear fission and immediately going to a glove box and experimenting. It might work, but it certainly isn't an efficient use of his/her time. Don't get me wrong I love working digitally, the flexibility of exploration alone is light years ahead of the analog past, but that being said we also face a new problem that never existed pre-digital and that is a concentrated focus on "tools" rather than "skills." Those two terms are often conflated now as if they mean the same thing.

   Drawing improves cognition, helps you think through ideas, isolates relationships, and stages visual narratives so that when you move to digital, it's less about pulldown menus and software and more about executing and craftsmanship of the ideas you've already figured out pre-digital. Thus, analog improves digital work flows.

   If you prefer to draw digitally, it still taps the same cognitive advantages of physical pen and paper. The problem isn't the tools. The problem is lack of drawing whether analog or what I'd call hybrid drawing digitally via a Wacom for example. Prior to the digital age, drawing was always taught, not because they expected everyone to become full-blown illustrators, but rather there was an industry consensus that drawing was a key part of ideation, development, and craftsmanship of design and art. Rarely does a creative program have any content specifically focused on drawing now. So the problem in my opinion is lack of drawing, and thus instead of fully vetting ideas in analog, a legion of creatives now entering the industry go immediately to digital and become obsessive Toolers or noodlers, whatever title you want to give them.

Tools may have become digital, but drawing is still the design's most important skill.

2. **In your works, you talk about "not being a Tooler." Who is a Tooler and can you explain more on this?**

The creative arts industry is saturated with individuals who admire creativity, dream of doing creative work, watch tutorials, read books endlessly about methods, and tend to think that at some point through osmosis of this type of content, they'll be able to create at the level they see others doing.

The common denominator of these individuals is that they grasp at any software tool, plugin, pulldown menu that can make the process easy for them without actually having to invest the real effort, struggle, skill, and time to truly create at that level. I call them Toolers, and Toolers do not like to draw. Drawing is the antithesis of Toolers. When it comes to design, there are some styles you simply cannot achieve without using drawing to create it. Drawing is the skill that could actually help them achieve their dream, that they unfortunately avoid like the plague. There is no shortcut to improving your drawing skills, you just have to start and stick with it, and over time, you improve and will discover your own style.

Toolers are lazy though, and unfortunately our industry from education to software companies releasing software caters to them. Adobe specifically dumbs down software so Toolers will latch on to it. Because in reality anyone can learn a tool, it takes dedication and time to develop drawing skills, and you don't improve vicariously, but you improve by simply doing it yourself.

Principles of Design

In the earlier sections, we took a very detailed look at the various elements of art. Principles of design explain how to use these elements of art. Color, which is also a very important element of art, is covered in detail in the chapter on lighting. Just as you can use different kinds of threads of varying colors and knit them in different ways to form different kinds of clothing, you can arrange the different elements (of art) to create different end results (Figure 3.23).

The most recognized principles of design include:

- Balance
- Contrast
- Emphasis
- Movement
- Pattern
- Rhythm
- Unity

The judicious use and combination of the principles of design to employ the elements of art can create a brilliant and appealing composition. We will cover the principles of design in Chapter 10 on Composition.

FIG 3.23 Design elements.

Lessons from Nature: Ideation and Visual Expression

Before concluding the chapter, let us take a brief look as to how you can learn lessons about ideation and visual expression from the finest teacher there is. Nature is the best designer, artist, modeler, and animator. You can get all the inspiration and motivation you need, when you are looking for ideas for animation and modeling, by observing nature. The solution for many of the modeling challenges and perfect shape or form for your plot is just in front of your eyes. You just need to look with intent (purpose). Nature presents us with diverse examples, which can provide us with ample inspiration to learn from and apply in our modeling as well as animation. Let us just take a quick look at few important categories we have discussed thus far.

Shapes in Nature

There are many different shapes of leaves such as linear, oblong, elliptical, oval, cordate, egg-shaped, and fan-shaped. Figure 3.24 shows the shapes and outlines of different types of leaves.

When you look at the above leaves and their shapes, what does that remind you of? You can see the word "fan-shaped" next to one of the leaves, which implies that it is in the shape of a fan. What do the other leaves look like? Is there a leaf that looks like a human organ to you? Which is that? Reniform leaf looks like a kidney (reniform means kidney-shaped). Observe other different leaf shapes in your backyard or in a park. Remember that many of the man-made inventions have been inspired by nature. Your ability to see shapes and forms in nature will reflect in the quality of your digital craft (Figure 3.25).

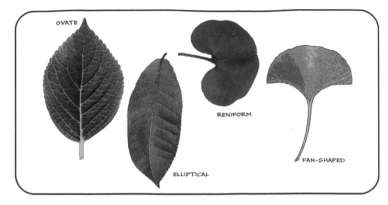

FIG 3.24 Different kinds of leaf shapes.

FIG 3.25 Complex shapes in nature.

Take a careful look at the animals in Figure 3.25 and when you look at their shapes, what does that remind you of? Revisit the Figure 3.9 and the Shape section earlier in this chapter, where complex shapes were created from simple shapes. How would you break these shapes into simpler shapes? Deconstruct these into simple shapes and then once again use the simple shapes to build the final animal shapes. Look at other commonly occurring objects around you and use the "break down to build up" approach to first disintegrate them into simpler shapes and then use the simple shapes to construct a bigger shape.

Look at how much mankind has learned from nature's designs and has been inspired by those to find the ingenious solutions (Figure 3.26).

An understanding of the "elements of art" will help you better "compose" your work. To be able to create a work that can compel and engage the audience, you need to have a grasp of the various visual "elements of art" and

FIG **3.26** Nature inspired inventions.

also the "principles of art." The elements are more like the constituents, while the principles are similar to the actual way in which they (the constituent elements) are used. For example, consider four circular shapes (elements) and see how the way in which they are arranged can lead to different visual expressions. Effective communication and visual expression entail the astute use of these elements of art.

We are surrounded by remarkable natural shapes and forms. Leaves, trees, landscapes, rivers, lakes, trails, mountains, and many other natural formations occur in a wide range of simple and complex shapes. We need to learn to observe these carefully and seek inspiration from these when trying to land on that perfect character or model for the animation plot. We can also include this kind of inspiration from nature to help during the "Imagination and Innovation" phase of the I5 technique we discussed earlier. Various aspects of animation and modeling including design, lighting, composition, and rigging are inherently interrelated to nature. As a matter of fact, natural things demonstrate intricate modeling and have plenty of texture on them. Natural objects are rich in detail that creating photorealistic-realistic 3D models of some natural objects is an extremely challenging task even for experienced modelers. Similarly, replicating or simulating natural movements is also a tremendously daunting task. Natural objects include varying levels of complex motions that happen with such rhythm, which may be so challenging to reproduce by artificial means.

Summary

Creativity is just connecting things. When you ask creative people how they did something, they feel a little guilty because they didn't really do it, they just saw something. It seemed obvious to them after a while.

– *Steve Jobs*

Animation and 3D modeling are interdisciplinary areas symbolizing the union of art, science, mathematics, and technology, among many others. As modeling and animation are visual art forms, they are inherently related to many basic aspects of design, drawing, color, layout, and composition. While, undoubtedly, digital tools and technology have simplified complex tasks, creativity and originality take precedence in modeling and animation. The process of ideation helps in the resourceful thinking process to ultimately yield innovative and appealing ideas. The initial stages of modeling and character modeling, especially the conceptual stages, can be quite abstract, and idea generation can be quite challenging during such times. In this chapter, we saw at some techniques that can be used to effectively generate ideas that can be successfully transformed into 3D models that are not just well aligned with the plot but will also contribute more to the plot's appeal and help engage the audience. Imagination, innovation, iteration, inspection, and interpretation are the five essential pillars of ideation. As one of the key aspects of ideation is to promote exploration, it is important that you think in a diverging manner. Imagination and innovation go hand in hand, especially during the ideation process. What authors and writers may call as the "fear of the blank page" can also be experienced when you initially do not know where or how to start. Mind maps are excellent tools for brainstorming that can be extremely fun to use. Mind maps can help you explore unexplored areas, recognize and categorize related areas, identify specific interests, and eventually narrow down. Iteration helps you exploit the earlier processes and narrow down further if you feel there is a need.

You can resort to collaborative I5 process wherein two or more members of your team work on the brainstorming processes (imagination and innovation) and perform interpretation and inspection (and iteration, if needed) in a collective manner involving all team members.

Chapter 3 Quiz

PART I

True/False (Circle the Correct Choice)

1. Balance, contrast, emphasis, etc. are examples of principles of design.
True False

2. Natural objects typically are characterized by curvilinear lines.
True False

3. Natural or free-form shapes are considered organic shapes.
True False

4. Shape denotes 3D objects and 3D composition.
True False

5. Value refers to the lightness or darkness of an object or its surface.
True False

6. Non-photorealistic renderings are so real-looking that the audience are generally not able to distinguish between the rendering and reality.
True False

7. Convergence is the depth cue that refers to the blocking of distant objects by those objects closer to us.
True False

8. Atmospheric perspective is the result of distant objects taking on the colors of atmospheric haze.
True False

9. In day-to-day life, objects seem to be different from their original forms and shapes, when we look at them from different angles.
True False

10. To be able to create a work that can compel and engage the audience, you need to have a grasp of the various visual "elements of art" and also the "principles of art."
True False

11. Mind maps can help you explore unexplored areas, recognize and categorize related areas, identify specific interests, and eventually narrow down.
True False

12. Remember that the rule for ideation is "there are no rules."
True False

13. The illusion of texture created in artworks is highly dependent on the "value."
True False

14. Typically, shapes are flat and have length and width as their two dimensions.
True False

15. It is good to be inspired but not to imitate.
True False

16. While, undoubtedly, digital tools and technology have simplified complex tasks, creativity and originality take precedence in modeling and animation.
True False

17. The overall ambience and the visual charisma of your digital rendering are greatly influenced by the choice and intensity (value) of light.
True False

18. Objects look quite different when seen from different points of view.
True False
Feedback: True. Objects look quite different when seen from different points of view.

19. The proper use of depth cues helps simulate the illusion of space.
True False
Feedback: True. The proper use of depth cues helps simulate the illusion of space.

20. Viewers tend to perceive the obstructed or blocked object as being afar or behind the object that blocks it.
True False

PART II

Multiple Choice Questions (Choose the Most Appropriate Answer)

1. Which of the following is not one of the steps mentioned in the 5I technique?
   a. Imagination
   b. Interpretation
   c. Iteration
   d. Inscription
   e. Inspection

2. _____ refers to the quality of an object's surface, both tangibly and visually.
   a. Shape
   b. Form
   c. Value
   d. Texture
   e. None of the above

3. _____ refers to the light reflected by an object and is defined in terms of hue, value, and intensity.
   a. Shape
   b. Form
   c. Value
   d. Texture
   e. Color

4. _____ color theory is the process that explains the color theory as we observe in case of pigments.
   a. Multiplicative
   b. Subtractive
   c. Additive
   d. Divisive
   e. None of the above

5. _____ color theory is the process that explains the color theory as we observe in monitors and electronic devices.
   a. Multiplicative
   b. Subtractive
   c. Additive
   d. Divisive
   e. None of the above

6. Colors that are opposite to each other on the color wheel are referred to as _____ colors
   a. Complementary
   b. Supplementary
   c. Composition
   d. Divisive
   e. None of the above

7. Which of the following is the last step mentioned in the 5I technique?
   a. Imagination
   b. Interpretation
   c. Iteration
   d. Innovation
   e. Inspection

8. _____ is the depth cue according to which edges seem to approach each other as they move away from the observer.
   a. Convergence
   b. Overlap
   c. Atmospheric perspective
   d. Foreshortening
   e. None of the above

9. _____ refers to the creation of depth by the use of shortened forms
   a. Convergence
   b. Overlap
   c. Atmospheric perspective
   d. Foreshortening
   e. None of the above

10. _____ texture indicates how things actually feel when you touch them or pick them up.
    a. Tangible
    b. Visual
    c. Atmospheric
    d. Shape
    e. None of the above

11. The chapter mentions which of the following as enemies of ideation?
    a. Impulsiveness
    b. Interpretation
    c. Inspection
    d. Iteration
    e. None of the above

12. When we are referring to the space occupied by 3D objects, we are referring to _____ ?
    a. Point
    b. Area
    c. Volume
    d. Circumference
    e. None of the above

13. _____ shapes are composed of unequal sides and angles.
    a. Isosceles
    b. Overlapping
    c. Irregular
    d. Regular
    e. None of the above

14. Renowned sculptor Erwin Hauer stated, "It is an important token reminder for the younger generation and their tutors, that above and beyond the abundance of electronic marvels, the human vision and _____ remains the most important element and...."
    a. Electronics
    b. Computers
    c. Analog devices
    d. Imagination
    e. None of the above

15. _____ said, "A man paints with his brains and not with his hands".
    a. Einstein
    b. Newton
    c. Michelangelo
    d. Picasso
    e. None of the above

16. Depth cues are also known as _____ cues
    a. Line
    b. Edge
    c. Distance
    d. Prospective
    e. None of the above

17. _____ refers to the phenomenon where parallel lines appear to taper or merge as they recede from the point of observation
    a. Convergence
    b. Overlap
    c. Atmospheric perspective
    d. Foreshortening
    e. None of the above

18. Which of the following are considered as enemies of ideation?
    a. Mind maps
    b. Creativity
    c. Impulsiveness
    d. Imitation
    e. Both c and d above

19. A reniform leaf is shaped in the form of the _____
    a. Heart
    b. Eye
    c. Kidney
    d. Hand
    e. None of the above

20. _____ refers to the phenomenon where the colors of far-off objects merge or blend with and take on some of the atmosphere's colors.
    a. Convergence
    b. Overlap
    c. Atmospheric perspective
    d. Foreshortening
    e. None of the above

Reference

Chandramouli, M. (2011). *A Ga-Enabled VR Framework for Generating Alternative 3D Interior Space Configurations*. Purdue University Dissertations – Purdue e-Pubs.

CHAPTER 4: Modeling – Part I: Categories and Approaches

Of all of our inventions for mass communication, pictures still speak the most universally understood language.

– Walt Disney

CHAPTER LEARNING OBJECTIVES

After carefully studying this chapter, you will be able to answer the following questions:

- What are some modeling categories and approaches?
- What are primitives?
- What is constructive solid geometry?
- What is Boolean logic and how is it useful in 3D modeling?
- What are meshes or polygonal meshes?
- What is polygonal modeling?
- What is the role of triangles and quadrilaterals in modeling?

DOI: 10.1201/9780429186349-4

- What is poly-count and what role does it play in modeling?
- What are the different elements of modeling with meshes?
- What is meant by deformations?
- How can deformations such as bend, twist, and taper be used for 3D modeling?
- What are the essential considerations in modeling?
- What is a scene hierarchy in a 3D scene?
- What is meant by parent–child relationship in a 3D model?

What Will You Learn in This Chapter?

In this chapter, you will continue to build the modeling skills you learned in Chapter 2. Earlier, you learned about the polygonal mesh modeling and the basic entities constituting the meshes such as points, lines, and faces. This chapter will discuss polygonal and spline modeling. This chapter will introduce different types of modifiers and deformers that can be used to quickly model complex shapes from simpler ones such as primitives. The chapter will then introduce another efficient and time-saving group of techniques collectively known as constructive solid geometry (CSG).

In this chapter, we will look at various modeling techniques and categories starting with primitives. Primitives are used to approximate simple geometric shapes and forms. Even though primitives may sound as something that could be used for basic models, by applying Boolean operations to primitive objects, many interesting models can be created quite efficiently. When employed creatively, Boolean operations can be time-saving. Complex 3D designs that could otherwise be extremely time-consuming can be created in much less time with a clever combination of Boolean operations. Then, we will discuss a modeling technique that is closely related to primitives called polygonal modeling. One common approach with polygonal modeling is to start with primitive geometric objects to make different kinds of objects. Polygonal modeling involves creating 3D models using meshes (also known as polygonal meshes). As the name implies, polygonal modeling involves combining many polygons to create the mesh that makes up the 3D model. When it comes to organic modeling (natural objects, animals, humans, etc.), polygonal meshes can also be quite useful and efficient. However, polygonal modeling can be time-consuming, especially when dealing with sophisticated designs requiring elaborate modeling. Especially, for highly intricate modeling, very small polygons may need to be used to avoid a faceted appearance. When a scene involves many such objects modeled intricately using polygonal modeling, the total number of polygons in the scene can increase manifold. We will look at some specific techniques that are applied using polygons. This chapter will cover deformations that can be applied to simple primitives to create complex, intricate shapes. Some examples of deformations include bend, displace, ripple, skew, and taper.

Modeling Categories and Approaches

There is no single way to classify all the different types of modeling currently used worldwide. Instead of focusing on a set of hard and fast rules to categorize the various modeling approaches, understanding the underlying mechanisms can serve to clarify the conceptualizations.

Generally, we all are good at taking what we already know and building on the information we already know. 3D modeling is not very different from some activities we did as children such as building using blocks of wood or plastic and carving things from a block of wood or modeling clay. In a broader sense, you can consider an additive approach or a subtractive approach. The additive approach goes from smaller to larger like adding blocks of wood to make a larger object, and the subtractive approach is similar to chiseling away pieces of wood from a larger block. This is similar to the way a stone sculptor creates 3D objects from stone. Various procedures, such as carving, chiseling, and scraping, are used in the process whereby the statue is sculpted from the larger piece or block. Whether using an additive or subtractive approach, modeling involves creating or recreating the shape of an object.

Modeling Techniques

Primitives

In computer graphics, a set of objects known as *primitives* are used to approximate simple geometric shapes. As the word suggests, primitives are basic or simple geometric objects. These can be as simple as a point or can be a 2D or 3D object such as a line or a face or a box. Some of the primitives (or primitive shapes) that are found commonly across different modeling software are cube (box), sphere, cylinder, cone, and so on (Figure 4.1).

Many of the common objects we come across in our daily life can be modeled using primitives. Figure 4.2 shows two tables created entirely from primitives only: one table created using box objects and the other using only cylinders.

FIG 4.1 Primitives.

FIG 4.2 3D objects created using primitives only (boxes and cylinders).

The perspective view on the right shows the whole objects, while the view on the left shows the individual boxes and the cylinders making the respective table objects. With creativity, you can model many different objects using just primitives.

You can also extend this ability to model using primitives further to model interesting characters. You do not have to always resort to complex modeling to create engaging characters. For instance, this character shown in Figure 4.3 was created fully from primitives (spheres) and using a bit of Boolean operations, which we will see later. The image on the right shows further modifying the character by adding additional spheres to create a slightly different looking character that is looking down (Figure 4.3).

The primitives we saw earlier such as box, cylinder, and cone serve as the starting point for many models. Look around the room at the many common day-to-day objects we come across, and try to break down these items in terms of basic primitives if you can. A modeling technique that is closely related to primitives is polygonal modeling. One common approach with polygonal modeling is to start with primitive geometric objects like the ones we saw above to make different kinds of objects. Now let us look at polygonal modeling.

FIG 4.3 Characters from spheres.

Polygonal Modeling

In polygonal modeling, the 3D scene objects are generated by putting together many flat surfaces, known as polygons or faces. Polygonal models are commonly used in graphics applications as they are not only simple to define in terms of storing within a database, but they are also easy to transform, manipulate, and display. Polygonal modeling involves creating 3D models using meshes (also known as polygonal meshes). In polygonal modeling, 3D objects are modeled using polygon meshes to recreate the surface that is being approximated. Typically, four-sided quadrilaterals or three-sided triangles are used. These are also known alternatively as quads or tris, respectively. In Figure 4.4, the actual 3D models are shown in the middle, and the wireframe model showing the quad-mesh is on the left and the triangular meshes are on the right. Each polygon is referred to as a face, line is also known as edge, and a point as vertex. In addition to tris or quads, polygons with more than four sides, namely n-gons, are also used for polygonal modeling

Generally, polygonal models are relatively more convenient to create and also to render. When it comes to organic modeling (natural objects, animals, humans, etc.), polygonal meshes can be quite useful and efficient. However, polygonal modeling can be time-consuming, especially when dealing with sophisticated designs requiring elaborate modeling. Especially, for highly intricate modeling, very small polygons may need to be used to avoid a faceted appearance. When a scene involves many such objects modeled intricately using polygonal modeling, the total number of polygons in the scene can increase manifold (Figure 4.5).

With polygons, you can also perform additional operations like extrude and bevel. An easy analogy to understand extrusion is to think of a circle and a cylinder, and visualize a cylinder being pulled out by adding height

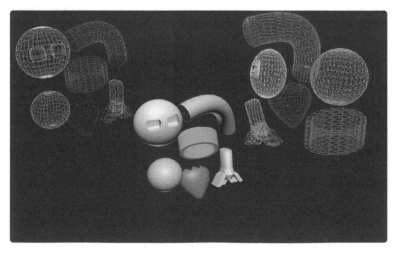

FIG 4.4 Quad Mesh & Tri Mesh.

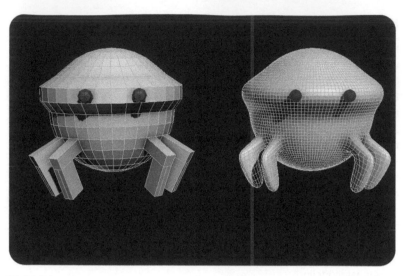

FIG 4.5 Polycount.

to the circle. Similar to that, extrusion involves pulling out (extruding) faces (polygons) in a direction at right angles to the polygon. Just as a polygonal surface can be pulled out, it can also be pushed inward. If polygonal meshes are created by pulling externally in one direction along an axis (say positive), then the negative equivalent can be considered as pushing inward to create an indentation.

However, there are also some disadvantages when polygons are used for modeling. The primary shortcoming with polygonal modeling is that to avoid the faceted appearance of the final models created, a large number of tiny flat surfaces and polygons are required. Remember that in polygonal modeling, there are a number of those quads or rectangles or squares or any other types of polygon, and this gives the smooth appearance to a model. However, the level of smoothed appearance that can be achieved with other techniques such as NURBS will require hundred thousands or millions of polygons. However, the use of so many polygons will create issues with rendering speed and time. For some cases, the level of smoothness through polygonal modeling can be achieved using NURBS curves with more efficiency.

Polygonal Mesh Operations

Just as polygons can be extruded, edges and vertices can also be extruded. While extrusion is done in a perpendicular direction to the surface being extruded, bevel involves performing the operation at an angle. Using the bevel operation, the modeler can create chamfered edges and corners on objects. This creates an effect to create an elegant appearance of smoothed-out edges for objects, which might otherwise look awkward and sharp. We frequently come across real-world objects such as glass objects, tables, playing dice, etc. whose edges may be beveled.

Extrusion

Extrusion refers to selecting a face from a polygonal mesh or an edge and pulling it out. Extruding a face or a polygon results in more polygons being created. Figure 4.6 (leftmost image) shows polygon extrusion applied on multiple polygons from a mesh.

Bevel

The beveling operation on polygons results in the creation of inclined surfaces. It begins similar to extrusion, and the extruded polygons are scaled down or up. This is also referred to as inward bevel (center image – Figure 4.6) or outward bevel (rightmost image – Figure 4.6). This is a quick way to generate slanted faces or polygons that are inclined.

Bridge

Bridging is an operation where the edges of the polygons can be bridged together to create objects by combining two 3D objects (Figure 4.7).

FIG 4.6 Extrusion, Inward Bevel, Outward Bevel.

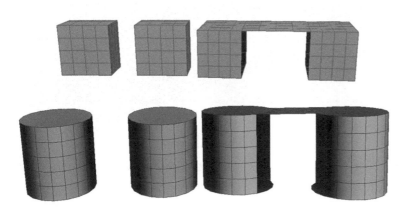

FIG 4.7 Bridge operation.

The basic difference between polygonal modeling and modeling with splines or NURBS lies in the way in which the 3D mesh calculation is carried out. We saw right in the beginning of the polygonal modeling section that 3D objects are constructed using flat plane shapes (polygons or faces), and hence, for polygon modeling, the computing process involves calculating polygons. However, in the case of NURBS, the computing to generate the 3D model involves calculations of splines. Since polygonal modeling involves modeling with faces (which are in turn made from straight lines), it is practically not possible to create an impeccably smooth model. But, by using methods such as subdivision and smoothing techniques, seemingly flat surface with awkward bends or sharp appearances can be made to "appear" smooth.

Constructive Solid Geometry

In CSG, Boolean operations are applied to primitive objects such as cylinders, cones, cubes, spheres, and pyramids to create complex designs and intricate shapes. Boolean operations in CG are founded on the Boolean logic introduced by George Boole.

The basic Boolean operations are referred to as

AND

OR

NOT

Figure 4.8 shows a 3D design for metal or wood work that was created very quickly using proboolean subtraction operation. Table 4.1 summarizes the information we discussed till now about the operators and their corresponding modeling terms with their symbolic notation.

FIG 4.8 Proboolean subtraction.

TABLE 4.1 Boolean Notations and Corresponding Graphics Operation

Notation	Graphics Operation
$A \cup B$	Union
$A \cap B$	Intersection
$A \setminus B$	Subtraction

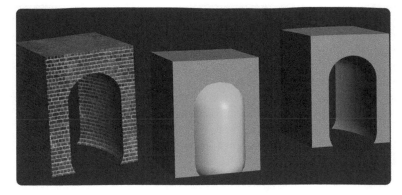

FIG 4.9 Arch shaped object using Boolean operations.

Boolean logic is used in many fields, including information theory, relay circuits, digital logic gates, control problems, and algebra, spread across diverse disciplines such as computer science, mathematics, and engineering. In graphics modeling, *addition*, *subtraction*, and *intersection* are common Boolean operations applied on primitive shapes. Addition is referred to as union, subtraction is also known as difference, and intersection is referred to as sharing. The intersection operation retains the portions common to both objects.

When employed creatively, Boolean operations can be time-saving. Complex 3D designs that could otherwise be extremely time-consuming can be created in much less time with a clever combination of Boolean operations. Figure 4.9 illustrates a 3D model created from Boolean subtraction. The same final model could have been laborious and time-consuming if it were to be created by conventional graphic modeling methods.

In this manner, you can use different primitives with a combination of Boolean operations such as addition and subtraction, and you can create a wide range of interesting characters as well. Many 3D software offer primitives such as:

Cube	Prism
Box	Pyramid
Cylinder	Cone
Tube	Sphere

Before we look at few other types of modeling, let us take a look at applying texture maps to 3D models. This can be used to create photorealistic 3D models, which means that the appearance of these 3D models resembles that of real-life objects.

Texture-Mapped 3D Models

In the real world, we often come across objects whose appearance attributes, especially surface properties, are not exactly the same at points (on their external surface). In fact, various properties such as roughness, coloring, glossiness, luminosity, reflectivity, refractivity, and transmittance continue to vary across the surface of an object. In fact, these subtle variations are found commonly in sceneries surrounding us and elements of such scenes such as trees, birds, plants, flowers, and grass. We are surrounded by innumerable textures, both in the natural and man-made objects we encounter in our daily life. When we use words such as shiny, rough, smooth, and glossy to describe the appearance of an object, we are referring to the texture. As you see from Figure 4.10, the textures show subtle and/or stark variations in proportion, size, shape, form, structure, density, etc.

Photorealistic rendering refers to the kind of rendering wherein the resulting image looks as close as possible to a real-world representation. In other words, the rendering is so realistic that it almost looks like a photograph of the real-world objects. One common method employed to create such realistic 3D models is to use texture and map (apply) them onto the 3D-modeled objects.

Figure 4.11 shows three box models. The leftmost 3D box model has a uniform color applied to it creating a non-realistic appearance, which is also known as non-photorealistic rendering. The other two show stone and rock textures applied to the box object. The raster images give a realistic appearance to the objects.

To recreate the variation in surface properties of the real-world surfaces, the surfaces of the 3D digital models are mapped with textures. These textures can be images from the real world, which are applied to the surfaces of the objects within the 3D objects. Just to get an idea of texture mapping, let us consider a very simple analogy of wrapping a gift paper on a gift box. While in the real world, an actual decorative paper is wrapped onto a gift box, in the digital world, a texture (image) is wrapped onto a 3D model. However, in the

FIG 4.10 Textures.

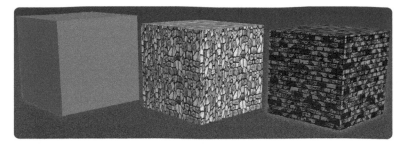

FIG 4.11 Textures on box object.

digital texture mapping process, there are more details to the actual process to ensure that the final model is realistic looking.

Even in the real world, the process will be very simple only if we are going to take a flat piece of decorative paper and paste it to an absolutely flat surface like applying a wallpaper to a wall or applying a plane printed image to a billboard. However, we may not only be dealing with exactly planar surfaces or box-shaped surfaces, but we come across curved objects as well. Just as wrapping a flat (planar) sheet over a spherical object in the real world can be tricky, applying planar textures over differently shaped 3D models also needs to be done in a specific manner. This is also known as image warping, wherein the original image texture is mapped on the target object (3D model) appropriately.

When dealing with a variety of 3D models with many different shapes, a clear and organized procedure is required for properly performing this mapping process (of the texture onto the model). Earlier we saw how the x-, y-, z-axes of the Cartesian coordinate space are used to position objects in 3D spaces and perform transformations. Similar to the x, y coordinates for object placement, a system of coordinates called u, v coordinates (known as UV mapping) is used for properly placing textures on to 3D models. This is

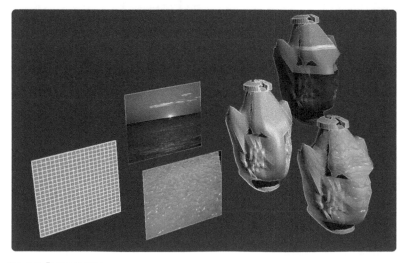

FIG 4.12 Texture mapping

also sometimes referred to as UVW when a third dimension W is wrapped in complex ways onto uneven and asymmetrical surfaces. However, here our discussion will focus mainly on UV mapping.

In UV mapping, U refers to the horizontal component of the texture and V refers to the vertical component. For the sake of simplicity, imagine if you were able to make the model's surface as a planar object. In other words, imagine if you were able to flatten the 3D model, which involves spreading out all the polygonal faces of the 3D model on a flat two-dimensional plane. This is known as *unwrapping*. You can think of this as unfurling a rolled flag or unfolding a folded object.

A common example used to demonstrate this unwrapping is the 3D cube primitive. Figure 4.13 shows an unfolded or unwrapped 3D cube model. Just as it can be done for a cube object, this unwrapping can also be done for a curved or a spherical object.

You should note that a cube is made of rectangular (square) faces that easily lend themselves to unwrapping and spreading on a flat plane. However, as you can imagine, organic and curved objects will be slightly different and hence will involve additional adjustments. One of the most common examples that demonstrates the successful accomplishment of this kind of representation between 2D and 3D is the common "map" (Figure 4.14). A map of the Earth is

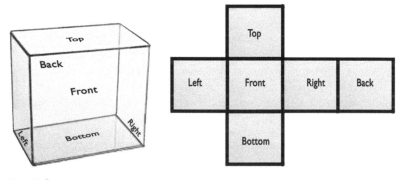

FIG 4.13 Texture unwrapping

FIG 4.14 Map (2D) and Globe (3D)

actually a 2D representation of a 3D object, the Earth. If you were to take a map printed on a sheet of paper and try to wrap it onto a spherical object, you will still have to do some pinching at the corners to make it fit.

Fortunately, procedures such as UV mapping offer a more standardized way of performing this mapping process of a 2D texture on 3D models. As a rule of thumb, proper UV mapping depends on proper modeling and good topology. Color is only one attribute of appearance, and there are various other characteristics such as surface roughness, shininess, transparency, refractions, reflections, and transmission. Listed below are some kind of image maps that can be used to recreate or simulate these properties:

- Transparency maps (used to modify the transparency of an image's texture)
- Displacement maps and normal maps (used to modify depth or height)
- Bump maps (used do simulate roughness, especially on surfaces of smaller objects such as oranges and golf balls)

To create realistic looking surfaces, imagine if you were to show all the surface variations or roughness by creating them in the 3D model itself. Then you will end up with a scene with an innumerable number of polygons. However, by using maps, we save a tremendous amount of rendering resources including time while still creating a highly photorealistic appearance on the 3D models. Also, you should note that these kinds of bump maps do not modify the actual size or the shape of the 3D-modeled object. They just accomplish the bumpiness effect by modifying how the object reacts with the lights in the scene and simulate reflections, refractions, and transmissions to *simulate* an appearance of surface roughness. Now, let us continue to look at few other modeling techniques.

Box Modeling

Box modeling is a common technique for 3D modeling compound scene models that are composed of multiple parts. Typically, box modeling involves starting with a standard primitive object such as a cube and then working with the sub-objects like faces and edges by transforming and modifying them in different ways. Box modeling can be used to create both organic models and hard-surface models. One of the obvious advantages of box modeling is that it can be used to create object geometries relatively easily starting with some simple primitives. On the other hand, achieving high level of precision with curved shapes and achieving good optimization are challenging with box modeling.

With box modeling, start with a primitive shape as a reference and continue to create the final model through a series of repeated steps and iterative refinement. Basically, this is similar to starting with something abstract and adding more and more details as you keep working. It is important to note that as you are working on your box modeling process, you should keep in mind the level of detail you are expecting with the finished model. This depends on what you are going to be using the model for and what kind of animations you plan to perform with it. You do not have to aim for a high level of precision if it is not required according to the plot. However, if this is a model that is going to be used often in the animation and needs to be shown with a high level of detail, you must focus on the accuracy, and the geometry should be capable of allowing the model to perform intended actions.

As you can see from Figure 4.15, starting with a simple box model (leftmost model), by operations including division, extrusion on selected polygons, and refinement, the final table object with four legs is created. In this case, quadrilaterals, polygons having four sides, are used. These are known as quads and are often employed in different modeling techniques. Figure 4.16 illustrates another example where the final shape is created from a simple box model. However, for purposes such as rendering, the graphics platforms and rendering engines may convert these to triangles. This is known *as triangulation*. The reason this is done goes back to the concept of planarity explained in the earlier chapters. It is very much possible that a quadrilateral may not be planar as there may not be a single plane in which all four vertices are present. However, for every three vertices, we can find one triangle (on a plane) that passes through the three points. As triangles are easily processed and organized (due to their planar property), the rendering engines employ triangles for surface generation.

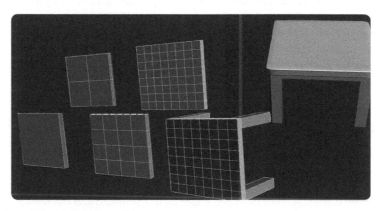

FIG 4.15 Table object using box modeling

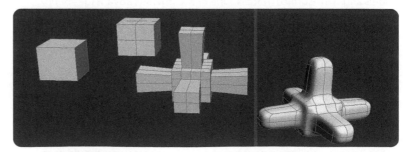

FIG 4.16 Box modeling variations

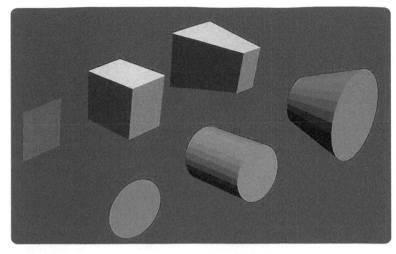

FIG 4.17 Extrude and bevel operations

The earlier box modeling operation was based on extrude. Let us see one based on bevel. Bevel involves extruding shapes into 3D objects, wherein a circular or flat bevel is applied to the edges. Bevel operation can be used to create chamfered edges. Figure 4.17 shows a rectangular (square) polygon on top and a circular polygon on the bottom. Extrude and bevel operations have been applied to both of them.

With extrude you can see that with both the square shape and the circular shape, the cross section remains the same. However, with bevel, the cross section continues to change. Cross section refers to the section (area) obtained when a three dimensional object such as a cube or a cylinder is cut across or sliced through at right angles to an axis. Obviously, when you slice a cube, you will end up with a square, while a circular shape is obtained when you slice through a cylinder. In this case, with extrude, you can see that the cross section remains the same. However, with the square shape, the bevel proceeds inward (towards the center) as we move along, and with the circular shape, the bevel proceeds to move away from the center.

Figure 4.18 illustrates more examples of 3D models that can be created using box modeling. With practice and creativity, even organic objects that may otherwise take much longer to create can be created swiftly and efficiently from primitives such as box.

In box modeling, the 3D model is made starting with a box and refining it. Another interesting approach to create a complicated model consisting of multiple components is known as part modeling. There are many objects that are made up of multiple smaller components such as cars, trucks, airplanes, refrigerators, and laptops. Even seemingly smaller objects such as cellphones and tablet devices are made up of numerous smaller components. Part modeling also saves time because recurring components within assemblies need to be modeled only once and can be reused as required.

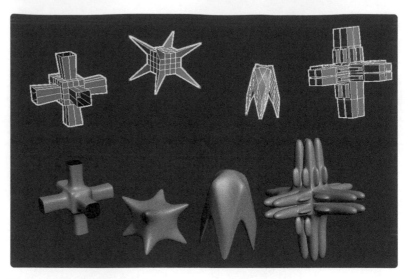

FIG 4.18 Box modeling and sub-objects

Part Modeling

Part modeling very much works like the usual modeling we have been seeing till now, wherein we use storyboards before starting the actual digital modeling. Similarly, sketches form the foundation in part modeling before actual assembly components can be modeled in 3D. As can be seen in Figure 4.19, part modeling has its application in the industry where compound parts and assemblies are involved. In the industry, especially when dealing with machine assemblies composed of intricate parts, dimensional accuracy is important. The threshold for accuracy can be very high when dealing with machine tools of specific diameter, angle, etc. and making threads in metal fasteners that need to fit precisely. 3D applications that are specifically designed for such purposes are used in part modeling when high level of precision is an important factor.

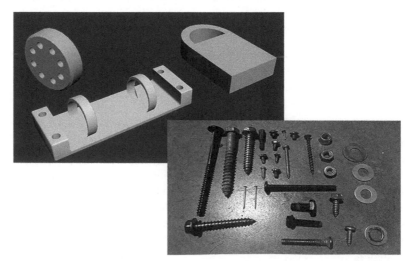

FIG 4.19 Part Modeling

Many Computer-Aided Design (CAD) applications in manufacturing, design, and many other engineering applications can use part modeling. This allows intricately and accurately designing components that serve as parts of large assemblies. Various procedures we saw till now including beveling, extruding, and Boolean operations can be used to create individual parts. This also gives the advantage of modifying components by easily adjusting their parameters if changes are required to designs.

When modeling parts and assembling them together, it is important to consider the hierarchy which involves parent–child relationships. This is not only relevant for part modeling, but is highly relevant to 3D modeling in general. Irrespective of the software or the modeling platform you may use, you need to understand how complicated 3D objects can be modeled by defining hierarchical relationships.

Hierarchy

Typically, 3D scenes are composed of 3D objects that are made by assembling or putting together smaller objects. For instance, a table object has a flat surface and is supported by four legs. This is an example of a relatively simpler assembly. On the other hand, the personal computer (PC) object is composed of several components such as the monitor, keyboard, processing unit, mouse, and PC stand, which are in turn assembled from smaller parts. Similarly, all the characters that you see in the animated 3D movies are made from smaller components. In other words, smaller shapes are joined together to form the hands, legs, torso, head, and so on, which are assembled together to form the complete model, much like how an automobile is built on the assembly line. How exactly these smaller objects are assembled within the program or the nature of the *relationship* or link between components of an assembled object manifests itself in two forms: grouping and hierarchy.

Grouping refers to the process when all objects constituting a larger object are "grouped" together to act as one single unit (or object). On the other hand, in a hierarchy, there is a specific order in which objects are assembled together. When looking at two bigger objects assembled together from smaller objects via grouping and hierarchical linking, you may not be able to tell the difference. However, the difference will be quite conspicuous when performing transformations such as translation and rotation. When objects have been merely grouped together, selecting any one object in the group selects the group as a whole and any transformation applied to any part of the group is applied to the entire group. However, when objects are linked in a *hierarchy*, the transformations affect the selected object and its dependent objects (Table 4.2). To understand how objects in hierarchical linking are affected during transformation, it is important to understand the nature of the relationships.

A discussion about hierarchical linking will not be complete without discussing the pivot. Simply stated, a pivot is the point about which something rotates. This is also referred to as the fulcrum in mechanical devices or as centroids in geometrical shapes and objects. The pivot represents a very important aspect of the animation hierarchy as the way in which transformations are executed

TABLE 4.2 Hierarchical Linking Terminology

Term	Description
Root	Topmost object in the hierarchical structure. The parent object that is above all other parent objects in the scene.
Node	All elements in a hierarchy are referred to as "nodes." Any object, either a parent or a child, is a node.
Branch	The hierarchical link or path that represents the association between a parent object and its child object.
Parent	A scene object that includes and controls one or more objects (children).
Child	An object in the scene that is dependent on (controlled by) a parent.
Sibling	Children of the same parent node. Note the difference between siblings and descendants (below).
Descendants	All children of a parent object (including all the child objects of its children).
Ancestors	All parents of a child object in a 3D model (including all the parent(s) of the child's parent object).
Leaf	The objects (nodes) that do not have any children. They represent the lowest level within the hierarchy.

depending on the position of the pivot. Pivot also is an important aspect when applying deformations such as bend, skew, and twist. By default, pivots are at the geometric center of the object. However, this can be selected and transformed (translated/rotated) as required. We will discuss more about pivots and joints later in Chapter 7 and Chapter 8.

Figure 4.20 shows an armature representing a dinosaur assembled from many minute components. Trucks, automobiles, aircrafts, helicopters, submarines,

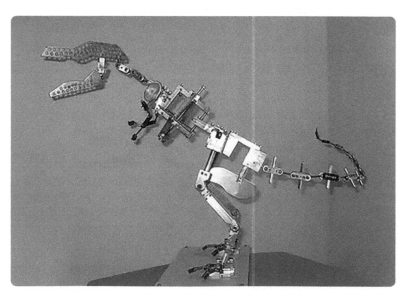

FIG 4.20 Armature depicting hierarchy (Image Courtesy: Tom Brierton)

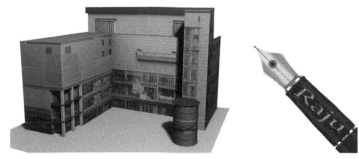

FIG 4.21 Components and hierarchy

and bicycles are all man-made machines that are made by putting together several smaller components. For each one of the above machines to function properly, the components must maintain their spatial relationships. In other words, all the components have precise measurements or dimensions that allow them to interact with each other coherently to produce the desired final motion (or effect). Being able to position things properly is a very important part of constructing things – be it an equipment or a larger space (metro interior). Placement of parts (components) is extremely important for these machineries to work properly. Wherever you are now, take a look around you and observe the objects in your environment.

Especially, look at all the man-made objects. If you are in a room, you might see objects such as a table, chair, television, lamp, desk, and shelves. Wherever you are, you will see so many objects around you. Irrespective of their size, many objects are made up of smaller objects. Be it a large object like a building or a small object like the nib of pen (Figure 4.21), measurements or dimensions are involved. The dimensions of a shelf in a refrigerator must enable it to fit perfectly within the refrigerator. The dimensions of a nib must be proportionate to the pen in which the nib will be used.

Deformation Operations

Just as Boolean operations can be utilized to create complex 3D models much efficiently, a set of processes known as deformation operations can be used to create complicated designs quickly even from simple primitives. Let us look at few of the common deformation operations that are commonly used in 3D modeling processes. Deformations are interlinked to the concept of transformation in the sense that you can apply a specific deformation along a specific axis and you can also constrain the values of allowable deformations. For instance, if you are bending an object, you can choose to allow the bending only within a specific range (say 30–90 degrees for instance). Earlier we saw how transformations can be used to translate, rotate, and scale. There are more advanced modifications that can be performed on 3D-modeled objects (Tables 4.3 and 4.4).

TABLE 4.3 Deformation Terminology

Term	Definition
Bend	Curvatures or turns in an object by an angle (up to 360°) about x, y, or z axis.
Skew	Affects the object's geometry by offsetting and controlling the magnitude of skew applied. This can be applied about a specific axis and also to the object in its entirety or just to specific elements within the geometry.
Slice	Generates new polygons, lines, and vertices by applying a plane that cuts into the object.
Stretch	This is a variant of the scale procedure to make the object skinny or thin around the center areas.
Displace	Pushes and redesigns an object's geometric form to achieve alternative configurations.
Lattice	Converts edges of objects into beam or girder or other similar shaped elements at the vertices.
Noise	Controls and confines the vertex positions of objects. Capable of generating different effects such as terrain and texture, and this should be applied along a plane (as a combination of axes, e.g., xy plane encompassing x- and y-axes).
Ripple	Generates a ripple effect on the selected object in a coaxial manner. This can be manipulated by regulating the number of ripples and the center of the ripple propagation.
Taper	Yields an elongated or narrowing effect on an object by scaling the ends in a contrasting manner; by scaling up one end or side of the object and scaling down the other end or side.
Twist	Curves an object about a selected axis; this can be controlled using the pivot point of application and using constraints on the axis.

TABLE 4.4 Operations to Fine-Tune the Modeling Process

Terminology	Operation Performed
Fillet	Molding or trimming applied at the point where two edges meet. Applying a smooth connection between surfaces.
Bevel	Removing hard edge between surfaces by substituting with a slanting edge or plane.
Round	A modified version of beveling, which rounds/smoothens the straight or hard edges using an adjustable number of facets. The number of facets/segments can be adjusted based on the degree of smoothing required.
Blend	Merging two surfaces using a new surface that is generated and controlled using control points.
Purge	Removing redundant vertices in the models generated using curved patches to reduce file size and the rendering time.
Fitting	Dragging noncontiguous model surfaces to fit and match their edges to eliminate minor gaps among surfaces.

As discussed earlier, pivot point also affects another set of operations known as *deformations*. By applying a deformation or a combination of deformations to simple 3D models (primitives), complex and intricate shapes can be created in a much less cumbersome manner, saving time. Some of the common deformation operations are as follows (Figure 4.22).

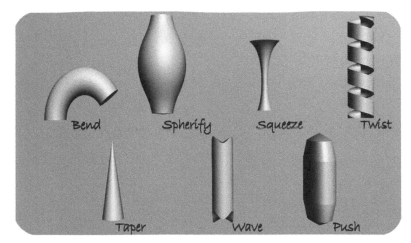

FIG 4.22 Deformations

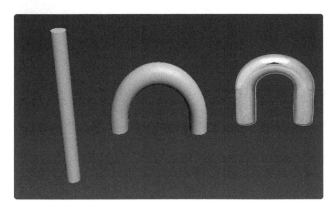

FIG 4.23 Bend operation

Bend

Bending is a term that we also use commonly in daily life. A road curvature is referred to as a bend. In manufacturing and other related industrial processes, bending refers to distorting an object (such as a cylindrical rod) about a specific axis. Figure 4.23 shows a cylindrical pipe that has been bent in different ways to create different kinds of final shapes including a U-shaped pipe.

Twist

Although the words twist and bend are used in colloquial language to refer to similar things, in 3D deformation operations, they refer to different operations. Twist operation is used to create a coiling or spiraling effect as seen in Figure 4.24.

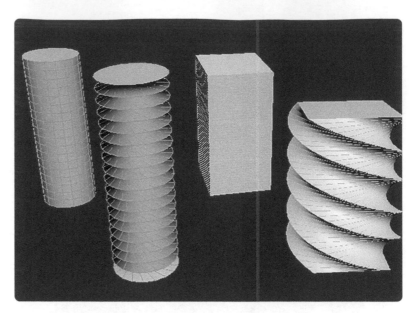

FIG 4.24 Twist operation

Squash

The squashing operation involves crushing or compressing an object along an axis. You may have been kids playing with some of those toys that squash or just consider a water balloon. A spherical kind of object when thrown on the ground or towards a wall flattens or spreads out very much like how a highly elastic rubber ball or a bubble gum behaves. 3D squash deformation can also be performed about a specific axis. Figure 4.25 shows the same object being squashed across different axes.

Stretch

Stretching involves elongating or expanding an object, as one can do with an elastic band. As you can see from Figure 4.25, the stretching operation makes the object thinner at the center.

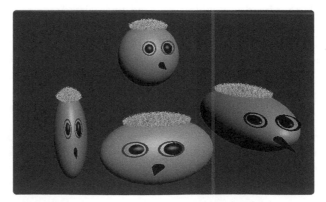

FIG 4.25 Squash and stretch

Taper

Tapering refers to making a 3D object progressively thinner as it approaches one corner or end. This is achieved by contracting and elongating the object about an axis. In the real world, when we refer to something as tapering, we are talking about the object being pointed or pyramidal.

External and Internal Navigation

By external and internal *navigation*, we mean whether the user is navigating inside or outside a structure. This is closely related to the poly-count and file-size considerations we discussed earlier. The creation of a 3D scene is driven by the purpose or objective of visualization. In case of some specific scenes, the 3D world is meant mainly to provide street navigation information to tourists or to help planning the urban landscape. In such a situation, a view of the overall landscape with buildings situated in it is important. In such a situation, it is just sufficient if the model depicts buildings as how they look from outside. On the other hand, if a virtual scene is for the use of an architect or an interior designer, the inside of a structure and its outside are equally important.

A typical example for external navigation would be navigating around a city (virtual-world representation), as in a virtual city to be used mainly for city planning purposes. This is a model developed to serve as a tool for landscape visualization and hence, for urban planning (Figure 4.26).

In such a case, the external appearance of the building is of utmost importance. In some cases, the interior model of a building or both the interior and exterior models are required. For instance, while planning or designing a new building, visualization offers excellent functionalities to facilitate the construction process. Different possible designs can be created, and the one that is most practical and also acceptable to the planners can be selected. This saves considerable time and expedites the construction process.

FIG 4.26 External navigation and internal navigation

High and Low Poly-Counts: Shaded and Wireframe Views
However, it will not practically be possible to infinitely increase the number of polygons in your model and scene, as it will burden your graphics processor and increase the rendering time. This is a major concern when creating photorealistic models of complex real-life objects such as trees. Besides the polygons, another thing a modeler needs to be mindful of is texture. As you will see later in the rendering chapter, the models combine high poly-count and textures to create a photorealistic 3D model. When you have such high poly-count models and more of them in your scene, this will cause a huge burden on your computer's resources and will lead to extremely high processing times.

Typically, the rule is the greater the number of polygons, the greater the time required to render them. When designing larger applications involving extremely detailed models or large-scale applications such as cybercities and other urban infrastructure applications, the number of polygons is an important consideration. For smaller applications containing fewer polygons, this would not be a big concern, but large-scale applications (e.g., urban infrastructure) may include a large number of polygons, and a reduction in the number of polygons would make a significant improvement. Also, textures often are draped onto polygons to give them a realistic appearance. These textures can be images (like raster images) that are applied onto the surfaces as material.

Raster images are covered in the chapter on composition (Chapter 10). Such textures also contribute to the overall file size, and displaying texture images with large file sizes also influences the rendering time. When there is a model with a large number of faces or involving very high-resolution textures, there may be a considerable time lag. This results in increased time for the browser window or software to display such polygonal faces and textures, and hinders the process of smooth interaction with the 3D model and navigation.

The number of polygons constituting a mesh normally determines the speed with which the mesh will be rendered. As a general rule, the greater the number of polygons, the higher the rendering time. Note that when creating complex 3D models that put a high demand on the graphics processor and the computer, *it is only the faces the user sees that really matter*. While modeling objects like roads, plane objects with two sides can be used instead of box objects with 12 sides (internal and external). The polygonal faces that cannot be seen by the user do not need to be rendered at all. Special capabilities or functionalities in 3D modeling languages can be exploited to accomplish this task. In a situation, where a model depicting a room is being built and will be viewed only from the outside, there is no need to model the internal faces of the object at all.

Raster image file formats (or *bitmaps*) can be, at times, very large in size. The formula to calculate the exact file size of any bitmap image is as follows.

$$\text{Image File Size}\left(\text{in Kilobytes}\right)=\left(\left(\text{Resolution}\right)^2\times\text{Width}\times\text{Height}\times\text{Bit Depth}\right)\div 8{,}192$$

(8,192 refers to the number of bits in a kilobyte).

For Instance, the file size for an Image 8″×9″ (width by heIght), with a bit depth of 24 bit, and a resolution of 72 dpi equals 1093.5 kb. Bit depth is also referred to as color depth. Bit depth refers to the number of bits used to represent the color of a single pixel, in a raster (bitmapped) image. One of the most common image formats, JPG, is often used for photographs and textures. Using such textures on models is an essential element of creating what are known as "photorealistic" representations. JPG images use 24 bits per pixel, and hence, their bit depth here is 24. Also, some models can be created without actually using textures involving only the colors (R, G, B).

In a Nutshell

With polygons and hence polyhedrons, all the required data needs to be explicitly specified and stored within the database. Generally, as a rule of thumb, the larger the number of polygons, the better the approximation of the curved surface. So, when hundreds of thousands are required to approximate an organic object involving curved surfaces, this totally amounts to a lot of data that should be stored. In 3D modeling, polygons are always viewed as having two sides, and the side of the polygon that is facing out is determined by what is known as the normal. In 3D modeling, the normal at a point on a surface (or face or polygon) is a vector that is at right angles to the tangent plane at that point. On a level (flat) surface, for any point on the surface, the perpendicular direction will be the same because it is flat. On the other hand, for a curved surface, one point's normal may be different from that of another point.

From the optical perspective, normals help to determine the polygon's orientation. For rendering, this helps in estimating how light is incident on the surface and how it is reflected. Consider a simple primitive such as a box. You can use this to represent a room.

Does the number of polygons matter? Yes. The number of polygons is referred to as *poly-count*. Ultimately, the number of polygons in your model or your whole scene is an important consideration when it comes to rendering your scene. There is no rule of thumb when it comes to the number of polygons that should be in a model. This varies based on your device, its rendering capabilities, and the quality you require. It is important to understand that when it comes to rendering 3D models, the issue of quality versus performance is always a key consideration.

Chapter 4 Quiz

PART I

True/False (Circle the Correct Choice)

1. A polyline is a closed figure.
True False

2. Triangles and rectangles are examples of polylines.
True False

3. Polylines have two distinct end points.
True False

4. In Boolean logic, subtraction is also known as difference.
True False

5. Area of a triangle$=\frac{1}{2} (b * h)$, where $b=$base, $h=$height from base.
True False

6. In polygonal modeling, 3D objects are modeled using polygon meshes to recreate the surface that is being approximated.
True False

7. Area of a circle$=\pi r^3$, where r is the radius of the circle.
True False

8. The intersection operation retains the portions common to both objects.
True False

9. The number of polygons is referred to as poly-count.
True False

10. Theoretically, a line can continue to extend infinitely in both directions.
True False

11. In Boolean logic, addition is referred to as sharing.
True False

12. The four vertices that make the corner points of a tetrahedron are planar.
True False

13. Rounding is a modified version of beveling, which rounds/smoothens the straight or hard edges using an adjustable number of facets.
True False

14. A triangle is made of three vertices, and these are always planar or co-planar.
True False

15. Trimming refers to the process wherein two surfaces use a new surface that is generated and controlled using control points.
True False

16. Purging involves removing redundant vertices in the models generated using curved patches to reduce file size and the rendering time.
True False

17. A polygon with more than four sides is called an n-gon in CG.
True False

18. Modeling is the process by which an image is created from a model.
True False

19. Area of a rectangle is a product of length and breadth.
True False

20. Beveling refers to removing hard edge between surfaces by substituting with a slanting edge or plane.
True False

Part II

Multiple Choice Questions (Choose the Most Appropriate Answer)

1. _____ are basic or simple geometric objects.
   a. Primaries
   b. Secondaries
   c. Primitives
   d. Tertiaries
   e. Cardinals

2. _____ is the polygon with the least number of sides.
   a. Hexagon
   b. Pentagon
   c. Square
   d. Rectangle
   e. Triangle

3. In Boolean logic, A $\cup$ B represents
    a. Union
    b. Intersection
    c. Subtraction
    d. Binding
    e. Outline

4. Hexagons have _____ vertices.
    a. 2
    b. 3
    c. 4
    d. 5
    e. 6

5. The geometric entities vertices, edges, and faces form the constituents of what is known as a _____ , which in turn is used to approximate a 3D surface.
    a. Mesh
    b. Triangle
    c. Edge
    d. Point
    e. Facet

6. In Boolean logic, A$\setminus$B represents
    a. Union
    b. Intersection
    c. Subtraction
    d. Binding
    e. Outline

7. A tetrahedron is a solid composed of _____ triangular faces.
    a. 2
    b. 3
    c. 4
    d. 5
    e. 6

8. Hedron means _____
    a. Face
    b. Fact
    c. Triangle
    d. Line
    e. Edge

9. In Boolean logic, A ∩ B represents
   a. Union
   b. Intersection
   c. Subtraction
   d. Binding
   e. Outline

10. According to Euler's formula, if the number of vertices of a polyhedron is four and the number of edges is six, the number of faces is _____
    a. 2
    b. 3
    c. 4
    d. 5
    e. 6

11. In polygonal modeling, the 3D scene objects are generated by putting together many flat surfaces, known as _____ .
    a. Polygons
    b. Primaries
    c. Primitives
    d. Faces
    e. Both a and d are correct

12. Vertices and edges in polygonal meshes that are common to more than one face (polygon) are known as _____ vertices or shared edges.
    a. Bridge
    b. Shared
    c. Divided
    d. Distant
    e. None of the above

13. In case of a_____ , the first vertex and the last vertex are the same.
    a. Geometry
    b. Primitive
    c. Primary
    d. Polyline
    e. Polygon

14. A polygon mesh that is completely flat is known as _____
    a. Nonplanar
    b. Triplanar
    c. Planar
    d. Singular
    e. None of the above

15. _____ winds an object around an axis based on the pivot point and axes constraints.
   a. Taper
   b. Skew
   c. Wrap
   d. Twist
   e. Axel

16. _____ involves pulling out (extruding) faces (polygons) in a direction at right angles to the polygon.
   a. Binding
   b. Bevel
   c. Extrusion
   d. Bridging
   e. Trimming

17. _____ is a variation of the scale operation resulting in the object being modified becoming thin around the center.
   a. Taper
   b. Skew
   c. Stretch
   d. Twist
   e. Axel

18. _____ produces an offset in the geometry of the object by controlling the amount and axis of skew.
   a. Taper
   b. Skew
   c. Stretch
   d. Twist
   e. Axel

19. _____ arches or turns an object by an angle (up to 360°) about a specific axis.
   a. Taper
   b. Bend
   c. Stretch
   d. Twist
   e. Axel

20. _____ involves pulling out faces (polygons) in a direction at angles that are not at 90° to the polygon being extruded.
   a. Binding
   b. Beveling
   c. Equivalence
   d. Bridging
   e. Trimming

CHAPTER 5: Modeling – Part II: Curve-Based and Other Modeling Techniques

I think by drawing, so I'll draw or diagram everything from a piece of furniture to a stage gesture. I understand things best when they're in graphics, not words.

– Robert Wilson

WHAT WILL YOU LEARN IN THIS CHAPTER?

- What are the common representations for curves in geometric modeling?
- What is a parametric curve?
- What are Bézier curves and B-splines and where are they used?
- What are NURBS?
- What are the common sweeping techniques?
- Is the final model made of submodels?
- How many levels of hierarchy are involved in the final scene?
- What is the level of complexity required for the animation?
- Is the model going to be used for internal or external viewing?

DOI: 10.1201/9780429186349-5

In this chapter, we will focus on splines, curves, and other modeling techniques which we did not discuss earlier. Splines are great tools that help in design and optimization, and are used in many disciplines besides graphics designs such as aircraft design, shipbuilding, and automobile design.

In the previous chapters, we discussed modeling approaches such as polygonal modeling, box modeling, constructive solid geometry, and part modeling. We also noted that the number of polygons required to represent highly curved surfaces and ornate designs properly may be quite high, and hence, alternative tools and techniques should be used for intensive curve-based modeling.

There are numerous 3D modeling software packages that are available in the market, some of which have been extremely successful and are used heavily in the game and movie industries. Such software packages give you a head start by providing you with ready-to-use, prebuilt models (both primitive and advanced) and help throughout the modeling and animation pathway. This can be extremely time-saving and can also help you focus on the creative aspect. However, what you need to understand is that there may be limitations to what can be accomplished with such tools, in which case you can write your own programs to accomplish what exactly you want to perform. So, whether to use programming tools or nonprogramming tools is a decision you need to make based on the requirements of your project and various other considerations of resources including time.

We will then discuss subdivision modeling, which involves originally creating a simpler model which is not very detailed and then creating a more organic smoothened version through subdivision. Typically, modelers create smoother 3D objects by applying subdivision modeling on quads or tris, since with n-gons subdivision modeling performs unsteadily. Different methods are available to perform subdivision modeling of surfaces to add detail to the modeled object such as approximation, corner cutting, averaging, and splitting.

Curved Lines

Curves are almost ubiquitous; they are found everywhere. From a computer graphics (CG) standpoint, curves are considered to be made of an infinite number of points or vertices. A curve's shape is controlled by points known as "control points." When you connect these points, they form a control polygon. We can find a lot of curves in nature: elliptical orbits, paths of comets, path of trails, rivers, many body parts like eyes and ears, animal tails, insects, butterflies, rainbow, etc. Many man-made objects also have curved and circular shapes: arches, wheels, automobile bodies, umbrellas, saucers, lens, etc. (Figure 5.1).

As we continue learning about more modeling techniques, we need to strengthen our understanding of curves and surfaces. In common language, a *curve* can be thought of as a smooth bending line that does not have any

FIG 5.1 Curves in natural and man-made objects.

sharp bends. One way to recognize and distinguish it from a straight curve is that it bends and changes its direction at least once.

In CG, there are three common ways to represent lines and curves:

- Explicit representation
- Implicit representation
- Parametric representation

Often times, it is much easier to understand terms that are seemingly complex by just looking at their basic meanings. In common language, the word explicit refers to something that has no uncertainty or vagueness and is straightforward or clear. However, implicit is something that is implied or hidden. Implicit refers to something that is understood but not directly or clearly described. Now, with this basic knowledge, let us try to understand explicit and implicit functions for lines and curves.

An explicit function is one which is expressed in terms of the independent variable. For instance, when you consider the function $y = x^2 + 5x$, y is expressed in terms of x. y is the dependent variable, whose value depends on the independent variable, x. When the value of x changes, the value of y changes accordingly. In this case, for any specific value of x, you have a specific value of y as defined by the function. In equations like the one above, the left-hand side (LHS) typically represents the dependent variable and the right-hand side (RHS) consists of the independent variable(s). y is a dependent variable as its value is dependent on (and is determined by) the value of x. You might have noted that when using explicit representation, multiple values are not attainable or possible.

With explicit functions for one specific value of x, only one value of y can be computed. As you can see in the table below, when the value of x is 1, the y value is 7. The equation $y = 2x + 5$ results in a straight line (Figure 5.2).

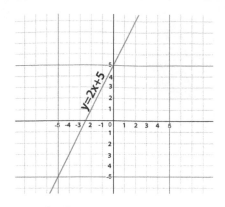

FIG 5.2 Straight line (equation y = 2x + 5).

x	y	(x, y)
−3	−1	(−3, −1)
−2	1	(2,1)
−1	3	(−1,3)
0	5	(0,5)
1	7	(1,7)
2	9	(2,9)
3	11	(3,11)

The equation $y = x^2$ results in a curved line (Figure 5.3).

x	Y (=x²)	(x, y)
−3	9	(−3,9)
−2	4	(2,4)
−1	1	(−1,1)
0	0	(0,0)
1	1	(1,1)
2	4	(2,4)
3	9	(3,9)

Note that in the above case, because the square of a positive number or a negative number results in a positive number, squares of −1 and 1 are both positive (+1). So, for both negative and positive values of x, y values are always positive, and hence, the curve remains in the upper two quadrants only.

The examples we saw above are for explicit functions. On the other hand, implicit functions are expressed both in terms of the dependent and independent variables. There are design situations or problems wherein it is not possible to describe something directly or explicitly. In these situations,

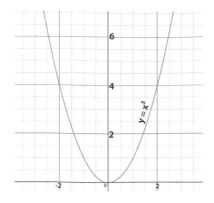

FIG 5.3 Curved line (equation $y = x^2$).

the dependent variable is not separately shown on one side of the equation (LHS). Unlike the explicit function that defined the dependent variable in terms of the independent variable, the implicit function is defined in terms of both the dependent and independent variables. This can be easily explained say with a circle's equation, $x^2 + y^2 - r^2 = 0$. In the case of explicit equations seen earlier, using the value of x, y value could be obtained. However, in this case, the solution to this equation cannot be found just with only x or y.

With implicit curves, the set of points on a curve are defined using a method to check if a point is on the curve. Figure 5.4 shows the representation for $x^2 + y^2 - 10^2 = 0$, where the radius is 10 units. In this case, y could have more than one value, and it could either be positive or be negative as shown below:

$$y = \sqrt{10^2 + x^2} \quad \text{or} \quad y = -\sqrt{10^2 + x^2}$$

With implicit representations, it is possible to have closed curves (like the circle above) and also multivalue curves.

Now, let us move on to the third form of representation, parametric curves. Just as with explicit or implicit, let us look at the basic meaning of the word parametric, which means referring to a parameter. In the case of

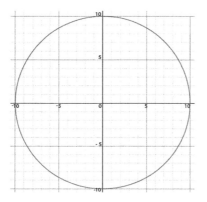

FIG 5.4 Circle (equation $x^2 + y^2 = 10^2$).

parametric representation, a parameter is used to define an ordered pair of x and y. For example,

$$x = t^2; y = 3t$$

In this case, for each value of the parameter t, we can get a value for x and y.

t	x	y	(x, y)
	$x = t^2$	$y = 3t$	
−2	4	−6	(4, −6)
−1	1	−3	(1, −3)
0	0	0	(0,0)
1	1	3	(1,3)
2	4	6	(4,6)

A *parametric curve* defines positions on a curve using parameters. Hence, mathematically, a parametric curve in x, y, z can be represented as follows:

$$x = x(t) \quad y = y(t) \quad z = z(t)$$

For any given value of t, a point in the three-dimensional space can be obtained using the above functions. You can think of parametric representations as a simpler way to generate coordinate values using the parameter values. They are a very useful tool for modeling smooth curves as they can generate a series of points for given values of t. In other words, a parametric equation takes parameter values as the input and output coordinate values. Earlier we saw how we can represent a circle using implicit representation. The parametric representation for a circle is as follows:

$$x = r\cos(\theta)$$
$$y = r\sin(\theta)$$

You may note one important thing with respect to parametric curves. Here, one coordinate is not described using another coordinate or in terms of another coordinate. For instance, the y coordinate is not expressed in terms of x as we saw earlier. Instead, both x and y are linked to this parameter which acts as a control variable.

Open and Closed Curves

Typically, curves that have two distinct end points are known as open curves, while curves that are closed do not have end points. In closed curves, the starting point and the end point are the same. Circles and ellipses are examples of closed curves. The closed curves encompass an area within them. If you consider the alphabets C and O, the former is an example for an open curve, while the latter is an example for a closed curve (Figure 5.5).

Simple and Nonsimple Curves

A simple curve, according to the definition of a curve, does change its direction, but it does not intersect itself while doing so. A simple curve can either be closed or open. On the other hand, a nonsimple curve intersects or crosses itself. We have two excellent examples of these two curves in the numerical system itself. Figure 5.6 shows the number zero and the number eight, the former being a simple curve and the latter being a nonsimple curve.

Upward and Downward Curves

A curve that points towards the upward direction is called an upward curve. An upward curve is also known as a concave upward curve. A curve that points towards the downward direction is called a downward curve. A downward curve is also known as a convex downward curve. The profiles of a spoon facing upward and downward are good examples of upward and downward curves (Figure 5.7).

FIG 5.5 Closed curve (left) and open curves (right).

FIG 5.6 Simple and non-simple curves.

FIG 5.7 Upward and downward curves.

Interpolating versus Approximating Curves

If the curve actually passes through the control points, it is known an *interpolating curve*. On the other hand, an *approximating curve* is one where the curve's path is near or very near to the control points but not necessarily through the control points.

Now that we have discussed about some important curve terminologies, let us look into splines in detail.

Splines

A spline is a curve in the three-dimensional space defined by a minimum of two points. Depending on the type of model being created, spline modeling offers an alternative to polygon modeling. Pierre Bézier, Paul de Casteljau, and many other pioneers contributed to splines and curve-based modeling.

As we will see in Chapters 7 and 8 on animation, historical developments over the centuries have influenced almost all aspects of modeling and animation. Similarly, splines can be traced back to several years before the advent of digital modeling when they were used in the shipbuilding industry. Let us take the points shown below as examples. Try to visualize a curve that passes through the points connecting the four yellow points (Figure 5.8).

Similar to the approximation shown above, in the earlier days of shipbuilding industry and for other drafting purposes, a pliable strip of wood or metal was utilized to create graphical representations like these. These were called splines. Builders used thin splints (splines) pulled into place by weights called knots. As you can see in the figure, the highly bendable spline (wooden strip) could be bent into specific curved shapes by moving ducks or changing their weights. Today, when we work with digital tools, we use control points instead of ducks used to vary the weights and hence the influence on the shape of the curve. We will look at this shortly when

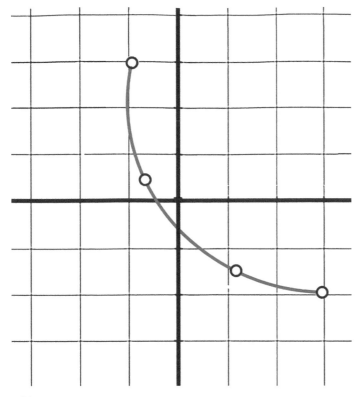

FIG **5.8** Spline.

we discuss control points. Splines were also used by draftsmen to create smooth-shaped curves for different kinds of applications involving detailed technical drawing. Back then, metal weights were used to control or bend a thin strip of metal or wood to create and draw smooth curves. In order to hold the spline thus obtained firmly against the drawing board, pieces known as *ducks* were used (Figure 5.9).

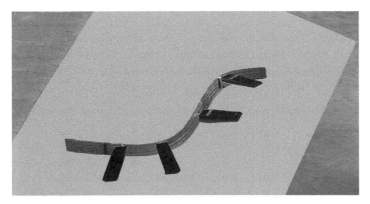

FIG **5.9** Spline Ducks.

In fact, this was an ingenious solution with the available resources during those times that allowed using the knots to control and generate very smooth curves. The use of weights was based on the fact that the effect of each particular weight is maximum at the original point of contact, which tends to decrease further down the path of the spline farther away from that particular weight. So, to exert greater influence or control, the builders used more weights. However, as you can imagine, this way of depending on physical weights creates restrictions in terms of both space and material availability, and hence, there was a need for describing curves using other means. This need was eventually met by the development of polynomials, which are not only significant in algebra and algebraic geometry but also in many other areas of math and science. There are different historical versions on the evolution of polynomials, but it can be safely said that polynomials evolved from the cumulative efforts of many people over the centuries.

Polynomials

Let us take a brief look at polynomials as splines are indeed curves constructed piecewise using polynomial functions. A polynomial is an algebraic expression composed of two or more terms represented by the product of a variable with a constant and raised to the power of an integer. The root poly means "many," and "nomial" refers to "terms." So, in essence, a polynomial refers to an expression made of "many terms." This is again referred to by piecewise in the term piecewise polynomial. Even though polynomials are considered to be quite efficient computationally, generating an optimal curve satisfies graphics requirements using single polynomials. So, the curve is broken down into segments or pieces, and each of these is represented by a polynomial function. Hence, the term piecewise polynomials as the final result is obtained by putting piecewise segments together. In the earlier chapters, we saw the distinction between a polyline and a polygon. A piecewise linear that is put together from a series of straight-line segments is referred to as piecewise linear.

Polynomials are generally represented using a standard expression such as:

$$f(x) = a_n x^n + a_{n-1} x^{n-1} + a_{n-2} x^{n-2} + \cdots + a_2 x^2 + a_1 x + a_0$$

In the above expression, $a_n, a_{n-1}, \ldots, a_2, a_1 x, a_0$ are all known as coefficients and x is the variable. Depending on the highest power of the variable, the polynomial equations are classified as linear, quadratic, cubic, etc. A linear equation is one where the highest power of the variable is one, and in quadratic and cubic equations, the highest powers are two and three, respectively.

It will be much easier to understand if we started with some simple, such as:

$$f(x) = 6x^2 + 9x + 3$$

Polynomials with just one expression ($6x$) are known as monomials. Polynomials with two expressions ($4x + 5$) are known as binomials, those with three expressions are known as trinomials ($6x^2 + 9x + 3$), and so on. Even constant numbers such as 3 and 5 can also be polynomials. In such cases, x is supposed to be raised to the power zero ($3 * x^0$), which is equal to 1. The degree of a polynomial is the maximum power of the exponential (only variables, not coefficients) within the polynomial equation. In case of an nth-degree polynomial, n represents the highest power of the exponent in the equation and n values can only be whole numbers.

Let us consider this polynomial for example: $3x^4 - 2x^3 + 3x - 5$.

The term with the highest power in the above polynomial is $3x^4$ and the highest exponent is 4. Hence, the degree of the above polynomial is 4.

If you consider this equation, $2x^2 + 3x - 2^4$, the degree of the polynomial is 2, even though the exponent of 2 is 4. As only the exponential power of the variables is considered for the degree of the polynomial, the exponent of the coefficient does not matter.

Now, let us come back to our discussion on how this discussion on polynomials applies to splines. A spline is actually a curve composed of curve segments that are connected together to form a continuous curve. Mathematically, this represents polynomial sections that have been merged together.

A spline is a piecewise polynomial that traverses through control points known as knots. These control points not only describe the spline but can also be used to modify and manipulate the spline. Mathematically, a spline is a function that matches the values at the points $x_1, x_2, x_3, \ldots, x_n$. A piecewise polynomial function $f(x)$ is obtained by dividing x into intervals and representing by a discrete polynomial interval. The polynomials are linked at the end point of the intervals. To understand how splines work, imagine trying to create a smooth curve using an elastic band by passing it through a set of points. In order to maintain the shape, obviously you may have to use something like tacks or pins to hold them in place as the elastic band passes through to produce a smooth curve through a designated set of points.

Bézier Curves

Bézier curves were popularized by French engineer Pierre Bézier who applied these curves to design and manufacturing applications, especially for automobiles. The Bézier curve was one of the early approximation methods employed in Computer-Aided Design (CAD) application that used splines to generate smooth flowing curves. Generally, with Bézier curves, the initial and final vertices lie on the curve, while the intermediate vertices are not actually on the curve. The idea is to approximate a polygonal shape formed by a set of vertices using a polynomial curve.

Bézier curves belong to the category of parametric curves that we discussed earlier.

Figure 5.10 shows two Bézier curves that use parameters to define the control and anchor points. These were created in an open source graphics programming language known as Processing© using a Bézier() function.

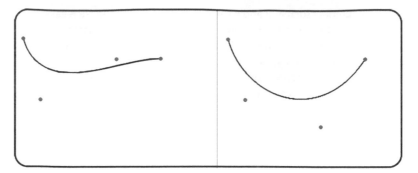

FIG 5.10 Control Points and Anchor points.

This function represents the control points and the anchor points using eight parameters.

$$\text{bézier}(m_1, n_1, a_1, b_1, a_2, b_2, m_2, n_2);$$

In the above function, (a_1, b_1) and (a_2, b_2) are the control points and (m_1, n_1) and (m_2, n_2) are the anchor points. Figure 5.10 shows the control points in blue and the anchor points in red for two Bézier curves. The anchor points for the two Bézier curves are the same, but see how the control points influence the shape of the Bézier curve.

Figure 5.10 shows the anchor points in red and the control points in blue. With the anchor points being the same, see how the position of the control points affects the curvature. Notice how the bent part of the curve is shifted as the control points are moved.

One of the problems frequently experienced with Bézier curves is the lack of precision in terms of the ability to control the curve. As the entire curve representation averages all the vertices of the Bézier curve, transforming any of the point modifies the curve as a whole. Thus, even transforming or moving a single control point globally affects the curve shape, which leads to instability. On the other hand, B-splines offer better local control compared to Bézier curves. *B-splines* are curve segments merged or linked to form a smooth shape. Owing to their adaptability, B-splines are considered more versatile than Bézier curves, even though B-splines themselves are a generalization of Bézier curves.

B-Splines

As we just saw earlier, B-splines can help overcome the limitations imposed by the Bézier curve wherein a change to any one control point affects the curve globally (the entire curve's shape is altered). B-splines tackle this problem by restricting the changes to the particular segment of the entire curve containing the control point being changed.

So, by manipulating the control point corresponding to the specific segment of the curve, the shape of that particular curve segment can be altered.

Isaac Jacob Schoenberg invented the term B-spline that is short for Basis Splines (Schoenberg, 1988). The B-spline, being a spline, is also a piecewise polynomial, and the points of intersection of these pieces are known as knots. In fact, the Bézier curves we saw earlier can be thought of B-splines that do not have any internal knots. B-splines are specified based on the number of their interior knots and their order. Different notations are used to refer to the knots and the order of the B-splines. N is a common notation for the number of knots, and as there are two end points for B-spline, the total number of knots will be $N + 2$ (where N stands for the interior knots).

The polynomials we discussed earlier under splines were extended later to B-splines. These, in turn, resulted in a new set of curve representations known as NURBS, which became quite popular. B-splines allow manipulating the curve with local control as the curve's shape can be controlled using each vertex. While they offer more flexibility and control, from the computational perspective, B-splines are intensive. Another type of curves are Bézier curves, in which the curve only goes through the end point and not actually through the intermediate points.

A B-spline curve is made up of segments which are joined together at points known as knots or knot vectors. If these knots are spaced equally or evenly apart from each other, the resulting B-spline is said to be uniform. In a nonuniform B-spline, these knots are not distributed uniformly or evenly across. When manipulated, the control vertices (CV) in B-splines only locally influence that specific region of the curve, unlike Bézier curves wherein they affect the entire curve globally. The scope of this book will not allow us go deep into computational geometry. So, having discussed Bézier curves and a general introduction to B-splines, let us now look at a specific category of B-splines known as NURBS, which have significant application in graphics modeling.

NURBS (Nonuniform Rational B-Splines)

NURBS are an excellent tool for creating smooth surface and representing organic objects. NURBS are used in popular 3D modeling software packages, such as CAD/CAM (Computer-Aided Design/Manufacturing) software, CAE (Computer-Aided Engineering), 3ds Max©, and Maya©, to design and model surface involving intricate curves. NURBS are a popular modeling tool as they facilitate good user interaction and can also be managed by CG modeling languages and software to create complex curves and surfaces. Figure 5.11 shows some NURBS curves.

To help you appreciate the reason behind the efficiency of NURBS, let us do a quick comparison with polygons. When using polygons, positions within the 3D coordinate system were defined using vertices (points), which were used to create lines (edges). Subsequently, polygons are created using these lines and points that together constitute the (polygonal) mesh. We had seen earlier that when approximating an organic (curved) surface or object, a large number of polygons are needed to create a smoother appearance.

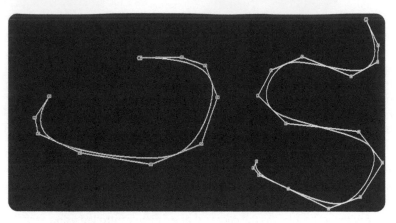

FIG 5.11 NURBS.

Otherwise, the object you create will have a jagged appearance. To achieve this, we can also perform polygon subdivision as we saw earlier. However, in case of a highly intricate organic structure, a lot more subdivisions will be needed, thus increasing the polygon count significantly. So, NURBS are more efficient in such circumstances. Figure 5.12 shows some extruded surfaces using NURBS curves. They are all extruded from the same NURBS curve, but the CV have been modified to generate the extruded models shown here.

Remember that each modeling technique has its own disadvantages and advantages. The knowledge of which tool to be used under what circumstance comes with experience and practice with different techniques. One of the biggest advantages of NURBS is that the designer or modeler need not necessarily completely understand the mathematical equation governing them in order to use them to model in 3D. We will now look at a number of methods and techniques that can take a NURBS curve and create complex surface from them. Typically, in advanced 3D modeling, a spline is converted into a NURBS before such sweeping operations can be carried out.

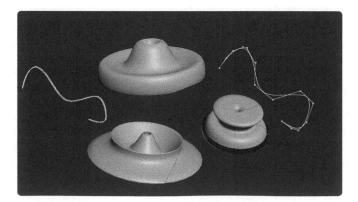

FIG 5.12 Surfaces from NURBS curves.

Another advantage of NURBS is that they create complex 3D shapes and surfaces starting from simple 2D splines and, more importantly, they can be modified interactively even after their creation. The user can interact with the basic spline object to fine-tune the model generated till final 3D shape is obtained.

This brings us to the next important topic of discussion, namely, sweeping techniques; here, we will discuss these in greater detail.

Sweeping Techniques

The basic notion behind sweeping involves taking a 2D shape (spline) and *sweeping* it to create a solid volume. Sweeping techniques such as extruding and lathing are extremely time-saving modeling techniques that are widely used to create intricate 3D objects efficiently. A cylinder can be considered as an extruded circle, and a box is an example of an extruded square or a rectangle. Figure 5.13 shows the basic 2D splines and the final 3D shapes extruded and beveled from the 2D splines. Photorealistic textures can be applied to these 3D models to give them realistic appearances.

Lathe

In machine tool operation, a *lathe* is a mechanical device that clamps or holds in position the material and spins it around an axis so that tools can be used on it to create the final product. *Lathing* creates a 3D surface by revolving the basic shape about an axis, which means that all objects created from lathing have symmetry about the axis of rotation. Figure 5.14 shows the 2D splines (left) and the final 3D shapes created by lathing. A 3D surface generated by lathing is known as a *surface of revolution*. If a closed surface is needed, typically the surfaces need to be swept by the complete 360°.

Otherwise, based on the requirements of the modeler, the lathing can be partial and the pieces thus created are known as slices. To understand this, imagine a whole apple as an object created by a 360° revolve operation and

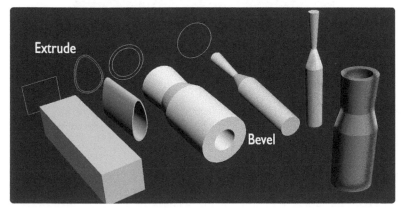

FIG 5.13 Extrude and Bevel Operations

FIG 5.14 3D objects from 2D splines.

FIG 5.15 Lathed 3D object with Photorealistic texturing.

a small slice of apple as one that has been swept only 30°. Figure 5.15 shows a lathed 3D model with a photorealistic texture applied to it and a light placed on the right side to accentuate the edges.

Loft

Let us consider a simple example of how splines can be used to effectively construct 3D objects which might otherwise be extremely time-consuming

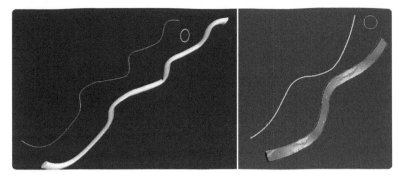

FIG 5.16 Lofting: Path spline and Shape spline

to create by looking at lofting. Lofting involves creating an intricate 3D object using two two-dimensional objects like splines. Typically with lofting, two splines are needed: One of these two splines serves as the cross section or the shape spline, and the other one serves as the path spline serving as the path along which the shape can extruded. Shown below is the image of a curved pipe object showing water flow. Figure 5.16 shows a non-photorealistic rendering of a lofted object on the left with the path and shape splines. The circle is the shape, and the curved spline is the path. The 3D object for the pipe was created using lofting. Note that loft is not to be confused with extrusion, even though they may seem similar. Extrusion works only along a straight line, while with loft, the path need not be straight.

In the preceding sections, we looked at various operations to create complex shapes using NURBS and other procedures involving sweeping operations to create intricate, esthetic shapes quickly and efficiently using various operations such as extrude, loft, and lathe.

Subdivision Modeling

As the name indicates, subdivision refers to dividing further or a subordinate division. Just as a polygon can be manipulated to modify the mesh, edges can also be modified to modify the mesh. Edges can be added or subtracted, which automatically causes a corresponding change in the number of vertices or polygons connected to those edges. Subdivision can be thought of an iterative refinement procedure wherein during each subdivision the number of polygons and hence the vertices keeps increasing on the model, thus enabling a smoother surface. As can be seen from Figure 5.17, an increased number of subdivisions create a smoother approximation of the curved surface.

The idea behind subdivision modeling is to originally create a simpler model which is not very detailed and then create a more organic smoothened version through subdividing. Typically, modelers create smoother 3D objects by applying subdivision modeling on quads or tris, since with n-gons subdivision modeling performs unsteadily.

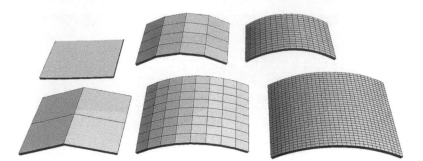

FIG 5.17 Subdivision Modeling.

Subdivision Surfaces

Subdivision surfaces (SDS) are unlike some of the curved surfaces we saw earlier in that they are not parametric. Characteristically, these are generated by a procedure that divides each of the surface into four by creating midpoints and then restructuring the vertices by averaging the local weights. SDS algorithms work by producing a smoother surface from a coarse mesh of polygons by applying multiple steps for fine-tuning with varying levels of precision as required by the model and the overall scene. The original rough mesh of polygons is referred to as the base mesh. The different methods to perform the subdivision of surfaces to add detail to the modeled object include Approximation, Corner Cutting, Averaging, Interpolation, Splitting, and Insertion. Now, let us look at few other classifications of modeling.

Organic versus Hard Surface Modeling

Organic modeling is a valuable tool to model organic (natural, life-like) character models. The term organic in the modeling context refers to something similar to living organisms and attributes of living organisms, especially from the external appearance and behavior. Deducing from this, an organic model can be representing an anthropomorphic (human-like) or other creatures. Organic models could also represent objects similar to living creatures or having forms similar to natural things. However, within 3D modeling, organic modeling is typically considered to be more sophisticated and involves greater attention to detail. Organic modeling may in fact involve a team of modelers and may account for a greater chunk of the time and resources in comparison to the rest of the modeling. Creating appealing organic models involves considerable time and effort involving studying many references as well as character anatomy and creating many drawings (Figure 5.18).

As you can see from Figure 5.18, creating a character inevitably involves some level of anatomical understanding of the anthropomorphic characteristics as well as the animal characteristics as the head depicts an animal face. Although organic shapes are modeled based on natural and living systems, organic modeling is not always used only in the context of creating models of

FIG 5.18 Organic Modeling.

FIG 5.19 Curved shapes in architecture.

creatures and characters. Organic modeling is also used in other areas such as design and architecture, especially those involving intricate carved structures (Figure 5.19).

Free-Form 3D Modeling

So far, we have discussed many modeling techniques to create 3D digital objects or models. However, most of these techniques follow a mathematical order or logic or pattern (revolving about an axis, extruding along a path, etc.). However, complex scenes involving extremely intricate models that include finer details cannot always be built using the other modeling techniques we discussed earlier. Under such circumstances, free-form modeling can be used. Free-form modeling, of course, can involve or be used in tandem with other modeling techniques we saw earlier. You can analogize free-form modeling to the building or molding of objects using modeling clay. When modeling a complicated model requiring intricate details (using modeling clay), you may have to perform operations like kneading, pushing, pulling, pinching, massaging, and so on. You can consider free-form modeling as the digital counterpart of such procedures in which you will be deforming (or manipulating) your 3D object in multifarious ways, which is the reason that free-form modeling is also referred to as free-form deformation (FFD).

We have now briefly discussed some of the prominent modeling techniques commonly used in CG modeling. Now, let us look at other important terms, procedures, and operations that are employed in 3D modeling to create multi-level objects composed of smaller objects.

In a Nutshell

In this chapter, we discussed about lines and curves in detail. We come across curved objects almost every day. Curves are applied in various areas including aerospace industry, packaging, automobile, and shipbuilding. So, having looked at many different modeling tools and techniques, here is an important question. Which modeling technique is the best? There is no single answer to that question. The same object can be created by multiple methods. It all comes down to efficiency, polygon count, modeling time, and also a matter of modeler's preference. However, the general preference should be for a similar-looking end result with a lesser number of polygons and in lesser time. If you can create a desired 3D model swiftly, you can use the time saved for modeling something more complex. Modelers around the globe use innumerable tools to help them with the modeling process.

While learning how to model is one of the primary learning outcomes of this book, before doing that we will cover mathematical, geometric, and trigonometric concepts applicable to 3D modeling. Knowing to use a modeling software tool is not the same as having a strong grasp of the foundational elements of modeling. Even though software tools and the vendors of such software may change over time, the basic concepts involving coordinate systems, transformations, curvature, polygonal modeling, and so on remain the same. Once you become knowledgeable and experienced in the fundamental aspects of modeling, switching between various modes of modeling will not be a problem at all. This is by no means an attempt to undermine the digital tools. Undoubtedly, digital tools and technology have made life much easier and more efficient.

We saw that splines are used in many design applications. Ship modelers and drafters utilized a flexible strip controlled or restricted by control points to create a smooth curve. The strip assumed the smoothest shape possible as determined by the flexibility of the spline materials and as limited by the constraints imposed by the control points. With Bézier curves, as the curve is the resultant blend from the constraints of all the control points, local control over a specific part of the curve is not easy to attain. Modern-day designers use these control points to interactively manipulate the shape of the spline to create intricate curved shapes. Earlier, we saw how transformations could be applied to 3D objects and models. Similarly, by applying transformations to the control points, spline curves can also be translated, rotated, and scaled. There are several kinds of spline curves, such as Catmull–Rom splines, Hermite splines, and B-splines.

Though tools may vary, the principles are the same. Whether you use a calculator, a computer, a cellphone, or just paper and pencil to find the sum of two numbers, you are performing the same operation, that is, addition. You are just using different tools to perform the operation. Calculators or computational devices allow performing complex additions quickly; however, everyone needs to know and understand how addition can be done. This is the reason that addition is among the fundamental things that are taught during elementary education. Likewise, for you to succeed in modeling and animation, you need to know the basic principles of modeling, which will be covered throughout this book. These include the fundamental aspects of geometry, trigonometry, transformations, projections, polygonal modeling, and so on. Once you gain mastery of the basic principles, you can choose to use any tool that suits your convenience and requirements.

In this chapter, we started with the fundamental representations for curves. The chapter discussed various types of curves and splines. The chapter covered some of the common operations that can be used on NURBS curves to generate surfaces such as extrude, bevel, loft, and lathe.

This brings us to the next important topic of discuss, that is, sweeping techniques. Subsequently, we discussed about CSG that involves applying Boolean operations to primitive objects such as cylinders, cones, cubes, spheres, and pyramids to create complex designs and intricate shapes. We discussed the difference between grouping and hierarchy before moving on to discuss terminology for hierarchical linking. We discussed parent–child relationships and what various terms such as descendants, ancestors, sibling, and leaf refer to. The importance of pivot and establishing this centroid for model objects was discussed in relation to performing transformations such as translation and rotation. When objects have been merely grouped together, selecting any one object in the group selects the group as a whole and any transformation applied to any part of the group is applied to the entire group. The chapter subsequently discussed how complex scenes involving extremely intricate models that include finer details cannot always be built using the other modeling techniques we discussed earlier. Under such circumstances, free-form modeling can be used in coordination with other modeling techniques.

Chapter 5 Quiz

PART I

True/False (Circle the Correct Choice)

1. When using explicit representation, it is possible to get multiple values.
True False

2. B-splines are a generalization of Bézier curves.
True False

3. Bézier curves offer better local control than B-splines.
True False

4. In NURBS, the control points are indicated as nonhomogeneous coordinates.
True False

5. You need at least two path splines to perform a loft operation.
True False

6. Loft and extrusion are exactly the same.
True False

7. Extruding and lathing, time-saving and prominent modeling techniques, are sweeping techniques.
True False

8. All elements in a hierarchy are referred to as *branches*.
True False

9. In parametric curve representation, one coordinate is not described using another coordinate or in terms of another coordinate.
True False

10. In closed curves, the starting point and the end point are the same.
True False

11. Ripple creates new faces, vertices, and edges by applying a cutting plane to the object.
True False

12. A nonsimple curve, according to the definition of a curve, does change its direction, but it does not intersect itself while doing so.
True False

13. The twist operation winds an object around an axis based on the pivot point and axes constraints.
True False

14. If the curve actually passes through the control points, it is known an interpolating curve.
True False

15. Mathematically, a spline can be thought of as polynomial sections that have been merged together.
True False

16. While Bézier curves offer local control, B-spline curves do not provide local control.
True False

17. In case of a Bézier curve, the curve goes through the end points and the intermediate points.
True False

18. NURBS can be used to create complex 3D shapes and surfaces from simple 2D splines.
True False

19. Owing to their adaptability, B-splines are considered more versatile than Bézier curves, even though B-splines themselves are a generalization of Bézier curves.
True False

20. NURBS are a popular modeling tool as they facilitate good user interaction and can also be managed by CG modeling languages and software to create complex curves and surfaces.
True False

Part II

Multiple Choice Questions (Choose the Most Appropriate Answer)

1. A/An _____ curve defines positions on a curve using parameters and is a very useful tool for modeling smooth curves.
   a. Explicit
   b. Implicit
   c. Parametric
   d. Isometric
   e. None of the above

2. An _____ curve is one where the curve's path is near or very near to the control points but not necessarily through the control points.
   a. Alternate
   b. Interpolating
   c. Arbitrary
   d. Approximating
   e. None of the above

3. A B-spline curve is made up of segments which are joined together at points known as _____ vectors.
   a. Segment
   b. Spline
   c. Knot
   d. Drawing
   e. None of the above

4. Some of the common operations that can be used on NURBS curves to generate surfaces include:
   a. Extrude
   b. Bevel
   c. Loft
   d. Lathe
   e. All the above

5. The basic notion behind _____ involves taking a 2D shape (spline) and sweeping it to create a solid volume.
   a. Anchoring
   b. Rendering
   c. Modeling
   d. Sweeping
   e. Surfacing

6. What is the smallest number of splines required for performing a loft operation?
   a. 1
   b. 2
   c. 3
   d. 4
   e. 5

7. A 3D surface generated by lathing the basic shape about an axis is known as a surface of _____.
   a. Rotation
   b. Transformation
   c. Translation
   d. Revolution
   e. Scaling

8. An _____ function is one which is expressed in terms of the independent variable.
   a. Explicit
   b. Implicit
   c. Parametric
   d. Isometric
   e. None of the above

9. Bézier curves were popularized by French engineer _____
   a. Paul Bézier
   b. Aiden Bézier
   c. Eigen Bézier
   d. Pierre Bézier
   e. None of the above

10. Polynomials with just one expression are known as _____
    a. Monomials
    b. Binomials
    c. Trinomials
    d. Constants
    e. None of the above

11. With _____, transforming any of the point modifies the curve as a whole.
   a. B-splines
   b. Binomials
   c. Bézier curve
   d. Segments
   e. None of the above

12. The topmost object in the hierarchical structure, the parent object that is above all other parent objects in the scene is called the _____.
   a. Root
   b. Branch
   c. Node
   d. Child
   e. Parent

13. Polynomials with two expressions are known as _____
   a. Monomials
   b. Binomials
   c. Trinomials
   d. Constants
   e. None of the above

14. In a B-spline, if the knots are spaced equally or evenly apart from each other, the resulting B-spline is said to be_____.
   a. Uniform
   b. Nonuniform
   c. Loose
   d. Normal
   e. None of the above

15. The shape of the alphabet O is an example of _____.
   a. Open curve
   b. Closed curve
   c. Rendering
   d. Bézier
   e. None of the above

16. The shape of the decimal number zero is an example of _____.
   a. Nonsimple curve
   b. Simple curve
   c. Rendering
   d. Bézier
   e. None of the above

17. The shape of the alphabet C is an example of _____.
    a. Open curve
    b. Closed curve
    c. Rendering
    d. Bézier
    e. None of the above

18. NURBS stands for _____.
    a. Nonuniform rational B-splines
    b. Nonuniform regular Bézier
    c. Nonuniform rendering B-splines
    d. Nonuniform rendering Bézier
    e. None of the above

19. The shape of the decimal number eight is an example of _____.
    a. Nonsimple curve
    b. Simple curve
    c. Rendering
    d. Bézier
    e. None of the above

20. NURBS are used in popular 3D modeling software packages, such as (Computer-Aided Design/Manufacturing) software, CAE (Computer-Aided Engineering), 3ds Max, and Maya.
    a. CAD/CAM
    b. CAE
    c. 3ds Max
    d. Maya
    e. All the above

Reference

Schoenberg, I. J. (1988). Spline functions and the problem of graduation. In *IJ Schoenberg selected papers* (pp. 201–204). Boston, MA: Birkhäuser.

CHAPTER 6: Animation – Part I: Brief History and Basics

… the only clue to what man can do is what man has done.

– R.G. Collingwood

Hand drawing on paper is the fundamental of animation.

– Hayao Miyazaki

CHAPTER LEARNING OBJECTIVES

After carefully studying this chapter, you will be able to answer the following questions:

- What is animation?
- What were some relevant early inventions that contributed?
- How are pottery, puppetry, and flip-books related to animation?
- What is motion and what are the basic aspects of motion?
- What do speed, velocity, and acceleration mean?

DOI: 10.1201/9780429186349-6

- What do force and momentum mean?
- What are some types of motion?
- Why is timing important in animation?

What Will You Learn in This Chapter?

In this chapter, we will take a brief look at the traditional forms of animation from a historical perspective. Animation as we know it today resulted from the conglomeration of several interesting inventions and scientific developments around the world over a long period of time. If we analogize digital animation to a puzzle, the various pieces of this puzzle were crafted by the works of many innovators over the past several centuries. Different aspects of graphics and animation have also been influenced by various major art forms including those in the iron and bronze ages, medieval art, renaissance art, modern art, etc. We will see how the humble flip-book forms a link between the earlier animation tools and techniques with the present-day methods, a tool that is quite popular even today just as it was among the early pioneers. We will look at how the ancient crafts such as pottery and puppetry influenced various aspects of animation ranging from modeling to performance animation. This will help better understand and appreciate the current techniques of animation. Some of the principles employed in these ancient art forms are still highly relevant to current forms of animation such as:

- Attractiveness (or Appeal: 12th Principle of Animation – Animation II)
- Emotional plea (Appeal)
- Delineation of shapes (Solid Drawing)
- Communicate the message clearly (Staging)

Consequently, many valuable inventions and contraptions were made throughout the 19th and 20th centuries that contributed to the development of animation. Irrespective of the device and the technology used, one common underlying feature among all the above animations was that they involved *change over time*. Subsequently, we will cover the basic principles that allow us human beings to perceive animation and the foundational aspects including the physics of animation. As motion is a basic aspect of animation, let us take a brief look at the very fundamental aspects behind motion. Understanding the basic physics behind motion can provide you a good foundation in your animation journey.

A Brief History: Standing on the Shoulders of Giants

Digital animation and modeling today have borrowed immensely from the various art forms such as opera, play, theater, puppetry, and comic arts. The word theater was derived from the Greek language indicating "to watch or behold" (Figure 6.1).

FIG 6.1 Theater.

Prominent Greek philosopher Aristotle defined a plot as "the arrangement of incidents," and he considered a plot as the most important feature of a dramatic or theatrical performance. Unlike today, wherein we have access to numerous resources and references, during the very early days of animation, the modelers and animators did not have much work that they could use as reference or learn from. Hence, these people were truly pioneers, because today we have lots of examples and earlier work to refer to. But, during the times when animation as a field was in the rudimentary stages, they did not have much to rely on or refer to. In other words, they did not have the innumerable digital tools and techniques that are available today to support the various pre-production, production, and post-production processes. For the most part, they were actually dealing with actual, physical equipment which were, often times, bulky to handle.

To animate means to give motion to or to make something move, which is related to the root of the word from which the term "animal" is derived. The ability to "move" is a distinctive feature of the animals (when compared to plants). In computer graphics (CG) terminology, animation refers to a digital representation of the movement of objects or processes.

Inherently numerous natural and man-made processes are animated. A football game, pumping of the heart, a movie, and games like tennis, table tennis, etc. involve movement. If we were to simulate such processes, then a single visualization would not suffice and hence we have to create dynamic representations that depict such dynamic phenomena and processes realistically. Applications involving such dynamic objects and occurrences demand that the virtual world also portrays them in a dynamic manner. For instance, a waterfall in the real world and phenomena such as earthquakes, volcanic eruptions, and debris flow are all examples of animation (Figure 6.2).

FIG 6.2 Animal movements.

In CG terminology, *animation* refers to a digital representation of the movement of objects or processes. All the celebrated cartoon shows such as *Looney Tunes®*, *Mickey Mouse®*, or *Tom and Jerry®* were animations. The fields of digital (computer) graphics and animation have probably been recognized as disciplines since the second half of the last century. Although much of the developments in animation have seemingly taken place in the last century or so, this is truly not the case. Animation is both an art and science. Animation has been in existence for a much longer time than digital animation. It was only around the 1940s that the work on the first electronic computers was finished, whereas recorded efforts concerning animation can be dated back to the earlier centuries. Before looking into the actual process of creating a digital animation, we will take a brief look at the traditional forms of animation from a historical perspective. This will help better understand and appreciate the current techniques of animation. Even a brief overview of the art forms that directly and indirectly contribute to shaping the field of modern animation will help you to build a solid understanding of the various aspects that you need to consider as an animator.

The study of CG and animation involves various diverse aspects including sketching, drawing, photography, form, composition, raster graphics, modeling, effects, lighting, shading, and rendering. Let us take a quick look at some of the significant developments in these and related fields that shaped animation into what it is today. The more relevant ones will be covered in more detail in Chapter 6. Table 6.1 shows a brief list containing some of the many significant inventions pertaining to animation along with the approximate years. The table shown is only a collection of few of the numerous milestones and is by no means an exhaustive list of all important achievements in graphics and animation.

Creation of a flip-book is an excellent example of how an animation works. In an animate cartoon or movie showing a dog chasing a cat or a train moving on tracks, in fact the characters (dog, cat, train) drawn in different positions at different points of time are being played (or flipped like a flip-book) to give the illusion of animation. If we break these scenes into constituent parts, then we will find that each scene is made up of numerous *still images*. These still images

TABLE 6.1 Important Milestones in Graphics, Arts, and Animation

Milestone	Time Period
Early art forms: stone/bronze/iron ages	BC
Block printing, movable-type printing	9th–15th centuries
Magic lantern/phantasmagoria	17th–18th centuries
Thaumatrope, stroboscope, zoetrope	1820–1840
Phenakistoscope, hyalotype, kinetoscope	1840–1890
Advertisement boom	20th century
Public demonstration of televised images	1925
Evolution and popularity of soap operas	1930s–1940s
Use of flight simulation training applications	1940s
Whirlwind project initiated at MIT	1943
First general-purpose computer: ENIAC	1946
CRT amusement device	1947
First graphic images on analog	1950
Blackjack program on IBM computer	1954
Simulation training for space exploration	1960s
Era of advertising: spurred by super bowl	1967
Inception and evolution of home computers	1970–1980s
IBM PC/MS-DOS operating system	1981
Macintosh computer/mouse-based GUI	1984
Image editing program Image Pro© (Photoshop©)	1988
Adobe 1.0 release	1990
First fully computer-animated feature film	1995

are run or moved at a specified rate to produce a *moving picture*. This describes the essence of animation. Movies that we see in theater frames are being moved or run at some specific rate, such as 30 or 60 frames per second (fps).

Nanos Gigantum Humeris Insidentes

This Latin phrase means "to understand the truth from earlier findings." Let us take a quick look at some of the works and art forms that have inspired and contributed to the principles of animation as we know it today.

The inspiration of various aspects of animation can be traced back to arts and crafts that flourished in various eras, regimes, civilizations, and nations such as Mesopotamia, Babylon, Egypt, India, and China. It goes without saying that ancient cave drawings and paintings were the forerunners of all kinds of modern graphic forms including printing, press, and 2D and 3D graphics.

Humans have always been endowed with creativity as evidenced by the prehistoric cave paintings and other art forms discovered and verified

FIG 6.3 Cave painting.

by archaeologists and scientists. The tools and the media have changed significantly from charcoal, fat, or dirt on cave walls, to paint, dyes, and pigments on canvas, and now to digital tools on software platforms. Undoubtedly, creativity is one of the cornerstones of animation, as, among other things, animation is also an art.

Cave dwellers could possibly have been among the very first ones to depict motion. The oldest known cave paintings dating back to tens of thousands years are the oldest undisputed examples of figurative cave paintings (Figure 6.3) and stick figure drawings to demonstrate simple geometric shapes.

A good number of these included portray of simple and basic human as well as animal movements; they also provide insight into the kind of tools used in the earlier days.

Another early form of representation used for communication was the hieroglyphics. Typically, hieroglyphs consisted of symbols and pictures of objects from Egyptian life. Hieroglyphs, unlike today's form of writing in the English language, could be written in columns as well as rows and from left to right as well as from right to left. The different media used for hieroglyphs included papyrus, stones, and walls, and they were also to embellish various objects used in daily life. Both the cave paintings and the hieroglyphs demonstrate examples of nonverbal communication (Figure 6.4).

The items in the list cannot be classified into a single category as animation and graphics have evolved from diverse sources and efforts. Different aspects of graphics and animation have also been influenced by various major art forms including those in the iron and bronze ages, medieval art, renaissance art, modern art, etc.

Pottery, the art of molding and shaping clay into various forms, can be analogized to the various types of 3D modeling. (*Modeling*, in the context of computer animation, is the process of recreating the physical shape of objects within digital environments.) Pottery developed and flourished in various parts of the world at different time periods. Varying forms of pottery ranging from utilities, such as pitchers, receptacles, bowls, spoons, or ladles, to craft items, such as statues or figurines, were made in diverse locations

FIG 6.4 Hieroglyph. (Creative Commons Attribution-ShareAlike 3.0 Unported (CC BY-SA 3.0) https://creativecommons.org/licenses/by-sa/3.0/deed.en.) https://commons.wikimedia.org/wiki/File:Hieroglyph_representing_the_infinite._Karnak,_White_Chapel_of_Senusret_I.jpg

FIG 6.5 Pottery. (Creative Commons CC0 1.0 Universal (CC0 1.0) Public domain dedication.) https://commons.wikimedia.org/wiki/File:PotMaking.jpg

during different time periods. Artifacts unearthed over the years dating back to different historical periods demonstrate intricate and aesthetically pleasing designs crafted with precision. The ability to envision, conceive, and finally extract such striking designs in pottery and similar fields requires creative talents just as the 3D modeling process does (Figure 6.5).

TABLE 6.2 Comparison of Ancient Art Forms with Modern Digital Operations

Ancient Version	Animation/Modeling Equivalence
Painting/drawing	Graphics
Pottery	Modeling
Coloring/painting/dyeing	Texturing/mapping/shading
Stage lighting	Digital lighting
Dancing	Motion choreography
Puppetry	Rigging/animation

Besides the geometric elements involved in painting (plane/2D) and pottery (3D), there is much to learn in terms of the pigmentation and coloring employed. Various pigments and dyes were used to color and decorate the paintings and pieces of pottery, which formed the basis of our understanding of color theories and light models. The use of various kinds of colors, dyes, and pigments to embellish the paintings and pottery might have piqued the interest in light and color which led to various contentions, arguments, and hypotheses that paved the way for our understanding of the additive and subtractive color models (Table 6.2).

Another important area that has influenced the growth of various elements of digital graphics and animation is performance arts. *Performing arts* is a huge umbrella term that is used to refer to different art forms (Figure 6.6).

The various components of performing arts such as staging, motion choreography, and lighting played a major role in shaping the principles of their corresponding equivalents in graphics and animation. Digital lighting and rigging have drawn inspiration from and have developed immensely grounded on the knowledge base obtained from performing arts. Do you

FIG 6.6 Anthropomorphic (human-like) wooden puppets.

recall seeing the central light used to emphasize an on-stage performance, a stand-up comedian, or a singer? The primary source of light that serves as the main scene illumination is referred to as key light, as in the three-point lighting that is used in digital photography and digital rendering as well. Three-point lighting has been prevalently used in theater to communicate varying moods and varying mood intensities. This is the goal of digital lighting and rendering exercises that endeavor to create a good composition.

Another art form that greatly influenced the craft of animation as we know it today is puppetry. Puppetry, an ancient form of art, is believed to have originated thousands of years ago. Over the centuries, puppetry has remained a highly successful medium used to entertain and communicate ideas using *animation*. In puppetry, a puppeteer controls or manipulates puppets to create an engaging performance. Puppets are typically objects resembling human beings (Figure 6.6) or animals, or they can be any other object that can be used to serve the (specific) purpose of communication or entertainment. Puppeteers used strings to control the hand and leg (limb) movements and the motion of the character as a whole. Puppets are known to have been made from different materials including wood, clay, and even ivory. Various forms of motion capture and performance animation are grounded on the basic principles of puppetry that involved a character into limbs and used the joints (as pivots) to control their delicate movements precisely. Motion for computer animation also involves a segmented approach, wherein the character's body is divided and subdivided into various parts, which are controlled using limbs and joints that act as pivots when applying transformation. Digital puppetry, which involves manipulating puppets (characters) in a digital environment, has derived extensively from traditional forms of puppetry. Motion Sesame Street/Elmo's© World is a remarkable example of digital puppetry that has gained wide acclaim and employs real-time performances as well. For instance, as we will see later in Chapter 9 on lighting, with digital software, one can easily switch between different types of CG lights and easily position key and fill lights, and this was an ordeal in earlier days. Not only were these lights cumbersome, but they also used to get quite hot (even today when such lights need to used, those who handle it use special gloves to protect their hands). Also, when performing on a stage, there is much less latitude for mistakes unlike a movie, wherein the actors can do as many shots or takes as they feel required before the director is completely satisfied. Puppets seem to have been used in India approximately 3,000–4,000 years ago. Archaeologists have excavated remnants of dolls with strings (for controlling their movement) dating to well before 2000 BC. Countries including India, China, Egypt, Turkey, and Burma and many other countries including many European and North/South American countries have contributed immensely to craft of puppetry (Figure 6.7).

Shadow play, another related art form, is an early form of storytelling that employs shadow puppets, which can be simple or elaborate flat cutout. Puppets are held against a luminous see-through background, which may be illuminated by light sources. The shadow puppets typically are shapes cut

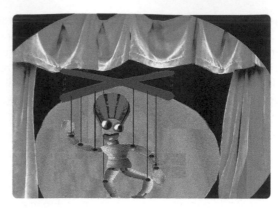

FIG 6.7 Puppetry.

FIG 6.8 Shadow play using a lit background.

out to resemble various types of objects depicting a wide range of shapes including animals, birds, trees, and humans. Puppets can range from very simple to highly complex and realistic ones that can be made from a gamut of materials

Combined with appealing storytelling, experienced puppeteers can make the puppets perform a wide range of actions including walking, flying, talking, laughing, or as required by the plot.

Shadow play (Figure 6.8) and puppetry are customary in numerous countries, and historical records show the prevalence of these arts in various cultures around the world. In some cultures, puppeteers are also known to lend voices to the characters represented by the puppets to create a more stimulating entertainment (Figure 6.9).

In fact, puppetry is considered to be one of the earliest known and most advanced forms of today's animation known as "performance animation." In the above image, the shadow puppets show anachronism, referring to the inclusion of a creature (dinosaur) belonging to an ancient period juxtaposed with other animals from current times. In ancient puppetry, the limb

FIG 6.9 Shadow play indicating anachronism and use of simple cutouts for engaging storytelling.

movements of the puppets were controlled by strings or rods as seen in the above image. Accomplished puppeteers were highly skillful in using rods and strings to precisely control the movement of various body parts including the mouth and eyes to create very realistic performances.

Early Innovations in Animation

In addition to the range of ancient arts and crafts we discussed earlier, animation was also shaped by the works of various innovators, a few of which we will see briefly. All the following gadgets and contraptions reflect the immense creativity of the pioneers. Although concerted efforts towards making animated films were seen towards the end of the 19th and the beginning of the 20th centuries, their foundations were laid few centuries earlier. Two of the critical inventions were the Camera Obscura and the magic lantern (Figure 6.10).

FIG 6.10 Camera Obscura. (Commons Attribution-ShareAlike 3.0 Unported (CC BY-SA 3.0). https://creativecommons.org/licenses/by-sa/3.0/deed.en; https://commons.wikimedia.org/wiki/File:Camera_obscura_2.jpg.)

The Camera Obscura is a significant invention that paved the way for photography and eventually led to various advances in animation. It is a very simple device consisting of a box with a small hole on one side, and the inverted image of the scene is formed (Figure 6.11). The box creates a dark compartment wherein the image of a real-world object is projected on a surface. As can be seen from Figure 6.11, light from the scene is transmitted through the hole and the inverted image of the scene object is formed. This creative device was used to study eclipses safely as viewing the actual phenomenon is considered to be harmful to the eyes, and hence, the images formed using this pinhole device were used to study the solar eclipse without risking exposure. This was also used by artists, who projected images that could be traced or copied.

The magic lantern is considered a predecessor to the projector. In this device, painted pictures on transparent glass plates were projected onto a medium using a light source. Even though used for entertainment initially, it was also adopted later for educational purposes. In addition to painted pictures, photographed and printed images were also projected using the magic lantern (Figure 6.12).

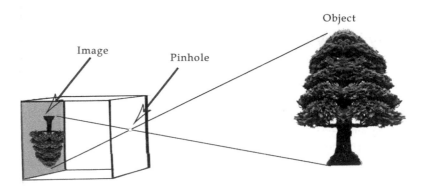

FIG 6.11 Pinhole camera mechanism.

FIG 6.12 Magic lantern attribution-ShareAlike 3.0 Unported (CC BY-SA 3.0). https://creativecommons.org/licenses/by-sa/3.0/deed.e.; https://commons.wikimedia.org/w/index.php?curid=2410766.)

Theaters based on magic lantern, known as phantasmagoria, took this to the next level and engaged audience by projecting scary images on semitransparent screens. Some of the important features employed later in phantasmagoria included the use of portable projectors as well as rear projection. While rear projection kept the magic lantern out of sight from the audience, the mobile projection facilitated image motion and image scaling.

Some of the pioneering inventions during the past several centuries were (not listed chronologically) the zoetrope (Figure 6.13), the thaumatrope (Figure 6.14), the praxinoscope, and the phenakistoscope, each one of which either improved the earlier one or contributed a whole new line of thinking.

The thaumatrope used a small round disc with pieces of string and a disc with pictures on either side. When the strings are spun rapidly, the two images on the sides of the disk "seem to" merge or blend into one another. In this case, the bird is on one side of the disc and the cage on the other. When the actual spinning happens, it creates an illusion as though the bird is inside the cage, even though we very well know that they are on separate sides of the disc. Although the thaumatrope (Figure 6.14) was popularly known as a

FIG 6.13 Zoetrope. (https://commons.wikimedia.org/wiki/File:Zoetrope.jpg)

FIG 6.14 Thaumatrope. (https://api.creativecommons.engineering/v1/thumbs/1c3e2de8-64b1-4d8c-8518-9284cca0be8e)

toy, it demonstrated a widespread notion behind the human perception of animation known as "persistence of vision."

Scientists and researchers have indeed put forth several different explanations regarding this, and there were serious contentions to the validity of the persistence of vision in explaining the human perception of motion. However, this was considered as a plausible explanation to the human perception of "motion." According to persistence of vision, an image persists (continues) to appear to human eyes even after we stop looking at the actual image, which enables us to perceive the motion as being continuous.

Another significant milestone in the history of animation was the highly acclaimed device known as phenakistoscope. Considered to be one of the foremost systems to create the illusion of media in motion, this device eventually played a critical role in the animation industry, especially motion picture industry. Like the other devices, this included a series of images, and these were drawn (or printed and pasted) around one disc. But, this also included a second disc whose movements were synchronized with the first disc. This other disc had windows placed apart from each other at equal distances for the viewer to observe. When observed on the mirrors through the slots on one disc, the images on the other disc seemed to be in motion due to the synchronized motion of the windows and the images

There are numerous other inventions made around this time period that have influenced and shaped the field of animation as we know it today. However, we will conclude our discussion on this topic with a couple of other milestones following the invention of the camera (Figure 6.16).

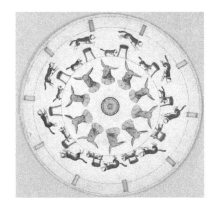

FIG 6.15 Phenakistoscope. (https://commons.wikimedia.org/wiki/Category:Phenakistoscope#/media/File: Optical_Toy,_Phenakistiscope_Disc_with_Cats_and_Donkey,_ca._1830_(CH_18607981).jpg)

FIG 6.16 Praxinoscope. (https://search.creativecommons.org/photos/b548ed29-9326-4075-b39d-012c53b21040)

In the zoetrope, a series of still images are displayed to the viewer in succession through a slender viewing strip (Figure 6.13). The zoetrope includes a cylindrical spinning device whose inner side includes a series of printed or drawn images showing various consecutive poses of animation. When the cylinder is in motion, the viewer observes the images through the vertical slits on the opposite sides.

A zoetrope resembles another device, known as the praxinoscope, which uses mirrors. In both the zoetrope and the praxinoscope, the animation effect is achieved via the spinning process wherein a series of pictures are shown in rapid succession. In the praxinoscope (Figure 6.16), mirrors are used instead of the narrow vertical slits, and as the spinning is started, the reflections of the images in rapid succession create the illusion of motion.

Kinetoscope

The kinetoscope was a significant development in the realm of images in motion, and it also took a step further by facilitating the recording of sound concurrently with motion. Kinetoscope, a sizeable apparatus, consisted of an enclosed box in which a looped strip of film was passed between a lens and an electric light bulb. There was an opening or a peephole through which the viewer could see the images in motion, which indeed created the illusion of animation, which resembled a realistic and animated depiction of things and/or people in motion. Later, the kinetoscope was also enhanced with headphones to facilitate listening to the musical or sound recording done for the animation.

These devices were capable of creating animation but did not allow for the user to interact with the mechanism. *Interaction* here specifically refers to the ability of the device to take an input from the user and respond to it (like what we all do when we are using our hand-held devices).

A significant invention, the cathode ray tube (CRT) amusement device made by Thomas T. Goldsmith Jr. and Estle Ray Mann, allowed interaction based on analog electronics. Using a control knob, the user or player was allowed to manipulate the location of the beam from the CRT and make it overlap with an airplane. Eventually, one of the most influential inventions in the world of human–computer interaction (HCI) was made by Ivan Sutherland. During the course of his doctoral thesis at MIT, Ivan Sutherland designed *Sketchpad*, a device that allowed users to interact with a user interface (UI) with a light pen. Several noteworthy inventions followed, and all along, the disciplines of graphics and animation were propelled by the unquenched thirst and unrelenting diligence of aspiring innovators.

Flip-Book

The flip-book is an animation tool that signifies a connecting link between the earlier animation tools and techniques with the present-day methods. It is quite popular among kids (and adults) even today just as it was among the early pioneers. Similar to the zoetrope and the other devices discussed earlier, a flip-book consists of a series of images. When flipped, these images, which vary from one another slightly, create an illusion of animation. It is also known as the flick-book in some parts of the world, and one of its original names was the "Kineograph" (Figure 6.17).

In addition to their function as educational aids to children (as well as adults), flip-books have played a very important role in the field of animation and motion pictures. The image below shows a flip-book made from the images shown on the two pages included here. Each page has eight images and hence a total of 16 images (Figure 6.18).

These images were arranged one behind the other in a sequence and made into a flip-book as shown below. When the pages were flipped, it created an animation effect showing the movement of the birds in the picture.

As renowned Oxford professor R.G. Collingwood stated: "… the only clue to what man can do is what man has done."

FIG 6.17 Flip-book in action.

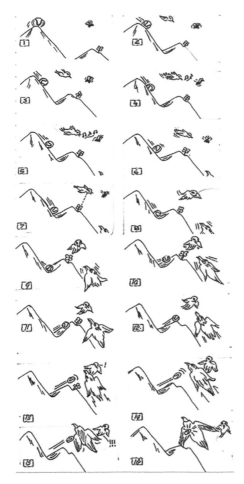

FIG 6.18 Flip-book. (Image courtesy: Nachiket, M.)

Digital animation is not very different from theater, opera, plays, and puppetry. How so? All these are, in essence, forms of communication. They communicate plots or stories or ideas. The primary distinction is the medium 3D animation uses digital tools and techniques, while theaters and plays use a stage. But, without an idea or the plot, there is absolutely nothing to communicate. You are thinking of two important things here: *What* and *How*? The story or the idea (*What*) conveyed is at the heart of any performance. Then comes the "how"? Once you have decided on the *What* (idea), your medium dictates the *How*? How to communicate things in a theater or play is different from how things are shown in a movie.

Most of the elements derived from still constitute the backbone of modern 3D modeling and animation. Digital lighting and rigging have drawn inspiration from and have developed immensely grounded on the knowledge base obtained from performing arts. The primary source of light that serves as the main scene illumination is referred to as key light, as in the three-point lighting that is used in digital photography and digital rendering as well. Three-point lighting has been prevalently used in theater to communicate varying moods and varying mood intensities.

Subsequently, many valuable inventions and contraptions were made throughout the 19th and 20th centuries that contributed to the development of animation. Irrespective of the device and the technology used, one common underlying feature among all the above animations was that they involved *change over time*. Something changed over time. As can be seen from the image below, in case of the tennis game, the ball's and players' positions change over time; in case of the clock, the minute and hour hands keep moving and their positions and orientations change over time

A notable explanation to the human ability to recognize animation or motion is put forward by the phi phenomenon, which states that when discrete (separate) objects are observed swiftly in sequence, an illusion of motion is perceived. However, delving deep into those will digress from the primary focus of this book, and hence, these are presented here very briefly for your information. To get a better understanding of these, think about the time your family had fun with sparklers. When moved in a circle, they create an illusion of a continuous line caused by the motion (Figure 6.19).

If the images change slowly, our brains perceive them as static images, but if they change rapidly enough, our brains do not process the change and

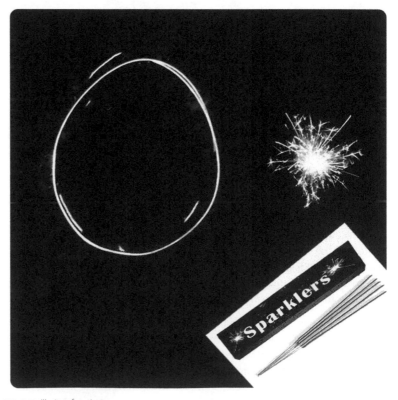

FIG 6.19 Illusion of continuity.

instead interpret the sequence as continuous motion. As a rule of thumb, images that change faster than 16 times per second are perceived as continuous motion. Movie projectors, which work on the same principle, use frame rates of 24 fps or higher for that reason.

You may even be surprised to know you may have already created an animation (without knowing it). One of the most common exercises that we did as kids and that we see kids do even today, the flip-book, is an excellent example of how an animation works. What we saw when one cartoon character was chasing another was in fact these characters are created in different positions at different points of time. If we delve into these scenes and break them into constituent parts, then we will find that each scene is made up of numerous "still images." These still images are run or moved at a specified rate so as to produce a "moving picture." This describes the essence of animation. All the movies we see today are frames that are being moved or run at some specific rate (say 30 fps) and so on.

As can be seen from the earlier sections, a vast majority of the modern techniques of animation are founded on the principles of the older forms such as hand-drawn animation and performance animation. The newer techniques can be considered as enhanced digital adaptations of the erstwhile techniques such as stop-motion animation, cel animation, and key frame animation. Ok. Now, let us look at these briefly.

Just imagine that you are sitting in a movie theater. Instead of showing you the "conventional" animated movie, you are provided the film rolls and a projector that can display the individual films one by one. It will consume a whole lot of time to see all the individual frames, and you will find it absolutely unexciting. This is because you would like to see the "animated version" of a naturally "dynamic process." What the individual frames altogether contain is human beings performing some action, and you would like to view the "action" and not the still constituents of the action.

Understanding Motion and Basic Physics

As motion is a basic aspect of animation, let us take a brief look at the very fundamental aspects behind motion. Understanding the basic physics behind motion can provide you a good foundation in your animation journey.

Time, Motion, and Speed

All actions we do in our real life, such as starting from home and reaching the shopping mall or office or university, start at a specific time and end at a specific time. They last for a specific amount of time (duration). Typically, any animation you perform involves motion. During animation, objects move over a period of time. This could be a small or a long duration of time.

Speed refers to the distance traveled by an object over a period of time. So, when somebody is driving at 30 mph, it means that they have traveled 30 miles over a period of 1 hour. Distance in this case is measured in miles and time in hours. There are varying units for measuring distance such as inch, foot, meter, and mile just as time can also be measured in seconds, minutes, etc.

Although speed and velocity are used interchangeably at times, they both do not refer to the exact same thing. While speed just refers to the distance traveled over a period of time, velocity indicates the distance over time in a specific direction. Considering the same example above, 30 mph refers to the speed of a car, but 30 mph in the southward direction refers to velocity. Speed, which only indicates magnitude, is referred to as a scalar quantity, while velocity, which includes both magnitude and direction, is a vector quantity.

While discussing the distinction between speed and velocity, let us also look at the distinction between distance and displacement, terms that are at times used interchangeably. Distance and displacement are not exactly the same thing. While distance is the measure of the actual path traveled by an object, displacement is purely the distance between the starting point and the ending point of an object. So, it is absolutely possible that an object that has traveled 200 miles has a displacement of "zero" (Figure 6.20).

Let us look at an example. In the above figure, assume that somebody walked along the boundary of the golf course (along the gray dotted line) and returned back to the starting point, indicated by the red dot at the bottom of the tree. The distance traveled by this person is equal to the total path (equal to the boundary) of the golf course, but the displacement is equal to "zero" as the person started and arrived back at the same point.

When an object is moving, say for instance a car, the velocity may change. This rate of change in velocity is known as acceleration. What causes this acceleration? The answer is "force." It is the "force" that causes and changes an object's motion. Words that we use commonly such as push and pull are actually forces. Earlier we saw that velocity is a vector, while speed is a scalar quantity. Force includes both direction and magnitude, and hence is a vector quantity. A common force that we all are familiar with is the "force of gravity."

The force of gravity attracts objects to the center of the earth. In fact, without gravity, we will all be floating around instead of walking or standing on the earth. The word gravity itself is derived from the Latin word gravitas meaning weight. You will be dealing with these jargon and concepts quite a lot in

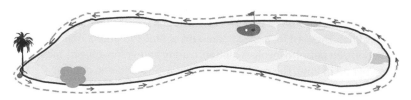

FIG 6.20 Distance versus displacement.

animation. We are not getting into theoretical physics or anything advanced. Let us have just a glance into some basics so that you can understand and appreciate the difference between these common physics terms as relevant to animation.

We need to take a step back and look into yet another pair of scalar quantity and a vector quantity, namely mass and weight, respectively. Mass represents the amount of matter contained in an object. This does not change depending on the place. For instance, you may recall from a science museum visit or field trip about how your weight is different on the moon than on the earth. Yes. Your weight changes. But, not mass. Mass remains the same. Weight changes because weight is a force which represents the product of mass and gravity. Weight=Mass * Gravity. The gravity on the surface of the earth is approximately six times stronger than that on the surface of the moon. In other words, a person who weighs 100 pounds on the earth would weigh only 16.5% of that (16.5 pounds) on the moon. This is because weight is obtained by multiplying mass with gravity and because the gravitational pull of the moon is only 16.5% of that of the earth. Thus, a person's weight would be much lighter on the moon than on the earth. Now, we know that weight is a force, which is a vector quantity since it has both magnitude (mass) and direction (from the gravitational pull). Having clarified that, let us get back to force and understand it using a very simple example of a soccer ball being kicked (Figure 6.21).

In the image above, you see a soccer ball being kicked rise up and reach a maximum height and then come down to the ground. The path followed by the ball during the course of its motion is known as a trajectory. The force of the kick makes the ball to accelerate and rise up. As the ball is rising into the air, it is not only subjected to the gravitational pull of the earth but also the frictional force exerted on it by the air. Hence, even though the force of the kick causes the acceleration resulting in the ball rising up, the other forces (friction and gravity) decelerate it and pull it down. As an animator, you must be aware of the forces in action when you are animating your scene objects.

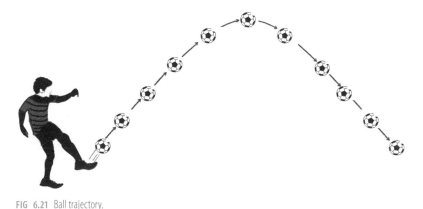

FIG 6.21 Ball trajectory.

While animating, you need to consider not only gravity but several other forces as applicable to the scene you are animating. We looked at friction briefly in the earlier passage. But, friction is an essential and fundamental force that is applicable in many common situations. Even though friction may be used in negative connotations such as wear and tear, friction is in fact highly important because our actions including walking, running, driving, grasping objects, and even writing would not be possible without friction. When you roll a ball on a surface, it is the frictional force that eventually brings the ball to a stop. That is why, you will find that a ball rolls on for a much longer time on a smoother surface than on a rough surface. The rough surface offers more resistance to the ball than the smooth surface. Hence, bowling lanes are treated to be very smooth and slippery to facilitate the ball to travel down the lane with less resistance.

Motion is the process wherein an object undergoes a change in its location or position. Typically, this change in location is caused by force(s) acting on the body. All the aspects of motion we saw earlier play a very important role when you are animating your scene using key frames, which we will cover in the next chapter. Key frames are specific frames establishing well-defined positions at specific points of time (frames). Timing is of foremost importance in animation. This involves two aspects: the specific moment when an action starts and how long it lasts. We will look at timing in detail later in the 12 principles of animation.

Momentum is another concept closely related to this discussion. Momentum is equal to velocity multiplied by the mass of an object. As velocity is involved, momentum is a vector quantity, which is directly proportional to both the mass and velocity. This means that an object traveling at a higher velocity has higher momentum than an object traveling slowly. Similarly, an object with greater mass has more momentum than an object with lesser mass. Again, these are essential considerations when animating objects so that you animate the objects in accordance with their mass, size, and velocity. If a car and a huge truck traveling at the same speed crashes into a wall, the momentum in case of the truck will be much higher than that of a car (Figure 6.22).

FIG 6.22 Varying momentum between objects of varying masses.

Translatory or Translational Motion

Translational motion refers to the case when an object moves along a path or a line in such a way that any point within this moving object is facing the same direction. The motions of a car, train, airplane, falling objects, etc. are all examples of translational motion.

Translatory motion is also referred to as linear motion; all the constituent parts of the moving object or even each particle on the body ends up traveling the same distance within the same amount of time.

In rectilinear motion, the path is straight, and in curvilinear motion, the path is curved. Let us try to connect the notion of trajectory we discussed earlier with the motion of the objects, parts, or particles. In rectilinear motion, the trajectories of all particles within the object are parallel. Elevators moving up and down their shafts and objects falling freely under gravity are examples of rectilinear motion. In curvilinear motion, the particle trajectories are curved. The motion of a soccer ball kicked across the field and that of a discus thrown by an athlete are examples of curvilinear motion (Figure 6.23).

Circular Motion

Circular motion refers to an object's motion in a circular path. Planets revolving around the sun and a toy train on a circular pathway are examples of circular motion. Based on whether or not the object moves at a constant speed, circular motion can further be classified into uniform circular motion and nonuniform circular motion.

In uniform circular motion, the objects move along a circular path in a constant speed. On the other hand, when an object moves along a circular trajectory with inconsistent speed, it is known as nonuniform circular motion.

When a body rotates, the line about which it turns or rotates is known as the axis. The axis along which the circular motion occurs offers the distinction between circular motion and rotary motion. In case of planets orbiting around the sun or a rider on carousel, the axis of rotation is not traversing through the object. For a planet moving around the sun or a rider in a carousel, the axis about which they rotate is not passing through them, but

FIG 6.23 Translatory motion.

FIG 6.24 Rotational motion (about axis).

it is outside. On the other hand, if you consider a figure skater or a spinning top, as they spin, they rotate about themselves. These are examples of rotary motion (Figure 6.24).

Interview with Justin Green

1. **What is rendering and from an industry perspective, how is it important?**

    3D rendering refers to the process by which graphical content is created via the use of 3D software technologies such as Autodesk Maya, Autodesk 3DS Max, and Cinema 4D. It is often used synonymously with other terms such as Computer-Generated Imagery (CGI), 3D graphics, and 3D visualization. The actual rendering process consists of complex mathematical calculations in which the computer calculates a number of user-defined settings such as lights, cameras, global illumination, and material surfaces in order to produce or render an image. If some of these terms sound familiar, it may be because in many ways 3D rendering is similar to traditional photography. It's therefore important for 3D artists to be familiar with the concepts of traditional photography, cameras, and lights.

Just like a photographer, 3D artists use their technical and artistic skills to set up virtual cameras, lights, environments, and several other variables required to get the desired shot. The obvious difference is that, unlike photography, 3D artists work in a simulated environment, and are not constrained by the laws of physics. This allows the 3D artist to create truly unique and spectacular images with the only limitation being one's imagination. Furthermore, the technology allows for an unprecedented level of control in regard to the style and quality of the image. Every shadow, every reflection, and every surface can be tweaked, modified, and adjusted on the fly. Thanks to modern rendering tools such as V-Ray, created by Chaos Group, and Luxion's KeyShot, 3D artists are able to work faster and produce higher quality results than ever before. This flexibility and level of precision is one of the main reasons why 3D rendering has become particularly popular in the consumer product industry.

2. **What is the role of creativity and imagination in a technologically advanced digital work environment?**

Creating designs only from memory is never a good idea. As a 3D artist, you will also want to gather as much reference as possible. The first question you need to ask yourself as a 3D artist is, how is your 3D model going to be used? If you're creating models for a video game, you'll want to create optimized, low-poly (or low-resolution) models that take into account the technical limitation for whatever platform the game will be running on. If, however, you're creating models for product rendering purposes, you'll want to create detailed, high-poly (or high-resolution) models that don't need to account as much for hardware limitations because the end results are images. Additionally, you also want to take into account whether your model will be static or animated and whether it will be seen close up or just in the distance. All of these details are immensely important because different workflows apply for different purposes.

No matter the area of production, as an artist, it's always essential to gather as much reference material as possible and understand how the model will be utilized once it's been completed.

An experienced 3D artist will always try to determine the most efficient workflow that does not sacrifice any noticeable quality. If the asset being modeled doesn't need to be animated, then fundamentals such as edge flow aren't as important to focus on. Similarly, if the model is only going to be seen in the background, it won't be as necessary to add the same amount of detail as if the model was going to be featured front and center on a poster or in a magazine. A good rule of thumb is to only create what's absolutely necessary and nothing more.

As should be the theme here, there's no one particular approach or one correct answer for any scenario. Everything is dependent on the specific details of what's required, and each artist will have a different preference regarding their approach. A truly experienced artist will have the ability to understand what the best workflow is for them from the beginning, and be able to properly plan ahead and account for potential challenges before they occur in the production process. The important thing is to develop a workflow that allows you to produce content intelligently and efficiently while maintaining a level of quality that will suffice for whatever the needs may be.

3. **Why should computer graphics students and 3D modelers should learn the concepts and theory? How does this knowledge help them succeed in modeling and animation?**

For 3D modelers, it's imperative to have a strong understanding of topology, which refers to how the edges flow across the model. 3D models are made up of three fundamental components: faces/polygons, edges, and vertices. As a whole, these components are also referred to as a mesh or geometry. An edge is basically a line made up of two vertices and three or more edges make up a face.

When creating a 3D model for animation purposes, it's incredibly important to make sure that the model contains proper topology meaning that the faces should be quads (four sides) and there should be a sensible flow regarding the edges, or topology, of the model and how the model will animate. Wherever the model will deform, extra edge loops should be added so that there is enough geometry for the model to deform smoothly. For static models, proper topology isn't very important, but it definitely makes things easier. When constructing a model for static or animated purposes, it's good practice to avoid Ngons and keep triangles (three-sided polygons) to a minimum. It's also important to try to keep all polygons somewhat evenly spaced and to avoid having any that are overly stretched. The most common 3D modeling techniques are polygon modeling and spline/NURBS modeling.

How the model was constructed and whether the model will be animated help to clarify the difference between organic and hard surface models further still. Organic models have very clean topology and edge flow, making them ideal for animation, while hard surface models contain Ngons (polygons with more than four sides) since they'll never need to deform. Organic models are often created using NURBS (nonuniform rational basis spline) or spline modeling techniques, while hard surface models are generally created using polygon modeling techniques. It's common for 3D modelers to specialize in either organic or hard surface modeling, depending on what interests them the most. Whichever they choose, it's still good to have a general knowledge of all areas, as you never know which technique might apply for any given project. At the end of the day, what really matters is whether the final design was constructed properly for the purposes that it will be used and less about the actual categorization.

In a Nutshell

This chapter provided an overview of the evolution of animation over the centuries by explaining how animation as we know it today resulted from the conglomeration of several interesting inventions and scientific developments around the world over a long period of time. The chapter covered how different aspects of graphics and animation have also been influenced by various major art forms including those in the iron and bronze ages, medieval art, renaissance art, modern art, etc. We looked at the early crafts such as pottery and puppetry and their influence on various aspects of animation ranging from modeling to performance animation. We saw how the common three-point lighting employed today was derived from the earlier performance arts and theater.

The basic idea behind covering these earlier discoveries and inventions is to better understand and appreciate the current techniques of animation. The many valuable inventions and contraptions made throughout the 19th and 20th centuries have contributed immensely to the field of digital modeling animation. Irrespective of the device and the technology used, one common underlying feature among all the above animations was that they involved *change over time*.

Subsequently, the chapter covered the basic aspects of the physics of animation as this can provide a good foundation in creating meaningful and powerful animations to support the plot. We looked at common terminologies used in animation such as speed, mass, force, and momentum. We also saw the distinction between the scalar and vector elements such as speed and velocity, mass and weight, and their role in animation. It is important to understand these fundamental concepts such as knowing the basic difference between commonly confused terms such as distance and displacement as these are most commonly used in the process of animating objects.

Finally, the chapter covered various types of motion such as linear motion, circular motion, and the subdivisions therein, namely, rectilinear and curvilinear motion, rotary motion, uniform and nonuniform motion, etc.

Chapter 6 Quiz

PART I

True/False (Circle the Correct Choice)

1. Animation has been in existence for a much longer time than digital animation.
True False

2. Photoglyphs consisted of symbols and pictures of objects from Egyptian life.
True False

3. The thaumatrope used a small round disc with pieces of string and a disk with pictures on either side.
True False

4. The kinetoscope included a series of images, and these were drawn (or printed and pasted) around one disc and it also included a second disc whose movements are synchronized with the first disc.
True False

5. Over the centuries, puppetry has remained a highly successful medium used to entertain and communicate ideas using animation.
True False

6. The flip-book is also known as the flick-book in some parts of the world, and one of its original names was the "kineograph."
True False

7. Momentum refers to the distance traveled by an object over a period of time.
True False

8. Pottery, the art of molding and shaping clay into various forms, can be analogized to the various types of 3D lighting.
True False

9. It is a very simple device consisting of a box with a small hole on one side and the inverted image of the scene is formed.
True False

10. Various forms of motion capture and performance animation are grounded on the basic principles of painting and lighting.
True False

11. According to theory of "persistence of motion," an image persists (continues) to appear to human eyes even after we stop looking at the actual image, which enables us to perceive the motion as being continuous.
True False

12. Force includes both direction and magnitude, and hence is a vector quantity.
True False

13. The gravity on the surface of the moon is approximately six times stronger than that on the surface of the earth.
True False

14. In live motion capture, the motion data from the performers of the dance or stunt sequences is first obtained and then refined.
True False

15. The 12 principles of animation were originally developed around the 1930s by animators in the Disney© Studios
True False

16. Force is equal to velocity multiplied by the mass of an object.
True False

17. Speed refers to the distance traveled by an object over a period of time.
True False

18. Distance and displacement are exactly the same thing.
True False

19. Velocity is considered as the corresponding vector quantity for the scalar quantity speed.
True False

20. Velocity is the product of mass and gravity.
True False

PART II

Multiple Choice Questions (Choose the Most Appropriate Answer)

1. Which o0f the following was not used for painting or coloring in prehistoric times?
   a. Charcoal
   b. Dirt
   c. Fat
   d. Synthetic paint
   e. None of the above

2. _____ is a very simple device consisting of a box with a small hole on one side and the inverted image of the scene is formed.
   a. Camera Obscura
   b. Camera
   c. Kaleidoscope
   d. Phenakistoscope
   e. None of the above

3. The _____ used a small round disc with pieces of string and a disk with pictures on either side.
   a. Thaumatrope
   b. Zoetrope
   c. Phenakistoscope
   d. CRT amusement device
   e. Kinetoscope

4. In _____ motion, the objects move along a circular path in a constant speed.
   a. Uniform tangential
   b. Uniform circular
   c. Non-uniform tangential
   d. Non-uniform circular
   e. Kinematic

5. _____ was invented by Thomas T. Goldsmith Jr. and Estle Ray Mann which allowed "interaction" based on analog electronics.
   a. Thaumatrope
   b. Zoetrope
   c. Phenakistoscope
   d. CRT amusement device
   e. Kinetoscope

6. Ivan Sutherland designed _____ , a device that allowed users to interact with a user interface (UI) with a light pen.
   a. Thaumatrope
   b. Zoetrope
   c. Sketchpad
   d. CRT amusement device
   e. Periscope

7. Which of the following is most relevant to motion capture and animation?
   a. Painting
   b. Pottery
   c. Drawing
   d. Coloring
   e. Puppetry

8. Which of the following is not a material that was used to make puppets in ancient centuries?
   a. Wood
   b. Clay
   c. Ivory
   d. Plastic
   e. None of the above

9. Which of the following country/countries have contributed to puppetry?
   a. India
   b. China
   c. Turkey
   d. Egypt
   e. All the above

10. The flip-book was also originally known as the _____
    a. Praxinoscope
    b. Kinetoscope
    c. Kinetophone
    d. Kineograph
    e. All the above

11. _____ was an art form based on the magic lantern, and it used projected images to create an interaction simulating animation.
    a. Theater
    b. Mime
    c. Vaudeville
    d. Phantasmagoria
    e. Opera

12. Pottery can be compared with which of the following.
    a. Storyboarding
    b. Scripting
    c. Modeling
    d. Animation
    e. Rigging

13. The _____ included a series of images, and these were drawn (or printed and pasted) around one disk and a second disk whose movements were synchronized with the first disk.
    a. Praxinoscope
    b. Phenakistoscope
    c. Kinetophone
    d. Kineograph
    e. All the above

14. The _____ , a sizeable apparatus, consisted of an enclosed box in which a looped strip of film was passed between a lens and an electric light bulb.
    a. Praxinoscope
    b. Phenakistoscope
    c. Kinetoscope
    d. Kineograph
    e. All the above

15. The word _____ was derived from the Greek language indicating "to watch or behold."
    a. Cinema
    b. Art
    c. Theater
    d. Parlor
    e. All the above

16. The sketchpad was invented by _____ .
    a. Isaac Newton
    b. Albert Einstein
    c. Ivan Sutherland
    d. Benjamin Franklin
    e. All the above

17. In _____ , puppets are held against a luminous see-through background, which may be illuminated by light sources.
    a. Shadow play
    b. Art
    c. Theater
    d. Parlor
    e. All the above

18. _____ is considered to be one of the earliest known and most advanced forms of today's animation known as "performance animation."
   a. Puppetry
   b. Art
   c. Pottery
   d. Parlor
   e. None of the above

19. The _____ is considered a predecessor to the projector.
   a. Thaumatrope
   b. Arkoscope
   c. Magic lantern
   d. Parlor
   e. None of the above

20. Which of the following is a unit for measuring distance?
   a. Inches
   b. Foot
   c. Kilometer
   d. Mile
   e. All the above

CHAPTER 7: Animation – Part II: Animation Types

You're not supposed to animate drawings; you're supposed to animate feelings.

– Ollie Johnston

After carefully studying this chapter, you will be able to answer the following:

- What is hand-drawn animation?
- How did computers influence the field of animation?
- Why are artistic skills like drawing and painting important even in the digital era?
- What is stop-motion animation?
- What are the different types of stop-motion animation?
- What is key frame animation?
- What is character animation?
- What is effects animation?
- What is camera animation?
- What are the 12 principles of animation?

DOI: 10.1201/9780429186349-7

What Will You Learn in This Chapter?

In this chapter, we will look into different forms of animation starting with hand-drawn animation that forms the foundation for the digital animation. The chapter will also briefly discuss the different kinds of popular stop-motion animation techniques such as clay animation, Lego© animation, and puppet animation. Next, we will move on to the process of creating animation using key framing (and in-betweening), which demonstrates how the parameters such as position and orientation (of an object or objects) change over a period of time. These discussions will evince how the advent of computer-based digital animation has made things much less cumbersome and time-consuming. To understand key framing, it is important to understand interpolation, which is key to the process of filling the frames between the key frames to ensure a smooth transition. Subsequently, the chapter will discuss kinematics, which is a branch of mechanics that deals with "object motion." We will discuss the variables involved therein such as position, orientation, time, distance, and speed and the two key categories of kinematics namely forward kinematics and inverse kinematics. We will see the use of a hierarchical chain of bones and joints that are involved in the kinematic calculations for obtaining a desired position. This discussion will be continued by rigging, wherein the bones and joints are used to create the many different poses that the model will be eventually animated into. Then, we will see how posing is important in character animation and the kinds of poses that are used to convey emotions such as anger, happiness, relaxation, and confusion. We will discuss two essential aspects of posing, namely, balance and symmetry. We will then look at the camera and camera movements before discussing camera animation.

Hand-Drawn Animation

One of the most common traditional forms of animation was the hand-drawn animation which was also known by other names including cel animation, classic animation, and traditional animation. The popular cartoon hits during the earlier decades of the 20th century were all, by and large, created using hand-drawn animation. The animation was made of a series of drawings wherein each image differed from the previous one slightly and when played in succession, these frames collectively created the illusion of animation. Figure 7.1 illustrates an example of drawings similar to those in the traditional animation. These traditional animations were typically two-dimensional (2D) where the characters were animated in a 2D space.

Another technique invented by the famous cartoonist Max Fleischer is rotoscoping. In this technique, the projection equipment (rotoscope) is used to project the images from the footage to a glass panel for tracing or redrawing. This was used in many of the hit cartoon movies during the 1940s and was also used to study anthropomorphic (human) and animal movements. Let us look a little bit deeper into the steps involved in hand-drawn animation as many of these steps also form the foundation for the digital animation that you will be learning subsequently.

1. Honey bee spotting a bud.

2. Waiting patiently for the bud to bloom.

3. Happy to see the bud finally blooming.

4. Bee confused to see something coming out of the blooming bud.

5. Startled bee looking at another bee coming out of flower.

6. Angry honey bee not so happy to learn that the little bee has eaten away all the nectar.

FIG 7.1 Hand-drawn animation. Image courtesy Vaishali M.

In the early days of hand-drawn animation, imagine how many frames had to be drawn assuming a rate of 24 fps (frames per second). If for 1 second it is 24 frames, think of the mind-boggling number of drawing that had to be made for a minute (60 seconds). We can only admire the infinite patience and diligence of the pioneers in creating a 5-minute cartoon show without any of the plethora of digital tools we have at our disposal today. Even though an animator may draw both the key frames and in-between frames, larger studios had key framer animators and in-betweeners. Key frame animators were the primary artists who mainly were responsible for the key frames, and the in-betweeners were the artists who hand drew the frames connecting the key poses created by the key frame artists. An animation involves drawing the layout, characters, background, effects, etc. As we now clearly know that animation involves motion depicting change, one frame can differ from the earlier frame in terms of the location or other attributes of a character that finally create the illusion of motion when played together in sequence. Therefore, transparent overlays known as cels were used for saving time and increase efficiency. Cel, representing celluloid, is actually a transparent sheet on which the characters are drawn against a stationary background. Animation productions involved hundreds of thousands of cels for creating feature films and cartoons. Having the still background separated from the character allowed for a smoother and more efficient production process as the characters could be modified separately and can just be superimposed on the background. Typically, it is the characters that are usually performing the animation such as running, walking, and jumping, while the background tends to be pretty much the same. For instance, in Figure 7.2, you can see that if we consider the boy on the skateboard as the central character, the boy's position changes, and also the body pose and orientation change; however, the background remains the same. So, based on that notion, the pioneers used the concept of cel, where they can reduce the number of frames being redrawn as well as the redrawing the same details in the frames like the background, thus saving time and increasing efficiency.

Of course, there are situations when the background objects had to be redrawn if they were broken or in any other way modified due to the characters' actions. By and large, cel overlays facilitated separating the different elements in an animation and provided greater control and efficiency over the animation production process. During the early stages, photographs of paper drawings were captured, and they were also used on the transparent cels as discussed earlier.

The advent of computers marked a significant change from the earlier trends, even though drawing and painting skills continue to be of utmost importance even today in animation. However, computers and digital tools enabled artists to digitize the sketches or directly draw on digital media and then manipulate these digital works in numerous ways to create stunning results rapidly. However, today, 2D animators and artists also have a wide range of digital tools available for producing the characters, backdrop and settings, graphic effects, etc.

FIG 7.2 Background remaining the same while foreground (character) changes.

Summarily, digital tools can facilitate numerous advantages such as:

- Digital sketching capabilities
- Different brush sizes, stroke weights, and stroke angles
- Coloring capabilities
  - Adjusting hue
  - RGB or CMYK values
  - Brightness
  - Contrast
  - Saturation
- Texture and texture modifications
- Changing emotions
- Time savings

Let us see a very simple demonstration of how digital tools can save a lot of time and increase the overall efficiency. Figure 7.3 is a simple hand-drawn image.

Now, let us see how many different modifications were made to the earlier image you saw using digital tools and techniques (Figure 7.4).

Frames (drawings) can be created digitally, and the final 2D animation can be created by animating multiple digitally drawn frames. Changes to the drawings in the digital environment can be made relatively easily. For instance, if the color or stroke weight of a character needs to be changed, the original image can be copied and the fill or the path attribute can be modified. Similarly, variations can be made to the original drawing in multiple ways, and new poses can be created swiftly and efficiently. Key frame animators always need a good understanding and appreciation of previsualization tools such as thumbnails, storyboards, and demo reels (animatics). In today's production pipeline, successful key frame animators need to be able to work with various technical members and supervisors from lighting artists to technical artists. Key frame animators need to have a strong foundation in character design, development, rigging, and animation.

Typically, although not always in the same order, the basic steps in the traditional hand-drawn animation include the following:

- Storyboarding
- Key frames are created using penciled drawings

FIG 7.3 Hand-drawn character from alphabets. (Image courtesy: Vaishali, M.)

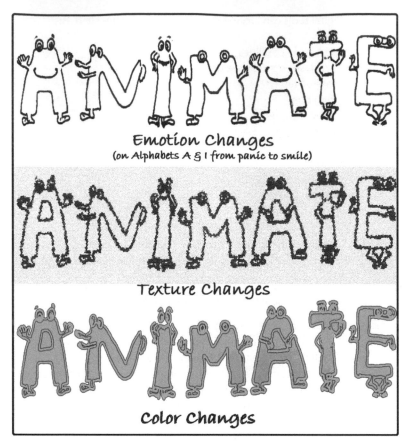

FIG 7.4 Changes in emotions, texture, and color using digital tools. (Image courtesy: Vaishali, M.)

- Pencil test (motion preview is created; key frames are coordinated to synchronize with the soundtrack)
- Enhancements are made, and the steps are repeated iteratively till the desired quality is attained
- Clean-up (finer attention to details and cleaning up the key postures of characters before transferring the drawings from the earlier steps into a new sheet of paper)
- In-betweening (is an exercise to "fill in" between the key poses)
- After clean-up and in-betweening, pencil tests are performed again
- Background (creation of the background or the sets on which the actual animation will occur)

Traditionally, transparent overlays (known as cels) were used to avoid the cumbersome of having to draw everything in each frame. The transparent nature of the cel facilitated only drawing the changes on the background (which remained relatively fixed), which was much less time-consuming. It is for this reason that the traditional hand-drawn animation is also known as cel animation.

Stop-Motion Animation

Stop-motion animation involves the use of real-world 3D objects that are photographed on a frame-by-frame basis to capture position (and hence changes in position). Different kinds of medium are used to create the jointed model. Figure 7.5 shows a stop-motion animation model (left) and clothing applied to the model (right). Figure 7.6 shows the individual pieces together making up the full final model.

The fundamental idea behind stop-motion animation is to use objects that are actually stationary or still to depict animation. So, when performing stop-motion animation, the animator photographs a puppet or a clay model (in one position corresponding to a specific frame) and then moves it slightly and again takes a photograph, and so on. Stop-motion animation is also hence known as stop-motion photography as these individual photographs are played back in sequence. In a type of stop-motion animation known as pixilation, the performers are actual people who slightly vary their positions between frames.

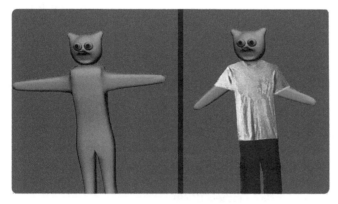

FIG 7.5 Clay model against gray background (with materials on right).

FIG 7.6 Individual parts made and assembled using clay modeling.

There is no specific best rate for stop-motion animation. It depends on the smoothness of the playback or animation that is required and/or desired for the particular piece of animation project. Different kinds of popular stop-motion animation techniques based on the medium used include:

- Clay animation
- Cutout animation
- Silhouette animation
- Model animation
- Lego© animation
- Puppet animation
- Pixilation

Stop-motion animation has its pros and cons, just as various other animation techniques do. One obvious drawback with stop-motion animation is the depiction of non-real movements, especially those defying basic laws of physics such as gravity. For instance, while with a simple drawing, almost any kind of motion can be shown, this is not practically possible with stop-motion as we use real-life objects as medium. It is not practical to show characters made of modeling clay floating among the clouds or Lego© pieces clinging to a ceiling of a room. If you take a look at the steps listed under hand-drawn animation, one major difference that you will find with respect to stop-motion animation is that stop-motion animation is about poses or positions of scene objects that change over time. These are just unique postures (Figure 7.5), and hence, there is no tweening or in-betweening represented in stop motion. James Stuart Blackton is widely recognized as a pioneer of stop-motion animation and is also considered a founding father of the animation industry. Different forms of stop-motion animation (puppet and cutout or a combination) have been used in films such as

- Alice in Wonderland© (1949)
- Rudolph the Red-Nosed Reindeer© (1964)
- The Emperor's New Clothes© (1949)
- Jack Frost© (1979)

And of course, King Kong© is one of the all-time hit movies based on stop-motion animation that made a tremendous impact on movie fans. Also, you need to note that a considerable number of movies have also been made in the 1990s and even after 2000 using stop-motion animation. One of the very famous feature films in this genre that was released in the past few decades is Gumby© (1995), which used claymation, a stop-motion technique that uses clay as the medium. Shaun the Sheep© and Bob the Builder© are other examples of popular TV series based on stop-motion animation.

Key Frame Animation

Animation can be considered as "change over time," and this change can be captured into "key" moments or postures, which can also be viewed as frames or shots in the actual animation. These key frames represent significant changes in the scene objects or models (representing characters, background, etc.). Depicting animation using key framing involves capturing how the parameters such as position and orientation (of an object or objects) change over a period of time. However, having only the key frames will not create a continuous and coherent animation. Let us say that you are preparing an animation that lasts 2 minutes and you are defining key poses at the following times: at 0th second, 15th second, 30th second, and so on… till the 180th second. Something has to happen between 0th and 15th seconds; otherwise, it would not be a smooth animation. Well, it won't be an animation at all. If you consider the animation depicted by the storyboard below, only the main events (key frames) are depicted here. However, the actual action is a continuous one and is not just discrete events as shown below. Actions such as the movements of the pencil should be continuous during the actual animation; this is accomplished through in-betweening (Figure 7.7).

In order for the viewer to get the sense of animation, it is important to show how the object (or objects) changes. The transition that occurs from the starting time to the ending time is defined by a process known as in-betweening. You can consider animation as being equal to *key framing + in-betweening*.

The advent of computer-based digital animation has made things much less cumbersome and time-consuming as the in-betweening aspect is typically by means of a technique known as interpolation. Interpolation is actually an approximating process (of a function) that involves using values at a given set of discrete points to create new data values within their range. Interpolation

FIG 7.7 Key frames. (Image courtesy: Nachiket, M.)

is hence a process of "filling in" or inserting something in between other given things. Is this not what is being done exactly with the animation we discussed in the earlier paragraph. We have "key" frames, and we need to "fill" in between. Thus, interpolation offers an excellent solution to this problem. Instead of laboriously having to draw everything by hand, computational methods of interpolation can be used to generate all the "in-between" frames.

However, despite these digital advances, some animators still employ hand-drawn animation as they feel appropriate. Even quite recently, a highly acclaimed work was created primarily using hand-drawn animation without relying on computer graphics (CG)-based modeling and animation techniques heavily as most modern productions do. Hayao Miyazaki, the Japanese director and animator, made Ponyo© in 2008 that included a mind-boggling 170,000 frames totally. In fact, it is believed that Hayao Miyazaki deliberately dismantled the computer animation branch of his studio so that Ponyo© could be created using hand-drawn animation. Well, now let us return back to computer-based interpolation to complete the rest of the discussion on key framing and in-betweening.

One Rate Does Not Fit All

Remember that in real life, oftentimes, different objects move at different speeds and accelerate and decelerate differently. In the case of a person biking on a road, rate at which the legs move when pedaling will not be the same as that of the movement of the head or the other parts of the body. When a bird is flying across a field towards a tree, the bird's speed will not be the same as that of any other birds which may be flying in the same or opposite direction and the rate at which the leaves flutter may be different from the motion of the tree.

So, when performing keyframing, you should not initiate all motion at the same key and end them all at the same time. Another thing to consider is that when multiple objects are involved in a moving scene, all objects do not come to a stop at the same time. When traveling on a bus or a train, even after the vehicle comes to a sudden stop, our bodies tend to continue moving forward. It is important to take into account all these factors when animating objects in your scene.

Frame Rate and Refresh Rate

While discussing both key frame animation and stop-motion animation, a basic knowledge of current frame rates employed in various applications is helpful. Frame rate, as used in CG and other digital systems, refers to the rate at which images are displayed or generated sequentially, and this is also referred to as frame frequency. Also, scanning is another important term that is used in this context. Scanning refers to the process whereby a frame in a video (rendering) is constituted by lines by scanning a display from one side to other.

Some of the commonly used frame rates for stop motion are:

- 12 fps
- 15 fps
- 24 fps
- 30 fps

The National Television System Committee (NTSC), which sets standards on the North American continent, employs a frame rate of 30 fps. The Phase Alternating Line (PAL), which is common in a number of European and Asian nations, employs 25 frames per second. The frame rate is at times confused with another term known as the refresh rate. While the **frame rate** refers to the rate (frequency) at which sequential images of an animation are displayed, the **refresh rate** is the frequency or the number of times a display such as a monitor gets refreshed. Frame rate is typically expressed as frames per second (fps), and refresh rate is expressed in hertz (Hz). When the refresh rate is low, blurs may be seen as the transition occurs from one frame to another frame. Smoother transition can be accomplished by using higher refresh rates. As a general rule of thumb, a device with a higher refresh rate can offer superior video quality. For example, if your television or gaming display has a refresh rate of 60 Hz, it means that it is refreshing the image 60 times per second. In other words, it means that the device is capable of drawing a new image 60 times in one second. However, recent advances have led to devices that are able to offer refresh rates such as 144 Hz or higher for enhanced viewing and gaming experience.

Refresh rates generally refer to the display device's or monitor's capability to display frames, while the frame rates are determined by your computer's hardware configurations including the processor and graphics card specifications. In order to have optimal viewing experience, proper synchronization (sync) is required between the frame rates and refresh rates. A viewer may not be experiencing the best results if the frame rate is much lower than the display's refresh rate. This results in what is known as "screen tearing," which refers to the case when the frame rate of the Graphics Processing Unit (GPU) and the refresh rate of the monitor are not in synchronization. Of late, with the advances in hardware, many different tools and techniques are available to achieve a good balance between frame rate and refresh rate to deliver optimal viewing and gaming experience for users.

Progressive and Interlaced Scanning

Scanning itself represents the process of digitally or electronically showing the pixels onto a digital display such as a monitor. To better understand how this process of scanning occurs, let us consider a simple common activity such as reading a book. As technically there are subtle variations in actually how the scanning occurs, do not take this literally, but just for your understanding. When reading a book, we start at the top of the page and then proceed reading a page from left to right and from top to bottom.

Similarly, in the display devices that we use, every second, rows of pixels (represented by numerous lines) are scanned horizontally, from left to right and top to bottom.

There are two common types of scanning employed: *progressive* and *interlaced*. You may have come across terms such as 720p and 1080i when dealing with video formats. The p in 720p stands for progressive scan, and 720 represents the number of lines. Similarly, i in 1080i stands for interlaced scan, and 1080 represents the number of lines of resolution. Interlaced scanning was the more popular video scanning method prior to the arrival of DVD (Digital Video Disc) and HDTV (High-Definition Television), which use progressive scanning.

In interlaced scanning, every other line of the image is drawn by interchanging between the odd- and even-numbered lines. Let us say that odd-numbered lines are drawn at first (lines 1, 3, 5, …) until the screen is completely filled, and then even-numbered lines (lines 2, 4, 6, …) are drawn. This is achieved by dividing or splitting each video frame into two equal halves, and then during each scan cycle, half of one frame is displayed. This half part of the video frame is referred to as a field. While the first field is made up of the odd-numbered horizontal lines consisting of the rows of pixels, the second field is composed of the even-numbered horizontal lines (rows of pixels). The total amount of horizontal lines is determined by the video resolution. Earlier we saw that 720i or 1080i refers to interlaced scanning. If the resolution is 1280×720 pixels, each field will contain 360 horizontal lines (720/2=360). With a refresh rate of 60 Hz, alternating rows of pixels (odd and even) are refreshed at 30 Hz each. However, the primary disadvantage with interlaced scanning is that images displayed may tend to flicker. The reason this technique was employed earlier was because of bandwidth limitation. The bandwidth that was needed for the display was reduced by this alternating displays of odd and even rows, which effectively reduced the number of pixels per cycle to be refreshed by half.

Progressive scanning is the method that is used for creating an image on computer screens that involves drawing lines in a sequence (one at a time). The complete frame is drawn 60 times per second (or every 1/60th of a second), thus facilitating the transmission of twice the amount of detail in the same quantity of time as interlaced scanning. In this way, with progressive scanning, video frames displayed consecutively are composed of all the horizontal lines (rows of pixels) that constitute the image. This creates a smoother appearance and hence animated sequences tend to be crisp or sharp. The primary drawback with progressive scanning is higher bandwidth requirement; however, with recent advances in video compression techniques and access to higher bandwidth, this may not be as big a concern as it used to be earlier.

Modern devices including DVD players and HDTVs use progressive scanning. Progressive scanning is a preferred method as it yields a more detailed image that is less prone to flickering than interlaced scanning.

Interpolation, Attributes, and Transformations

A character is after all made up of objects defined by attributes that govern its geometry and appearance. Below, you can see the key positions (poses) of the characters; however, as animation is not "static" but dynamic, the transition between the poses needs to be calculated. This is done by interpolation (Figure 7.8).

Let us consider an example of interpolation in its very simplest form using an example of the Cartesian coordinates that we have covered in detail in the earlier chapters. Consider two points, P_1 and P_2, in the Cartesian coordinate space represented by (x_1, y_1) and (x_2, y_2). Given these two points and their x and y values, a y coordinate for a third point can be interpolated from its x value. In other words, as seen from Figure 7.9, using linear interpolation, the value y_3 can be found for x_3.

In CG, interpolation is important for filling the frames between the key frames to ensure a smooth transition as the animation progresses from one key frame to the next. Interpolation also plays a key role in accomplishing

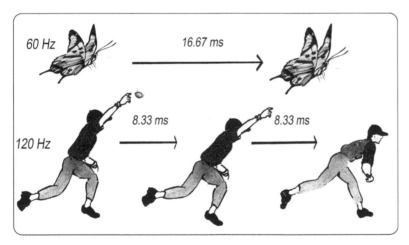

FIG 7.8 Key positions demonstrating actual pose. (Image courtesy: Dhruva, M.)

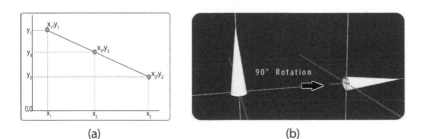

(a)   (b)

FIG 7.9 Interpolation.

transformation such as translation, rotation, and scaling. As can be seen from Figure 7.9a, If points (x_1, y_1) and (x_2, y_2) are provided, the value of (x_3, y_3) can be calculated by interpolation. Interpolation is used for calculating positions for many transformations. Let us consider that an object has to be rotated through an angle of 90° within a particular time frame, say over 30 frames. As shown in Figure 7.9b, at Frame 0, the conical object is oriented vertically and at Frame 30, after the conical object has been rotated through 90°. If not for interpolation, the animator has to painstakingly specify the orientation of the conical object for every frame (Orientation for Frame$_1$, Orientation for Frame$_2$, and so on) for all 30 frames. But, with interpolation, only the "key" orientations at the beginning and ending frames need to be positioned, and the rest of the intermediate values can be generated via interpolation. Whew ... that is easy, right?

Both linear and nonlinear interpolation techniques are used in CG for modeling with curves and splines. Earlier we discussed about the knots (knot points), and in such cases, cubic spline interpolation methods are used to obtain good results with deriving linear equations for obtaining the required values. From the animation perspective, interpolation is a fundamental technique that is used in key framing for the following purposes:

- In-betweening (between the key frames)
- Defining angular orientations at key frames
- Changing scale parameters
- Coordinate transformations

Motion Capture

Motion capture (mocap) refers to recording of the actions of human performers, animals, or even inanimate objects and transferring those movements to a digital character. In mocap, the motion of the objects or actors is tracked with respect to points of reference. As typically motion capture involves actors performing motion sequences such as dance or stunt sequences, it is also often referred to as performance capture. While there are different types of motion capture systems and several different classifications based on the types of markers used, we will examine four broad categories of mocap systems.

Prosthetic motion capture involves using devices known as potentiometers, electronic devices for calculating the joint angles based on the rotation at each link. *Magnetic motion capture* devices use receivers that can sense magnetic fields and magnetic fluctuations to ascertain their positional values. However, any external interference on the devices when the performance is being carried out can cause the values to change, resulting in erroneous measurements. In a similar way, *acoustic mocap* is based on the use of transmitters or transponders that calculate spatial location and orientation using radio signals. But then again, any kind of noise or external interference can cause the values to fluctuate and result in measurement errors.

Optical motion capture techniques use image-sensing devices that determine the subject's 3D spatial location. Optical sensors have no interference problems, as experienced with an acoustic or magnetic mocap system, and they also facilitate recording the performance of multiple performers simultaneously. Markers or reflective spots are attached to the clothing of the actors who perform the stunt sequences or choreography, and the rotational information is calculated by the triangulation values obtained from three or more sensors.

Based on whether the performance is captured in real time or not, performance capture is also classified as either live motion or processed motion capture.

As the name implies, *live motion capture* refers to the live recording of the movements in real time. This does not involve any kind of processing that is applied to the data. The movements of the performers are fed live to the CG scene objects. On the other hand, with *processed motion capture*, the motion data from the performers of the dance or stunt sequences is first obtained and then refined. That is, the original data captured is tweaked and edited to suit the requirements of the CG animation.

Camera Animation

Camera is a key component of the process of animation, especially as perceived by the audience. Simply stated, the audience sees what the camera sees. First and foremost, you need to realize that as a digital professional, you have a definite edge. In the real world, handling camera and related equipment precisely to capture the scene exactly as desired by the directorial team is indeed a challenging task. Furthermore, it involves huge costs and is a time-consuming process. However, in the digital domain, you can create any number of cameras in your CG scene and you can add any number of lights (we will see in the next chapter why that is not a good idea). But, the bottom line is that you have a greater degree of freedom to err in CG modeling (at least when you are learning and practicing) than one can in the real world. We will discuss cameras in more detail in Chapter 8 when we discuss rendering.

From the animation point of view, it is important to understand cameras used in CG and the terms associated with their movement. The camera is capable of performing a wide range of movements such as (Figure 7.10)

- Pan
- Tilt
- Roll
- Track
- Dolly
- Orbit
- Zoom

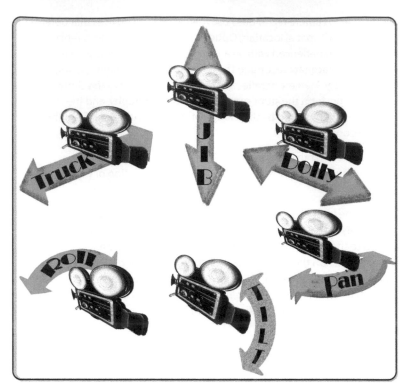

FIG 7.10 Camera movements.

Panning refers to the horizontal turning (rotation) of the camera from right to left and left to right. While panning is done in the horizontal direction, the vertical counterpart is referred to as *tilt*. Panning is more suitable for scenes that involve buildings lined against the horizon or other panoramic scenes. On the other hand, when the objects in a scene are vertically lined up –for instance sky scrapers or tall trees – tilting is employed. When the rotation is performed along the viewing axis of the camera, it is referred to as a *roll*. When the camera is moved along either the horizontal or vertical axis, it is referred to as *track*. *Dollying* is a popular term used in filmmaking and is used to refer to the movement of the camera mounted on wheels. Incidentally, the wheeled platform that involves the cart on which the camera is mounted is also referred to as the dolly (Figure 7.11).

Based on the distance of the camera from the scene or the model, the shot is classified as long, medium, or close-up shot. To understand this, imagine that you are looking at a real-world scene, a tourist attraction or a memorial or a monument. Now, envision seeing the monument from:

1. A very long distance
2. Moving closer and viewing it from not-so-far
3. Viewing the monument when standing extremely close

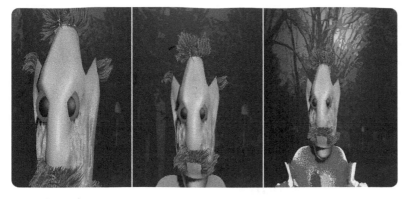

FIG 7.11 Distance from camera.

Now when you are at a very great distance from the monument, you see not only the subject (monument) but also a great deal of other things including the sky, trees, other buildings surrounding the subject, roads, and sign posts. Composing a shot using a camera in a CG scene is similar to this. The *long shot* will include the primary character (and secondary characters) and a considerable number of the background objects. The *medium shot* is even closer but still shows a good amount of the background. The *close-up shot* shows the head and torso of the character, placing strong emphasis on the emotions.

One important thing that you need to consider when recording animation with the camera is the *transition* or continuity. To establish proper continuity, you must understand the *line of action*. The line of action (Figure 7.12) is a hypothetical line in the scene that links your primary scene characters. This is an imaginary line along which your subject moves or looks. The basic rule when recording the animation with your camera is that one should not abruptly cut to a perspective from the other side than the one the camera is currently viewing, as that would result in viewers looking at the scene suddenly from the reverse direction than what the characters seemed to be facing earlier. This would cause confusion and disorientation, thus preventing a coherent flow of the story. As seen from the earlier discussion, it is important that the camera should continue to stay on one side of the

FIG 7.12 Line of action.

line, except when the director or the animator wants to cut across the line for specific reasons. By now, you should have understood that modeling complex real-life characters and fictional or mythological characters is quite a complex process indeed. When you are capturing your animation involving such complex models, camera animation plays a key role in properly capturing the diligently and meticulously created models. Hence, during the learning stages, one should experiment a lot with the camera positions and orientations. This involves exploring several views such as top view and side views, and trying various motions such as dolly, pan, or zoom.

Effects Animation

The term effects animation is typically used to refer to any animation that is not character animation, including background effects such as rain, storm, dust, fire, snow, and hail. Let us consider an animation showing a character rowing a boat on a lake surrounded by some vegetation. There are several things in addition to the character that needs to be animated. These include:

- Ripples or other small movements on the water surface as the boat moves
- Fluttering of the leaves on the surrounding trees
- Background movement of objects such as clouds
- Flying birds, butterflies, or any other insects to add to the scene reality

All the above are examples of effects animation as they do not directly deal with animating the character (the person rowing the boat). In addition to these, effects animation also includes lighting effects. Let us consider an animation occurs in an interior space such as a bar, restaurant, or if it involves a party or a discotheque. In such cases, special lighting effects can be used to create the proper ambience as required by the plot. With CG, you can create and use a creative combination of lights and also employ an interplay of shadows to create exciting results. As we will see in Chapter 9, lights are extremely powerful tools when dealing with creating an ambience and they have a high emotional influence on the audience.

We learned about the various tools and techniques to create animation. We looked at a wide range of techniques from traditional hand-drawn animation to the advanced performance animation such as motion capture (mocap). Now, let us look at some of the fundamental principles of animation that are inherently intertwined into any kind of animation, using any of these methods that we discussed.

Principles of Animation

The 12 principles of animation, which were originally developed around the 1930s by animators in the Disney© Studios (Thomas & Johnston, 1981), continue to help today's animators in making superior-quality animations.

Ollie Johnston and Frank Thomas explained these principles of animation in the book *The Illusion of Life: Disney Animation* (1981). Just as we saw earlier that the modern modeling tools such as splines and Nonuniform Rational B-Splines (NURBS) have their origins from the modeling techniques used centuries before, the development of animation as a craft over the decades has been inspired by numerous older disciplines including visual arts, opera, performing arts, and theater. The 12 principles of animation, even though they originally functioned as a reference tool for hand-drawn animation, are actually suited for any of the wide range of animation methods.

When learning the principles of animation, you need to bear in mind that many of these are inherently interrelated. For instance, you will see that exaggeration is related to squash and stretch, and anticipation is related to timing. Instead of treating each principle of animation as a discrete entity by itself, try to understand the 12 principles in their entirety, with the ultimate goal of creating an effective animation involving appealing characters.

These 12 principles are as follows (Thomas & Johnston, 1981):

1. Squash and stretch
2. Anticipation
3. Staging
4. Pose-to-pose and straight-ahead action
5. Follow-through and straight-ahead action
6. Slow-in and slow-out
7. Arcs
8. Secondary action
9. Timing
10. Exaggeration
11. Solid drawing
12. Character appeal

Remember that these principles of animation are highly interrelated to each other. They are not mutually exclusive but act in many different ways together to communicate the plot to the audience and help the characters convey the overall animation. The age-old saying that "a picture is worth a thousand words" implies that a picture can express a large amount of information that is difficult to express even using a thousand words. Going by that analogy, an animation can be much more powerful than a picture. However, when a lot of information is being conveyed, it is important to make sure that it is conveyed in the most appropriate manner so as to get the central idea unmistakably to audience.

The 12 principles play a significant role in this process of communication. Oftentimes, these principles complement each other and when used in correct combination help deliver a highly appealing animation to captivate the audience. Remember the most important rule with respect to these principles – there is no hard-and-fast rule. It all depends on what the scene

FIG 7.13 Squash and Stretch

FIG 7.14 Anticipation

demands especially in the context of the overall plot. Sometimes, just as you may have to combine two or three principles or overdo one specific principle, you may also have to completely do away with some principles if the scene dictates that. So, the use of these principles stems from the staging of the scene to express the idea in the larger context of the overall plot of the animation.

Squash and Stretch

The principle of squash and stretch deals with a character's volume as it affects its suppleness, pliability, or bendability. Squash and stretch may tend to exaggerate a character's actions to create different types of effects ranging from comical to serious. For instance, oftentimes in cartoon and CG movies, we see objects like buses and cars squeezing from their original size or stretching or expanding (when they start off from the start line for race). However, we know that this is not how things behave in the real world. For instance, in the image below, you can see the expressions of the ball as it is approaching the wall when it is about to hit the wall with a great speed. As it approaches the wall, it stretches, and upon impact with the wall, it squashes. This kind of effect is more pronounced in CG-animated movies and cartoons, and they help deliver the essence of the animation more effectively (Figures 7.13 and 7.14).

Anticipation

Anticipation, just as the literal meaning of the word implies, refers to expectation. This creates an expectation among the audience and prepares them for the upcoming main action. In the real world, most actions are preceded by other actions. For instance, a baseball player swings the bat back before hitting the ball. Before striking the keyboard key with a finger, the typist raises the finger up. A basketball player bends his knees before launching himself up to throw the ball. This is also closely related to other principles such as timing and secondary action.

Anticipation can also be used to explain subtle and not-too-visible actions, such as contemplation or the thought process, which are hard to directly express. Simple movements such as tapping fingers on a table or touching one's hat or bending over with folded hands on a table can be used to create anticipation among the audience, making the audience wonder about the next action of the character. Also, anticipation can be used to prepare the audience for something very intense that is about to happen. These can be highly related to timing as well. In movies, dramatic pauses before a critical scene in the plot are often employed to elicit anticipation and create the element of suspense or surprise.

Staging

Staging involves composing the scene in the best possible manner to convey the plot clearly to the audience. Effective staging entails effective scene composition. This involves grabbing the complete attention of the audience and is, in fact, the essence of animation. If you see the example below, the characters are very simple including a pencil, stapler, and an eraser working together on a writing. Together, they express the notion of well-formed writing through their combined effort (Figure 7.15).

Staging involves and spans across almost a wide range of elements along the production pipeline including proper pre-production and storyboarding leading to the other elements in the production process. These steps in production that contribute to effective composition and staging include optimal use of cameras, materials, colors, appropriate use of lights and three-point lighting, proper posing, and effects. Timing, another principle of animation, is of essence in staging. To ensure coherent flow of animation, the frames of animation should be carefully planned (preceding, present, and succeeding) so that the continuity is maintained to engage the audience. As we will see in Chapter 10 on Composition, colors and light play a critical role in this communication and composition. In view of the digital nature of the storytelling process, the characters and the effects (props/background) should go hand in hand and not overwhelm the viewer.

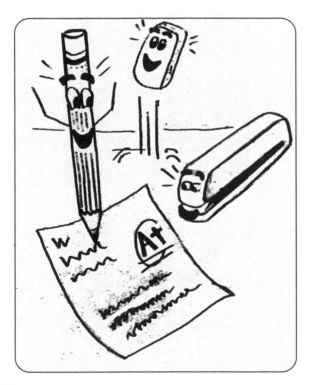

FIG 7.15 Staging

Straight-Ahead Action and Pose-to-Pose

These are two approaches to the creation of animations. The pose-to-pose method offers a more calculated approach where the entire scene is described using distinctly organized key poses. Hence, this offers greater flexibility through better control of the character poses by manipulating the overall size (volume) and the accompanying actions. As pose-to-pose method involves breaking down the overall animation into well-defined poses over the entire duration, it also offers good control in maintaining a proper timing (Figure 7.16).

Straight-ahead animation is more helpful with creating a spontaneous animation and was one of the essential aspects of hand-drawn animation. Straight ahead is better used for depicting motion of things like fire, water flow, etc., which tend to be more spontaneous and inconsistent. Straight-ahead animations facilitate spontaneity but have disadvantages with respect to tweaking or making changes, controlling the overall duration, etc. The image on the right (top) shows only the key poses (pose to pose), while the bottom images show all the poses (straight ahead).

However, there may be situations when these two approaches, straight ahead and pose to pose, may be used together. A combined approach allows exploiting the authenticity and extemporaneity of straight-ahead animation and the meticulous organization facilitated by pose-to-pose method.

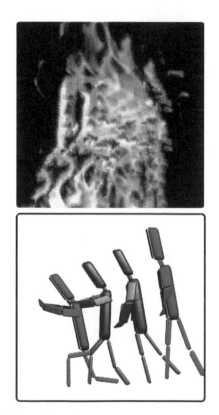

FIG 7.16 Straight-Ahead Action and Pose-to-Pose

Follow-Through and Overlapping Action

Follow-through and overlapping action are highly interrelated. In a way, just as anticipation helps prepare audience for the succeeding action, follow-through helps with the completion of an action and the associated motion(s). In the real world, actions do not cease abruptly or suddenly, but there are always associated motions that continue after the main motion has stopped. When a car comes to stop, our bodies continue to move forward. Similarly, if a character is skiing or jumping off a cliff, the clothes may still continue to move even after the character has come to a halt. Such actions actually complete an animation and make it more believable. When you show a character throwing a ball, it will be very unrealistic to stop the arm motion immediately when the ball is thrown. For more realistic and appealing animation, just as in the real world, the motion of the hand should continue to a reasonable time after the ball has been thrown from the hand.

In Figure 7.17 (left), you can see that after the ball has been released, the hand and the body of the baseball player continue to move. In Figure 7.17 (right), the image shows a robotic character that exemplifies overlapping action as it is carrying a tray on the right hand, listening to the headphone, and carrying another item on the left hand. As the name indicates, overlapping actions refer to action that "lap over" other actions. Overlapping action is the principle that represents how different constituent components of a larger object move at different speeds and perform different motions. For instance, while a car is moving along a straight path, the wheels continue to rotate about their axes.

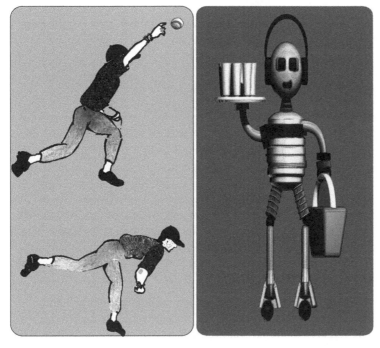

FIG 7.17 Follow-Through and Overlapping Action.

FIG 7.18 Slow-In and Slow-Out.

Slow-In and Slow-Out

Slow-in and slow-out is an essential principle in creating realistic motions that represents how many real-world motions happen. This is highly related to timing and appeal, among other principles of animation. Typically, objects tend to accelerate in the beginning of a motion and decelerate towards the end of the motion. When someone asks us what our average speed was when we drove to work today, we may say 30 mph (miles per hour). However, we never start at 30 mph and we cannot actually come to an abrupt stop from 30 mph when we stop (Figure 7.18).

This can be seen in many other examples of objects in motion, including automobiles, trains, and airplanes, all of which tend to speed up in the beginning and slow down as they come to an end.

Arcs

Arcs represent the essence of most of the things we see in nature and the world around us. Human body parts such as the eyes, ears, and nose have curved shapes. Animals, birds, and fish move along curved trajectories. Even when we walk along a straight line, the actual body parts involved in the motion such as our legs, feet, and other parts perform variable degrees of arc motion. Curved shapes and arcs are seen in natural bodies such as rivers, trails, and rainbows; shapes of birds, animals, and insects; shapes of seeds and flowers; and numerous other natural things. Not just the shapes of many natural organisms, but the actual motion of many phenomena (tornado, cyclone) and organisms (bees, wasps) and natural bodies (waves, rivers, etc.) follow a curved path (Figure 7.19).

As you can see from the above image, arcs are important both to the character design and to the motion. Arcs create a marked transformation to the overall nature and appeal of the entire animation by adding lucidity to the character's actions.

 FIG 7.19 Arcs

Secondary Action

A secondary action, as the name implies, is a subordinate or dependent action for the main movement or action. Secondary actions are the direct outcome of another action. In the real world, motions tend to be compounded or complex where multiple actions are involved. For instance, when we are reaching out to grab a cup of coffee, while the hand moving forward is the primary motion, our fingers tend to come together to grasp the object (secondary action). In the examples shown in the above image, even though the primary action is the kid's baseball posing for hitting, the other body parts, such as the head and legs, are turning and moving to overlap with the main action. Similarly, a person checking his cellphone while sipping a cup of coffee is an example of overlapping action. While swinging the bat to hit the ball is the primary action, the other actions including eye movements, head movements, and all other body actions can be thought of as secondary actions that support the main action (Figure 7.20).

FIG 7.20 Secondary Action

Together, the primary or independent (main) and secondary actions play a critical role in engaging the audience and creating a more believable and appealing animation. Secondary actions accompany and strengthen the main action to enhance the animation and make it more appealing. Sometimes, secondary actions tend to become the main action over time. The secondary motion, which started as a dependent motion (on the main or the independent action), may eventually become the independent motion itself.

Timing

Timing refers to the actual duration of an action as well as the exact time when something starts to happen. For instance, let us say that a jeep and a convertible cover a specific distance in 2 and 5 hours, respectively. We would

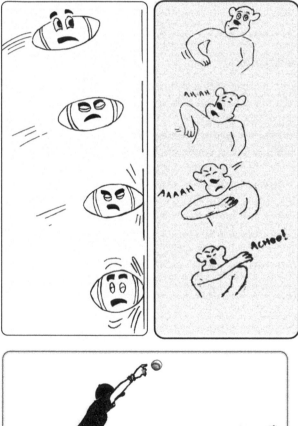

FIG 7.21 Timing

say that the jeep was faster because it covered the same distance in a lesser amount of time. But, there is more to timing than just the speed. Timing plays an important role in various aspects of the animation including the staging and also the character's traits and the overall appeal. Let us revisit the examples we looked at earlier to better understand timing (Figure 7.21).

In all cases shown in the image here, timing is important.

- How long does the ball fly before impact and at what time does it touch the wall?
- How long does it take for the entire sneeze to happen and when exactly does the sneeze occur?
- How long is the ball throw taking place and when exactly is it released from the player's hand?

In a 100-frame animation, for instance, a car may start moving at the 10th frame and continue to move till Frame 45. At the same time, another object (or more objects) in the scene may be moving (say from Frames 20 to 35). However, if the animation was to be tweaked and the motion of the car is from Frames 10 to 95, it will not only be gradual but can also be gentle. Timing is closely related to various other principles of animation including anticipation, staging, slow-in, and slow-out. In fact, timing is key to successful animation. Timing also is related to the rhythm or the tempo of an animation.

Exaggeration

In colloquy, exaggeration refers to an overstatement or a hyperbole. In animation, exaggeration involves modifying or transforming the physical characteristics or actions or poses of characters and actions for a comical and dynamic effect.

Simply stated, this involves making a strong character look even stronger, a tall character look taller, or a happy character look happier. The image below shows an example of exaggeration with an ant lifting a very heavy object (Figure 7.22).

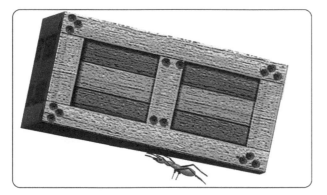

FIG 7.22 Exaggeration

We all may have seen the use of exaggeration in popular toons and animated movies such as

- Eyes popping out of the face of a character to express surprise, or
- A character splitting into smaller characters upon being hit, or
- A small character carrying a heavy weight to show abnormal strength, or
- A character's head transforming to a bulb on getting a good idea.

In all the above cases, the animation involves stretching beyond what is realistic and amplifying the character's postures and actions. This is intended to get the idea across to the audience instantaneously in a flamboyant manner. However, as with anything, exaggeration needs to be employed carefully so as to not muddy the scene or confuse the audience.

Solid Drawing

The principle of solid drawing is intended to build clear, well-defined character poses grounded in properties such as volume and weight of the character. This is also related to concepts in physics such as equilibrium and center of gravity, so as to evenly distribute the weight for balance and plausibility (Figure 7.23).

In posing, we saw how postures help in conveying the emotions and the intentions of a character. The principle of solid drawing involves proper drawing using lines to create appropriate shape, volume, or form. Solid drawing is essential to ensure that the character's volume and mass are consistent throughout the animation, thus conveying proper form and balance to the audience.

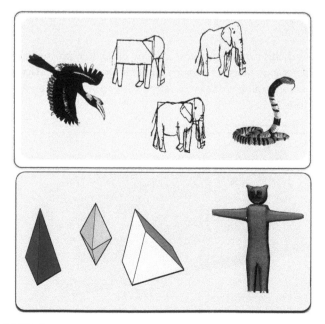

FIG 7.23 Solid Drawing

FIG 7.24 Character Appeal

Appeal

Appeal is about creating a character that is of interest to the audience, engages them, and serves as a proper medium to communicate the plot. While "to appeal" means to attract, captivate, charm, or enchant, it not only applies to the protagonist or good characters, but the bad characters or villain can also appeal to the audience. We may recall not just the main character or the hero from a cartoon or an animated movie, but we may also find many other supporting characters quite engaging. Characters of different background with different characteristics, appearance-wise and/ or behavior-wise, can be appealing. This requires studying the nature of the characters properly and their role in the plot before actually creating the 3D-modeled character. Characters with proper appeal are those that the audience are able to empathize with, not just the charming ones (Figure 7.24).

Irrespective of the tool or the software platform you are using for animation, these principles of animation help in creating good characters and communicating the plot clearly in an engaging manner.

In a Nutshell

In this chapter, we looked at different forms of animation starting with hand-drawn animation that forms the foundation for the digital animation. The chapter covered the different kinds of popular stop-motion animation techniques such as clay animation, Lego© animation, and puppet animation. Next, we moved on to the process of creating animation using key framing (and in-betweening), which demonstrates how the parameters such as position and orientation (of an object or objects) change over a period of time. These discussions evinced how the advent of computer-based digital animation has made things much less cumbersome and time-consuming. To understand key framing, it is important to understand interpolation, which is key to the process of filling the frames between the key frames to ensure a smooth transition. We then looked at the camera and camera movements before discussing camera animation. Finally, camera animation and motion capture were discussed before briefly outlining the well-known principles of animation (Thomas & Johnston, 1981).

Chapter 7 Quiz

PART I

True/False (Circle the Correct Choice)

1. Hand-drawn animation involves the use of real-world three-dimensional objects that are photographed on a frame-by-frame basis to capture position (and hence changes in position).
Answer: True False

2. In today's production pipeline, successful key frame animators need to be able to work with various technical members and supervisors from lighting artists to technical artists.
Answer: True False

3. The National Television System Committee (NTSC), which is used in North American continent, employs a frame rate of 30 fps.
Answer: True False

4. Orbiting refers to the horizontal turning (rotation) of the camera from right to left and left to right.
Answer: True False

5. Optical motion capture techniques use image-sensing devices that determine the subject's three-dimensional spatial location.
Answer: True False

6. Zooming is a popular term used in filmmaking and is used to refer to the movement of the camera mounted on wheels.
Answer: True False

7. Anthropomorphic animation is typically used to refer to any animation that is not character animation, including background effects such as rain, storm, dust, fire, snow, and hail.
Answer: True False

8. Magnetic motion capture devices use receivers that can sense magnetic fields and magnetic fluctuations to ascertain their positional values.
Answer: True False

9. Character animation primarily focuses on the effects such as rain or fog or background movement of objects such as clouds.
Answer: True False

10. The close-up shot shows the head and torso of the character, placing strong emphasis on the emotions.
Answer: True False

11. Acoustic motion capture techniques use image-sensing devices that determine the subject's three-dimensional spatial location.
Answer: True False

12. Force includes both direction and magnitude, and hence is a vector quantity.
Answer: True False

13. The gravity on the surface of the moon is approximately six times stronger than that on the surface of the earth.
Answer: True False

14. In interlaced scanning, every other line of the image is drawn by interchanging between the odd- and even-numbered lines.
Answer: True False

15. Animation can be considered as "change over time," and this change can be captured into "key" moments or postures, which can also be viewed as frames or shots in the actual animation.
Answer: True False

16. In live motion capture, the motion data from the performers of the dance or stunt sequences is first obtained and then refined.
Answer: True False

17. The first principle of animation is "Timing."
Answer: True False

18. The 12 principles of animation were originally developed around the 1930s by animators in the Disney© Studios.
Answer: True False

19. Progressive scanning is not a preferred method as it yields a more detailed image as it is less prone to flickering.
Answer: True False

20. The last principle of animation is "Character Appeal."
Answer: True False

PART II

Multiple Choice Questions (Choose the Most Appropriate Answer)

1. Rotoscoping was invented by _____ .
   a. Dave Fleischer
   b. Mark Newton
   c. Max Fleischer
   d. Max Colwell
   e. None of the above

2. Ponyo was directed by _____ .
   a. Akira Kurosawa
   b. Mark Fleischer
   c. Hayao Kurosawa
   d. Hayao Miyazaki
   e. None of the above

3. _____ scan is the method that is used for creating an image on computer screens that involves drawing lines in a sequence (one at a time).
   a. Dragged
   b. Interlaced
   c. Marginal
   d. Progressive
   e. None of the above

4. After the revision and approval of the key frames, animators known as _____ draw the missing frames occurring between the key frames.
   a. Tweakers
   b. Renderers
   c. In-betweeners
   d. Synthesizers
   e. None of the above

5. _____ refers to recording of the actions of human performers, animals, or even inanimate objects and transferring those movements to a digital character.
   a. CRT capture
   b. Key framing
   c. Motion capture
   d. Interpolating
   e. None of the above

6. _____ motion capture involves using devices known as potentiometers, electronic devices for calculating the joint angles based on the rotation at each link.
   a. Magnetic
   b. Prosthetic
   c. Optical
   d. Acoustic
   e. Live

7. _____ motion capture techniques use image-sensing devices that determine the subject's three-dimensional spatial location.
   a. Magnetic
   b. Prosthetic
   c. Optical
   d. Acoustic
   e. Live

8. The line of _____ is a hypothetical line in the scene that links your primary scene characters.
   a. Panning
   b. Positivity
   c. Thirds
   d. Edges
   e. Action

9. _____ motion capture refers to the live recording of the movements in real time.
   a. Magnetic
   b. Prosthetic
   c. Optical
   d. Acoustic
   e. Live

10. When the rotation is performed along the viewing axis of the camera, it is referred to as a _____
    a. Pan
    b. Zoom
    c. Tilt
    d. Roll
    e. All the above

11. In CG, _____ is very important for filling the frames between the key frames to ensure a smooth transition as the animation progresses from one key frame to the next.
    a. CRT capture
    b. Key framing
    c. Interpolation
    d. Motion capture
    e. None of the above

12. James Stuart Blackton is widely recognized as a pioneer of _____ animation.
    a. Stop-motion
    b. MOCAP
    c. Hand-drawn
    d. Motion capture
    e. None of the above

13. Shaun the Sheep© and Bob the Builder© are examples of _____ animation.
    a. Stop-motion
    b. MOCAP
    c. Hand-drawn
    d. Motion capture
    e. None of the above

14. NTSC stands for _____ .
    a. Storyboarding
    b. Scripting
    c. Modeling
    d. Animation
    e. Rigging

15. The _____ included a series of images, and these were drawn (or printed and pasted) around one disk and a second disk whose movements are synchronized with the first disk.
    a. Praxinoscope
    b. Phenakistoscope
    c. Kinetophone
    d. Kineograph
    e. All the above

16. The Phase Alternating Line (PAL), which is common in a number of European and Asian nations, employs _____ frames per second.
    a. 10
    b. 15
    c. 25
    d. 30
    e. 40

17. The NTSC employs _____ frames per second.
    a. 10
    b. 15
    c. 25
    d. 30
    e. 40

18. In _____ , the projection equipment is used to project the images from the footage to a glass panel for tracing or redrawing.
    a. Thaumatrope
    b. Phenakistoscope
    c. Rotoscope
    d. Camera Obscura
    e. None of the above

19. _____ animation involves the use of real-world three-dimensional objects that are photographed on a frame-by-frame basis to capture position (and hence changes in position).
    a. Stop-motion
    b. MOCAP
    c. Hand-drawn
    d. Motion capture
    e. None of the above

20. The cel in Cel Animation represents _____ .
    a. Cell
    b. Creature
    c. Cello
    d. Celluloid
    e. None of the above

Reference

Thomas, F., & Johnston, O. (1981). *The Illusion of Life: Disney Animation*, first Hyperion ed. Disney Editions (New York, NY: Walt Disney Productions).

CHAPTER 8: Character: Design, Rigging, & Animation

You're not supposed to animate drawings; you're supposed to animate feelings.

– Ollie Johnston

WHAT WILL YOU LEARN IN THIS CHAPTER?

- What is character design?
- What are some important elements of good character design?
- What is personality?
- What are different ways to create characters out of anything?
- What is rigging?
- What is kinematics?
- What is forward kinematics?
- What is inverse kinematics?
- What is posing?
- How to achieve balance in posing?
- What are the various considerations in character design and modeling?

DOI: 10.1201/9780429186349-8

- What are the various constraints in character design and modeling?
- What is meant by level of detail?
- What are other important considerations for appeal?

Good character design entails a proper understanding of the character's nature and role in the plot. Typically, designing the character is a collaborative effort involving personnel from pre-production, production, and sometimes even post-production stages. The main function of a character is to fulfill the role in the plot. The majority of the great characters that we have all seen on the screen or in video games over the years all started as simple sketches on paper. After completing the modeling, rigging is the process through which you prepare your model for animation. The primary purpose of rigging is to create a skeleton that can be used to operate, control, and animate the character. In character animation and rigging, there is a hierarchy, which refers to the order in which the bones are connected. A skeleton hierarchy consists of a succession of joints connected via joint chains. The nature of a joint defines (or restricts) the freedom that the character has in its movement at that joint. We will look at some important types of joints from our own skeletal system that are relevant in this context: ball and socket, pivot, hinge, gliding, and saddle.

Subsequently, we will look at kinematics, a branch of mechanics, which deals with studying the motion of objects, and it deals with the motion of a hierarchical skeleton structure. In forward kinematics (FK), the end effector's position is calculated from the joint parameter values. In inverse kinematics (IK), the joint parameter values are calculated from the end-effector position. Whichever method is being used, the ultimate objective is to attain good posing. Posing is the process of depicting the character in a specific way or "how" the character is postured. If this is done properly, then it will answer the "why" (the motivation – why is the character acting that way) and the "what" (what emotion is being conveyed). Good posing also sends clear signals about weight and balance. Keeping a pose balanced is very important. The body is simply a system of joints that is trying to stay in balance.

Finally, there are some kinds of considerations in the animation process and, most importantly, constraints and limitations within which we have to operate. Only in a Utopian or ideal environment, you do not need to care about system resources or modeling constraints and the other factors contributing to issue in lighting, rendering, animation, etc. However, in the real world, characters are modeled for a specific animation project and plot, with limited system and modeling resources, and under strict timelines and delivery requirements.

You Can Create a Character Out of Anything

In other words, you can basically convert anything into a character. Simple, day-to-day things we come across in our lives can be made into *appealing* characters (Figure 8.1).

FIG 8.1 Sample characters from common objects.

The majority of the great characters that we have all seen on the screen or in video games over the years all started as simple sketches on paper. As mentioned earlier in Chapter 3 on ideation, do not be restrictive of yourself, at least initially. Keep your eyes open and be willing to think outside of the box. You may get that awesome idea for your character basically from anywhere. With a lot of flexibility to create your character, it is important that you consider the following elements when designing a character so that the character fulfills its role in the plot and is appealing to the audience. We will look at this detail later in the section on elements of character design.

Rigging

After completing the modeling, rigging is the process through which you prepare your model for animation. Typically, when the audience look at a character, we see the external appearance, which is also referred to as the *mesh* or *skin*. But, what is actually used to animate a character is a set of bones and joints, known as the skeleton. There are no hard-and-fast rules for rigging either. But, by and large, character rigs typically consist of bones, joints, and the skin. This is similar to the human body where movement is enabled by the bones that are covered by the muscles and skin. Many software use IK handles and controls to manipulate the bones and joints, which in turn determines the degrees of freedom. The primary purpose of rigging is to create a skeleton that can be used to operate, control, and animate the character. Utmost care needs to be taken in building this skeleton that is composed of *bones* and *joints*. The skeleton design should be done in a way to allow the range of motions that the character should eventually be able to perform. For instance, in the real world, we are able to reach out and grab a cup of coffee from a table because of the upper arm and forearm movements combined with the bones of our palm. The joints in our shoulder, elbow, and the wrist allow us to make necessary movements to perform various day-to-day tasks. For instance, if there was no elbow joint, we would not be able to bend the hand at our elbow, and our entire arm from the shoulder to wrist would act like a single unit.

The degrees of freedom (DOF) is a measure of the number of independent movements of objects. You may recall the discussion we had about coordinate systems and axes in earlier chapters. If you consider an unconstrained object in the x, y, z coordinate system, it has six DOF as it can be translated along each one of the three axis and it can also be rotated around the x-, y-, and z-axes.

A well-built skeleton can be swiftly operated to accomplish any pose without much difficulty (Figure 8.2). Once the skeleton has been created, it should be capable of manipulating the character to present the final finished character in a truly engaging manner to the audience. In earlier chapters, we looked

FIG 8.2 Sample characters with joints for rigging.

at hierarchy, where 3D scenes are composed of 3D objects that are made by assembling or putting together smaller objects. For instance, a table object has a flat surface and is supported by four legs.

Similarly, in character animation and rigging, there is a hierarchy, which refers to the order in which the bones are connected. Considering the example of our arm again, when you move your upper arm, the lower arm and the palm are automatically moved because the lower arm is connected to the upper arm and the palm is connected to the lower arm. There are numerous examples of objects that function through such a connected hierarchy of links and joints. In 3D graphics, the pelvis is normally considered to be the root as it controls the center of gravity of an object. The center of gravity represents the position through which the whole weight of the object acts. A basic knowledge of anatomy can be very useful in character design and animation. The scope of this book will not allow us to go deep into anatomy. However, we will take a very brief look at basics of anatomy, especially some key aspects of bones and joints (Figure 8.3) as applicable to character design.

For rigging purposes, the hip or the pelvis is considered to take the weight of the upper body and pass it to the ground through the legs. A skeleton hierarchy consists of a succession of joints connected via joint chains. The nature of a joint defines (or restricts) the freedom that the character has in its movement at that joint.

There are many types and classifications of characters. Characters that are similar to human beings in form are referred to as *anthropomorphic*. Based on the number of legs, characters are classified as biped or quadruped. A biped refers to an animal with two feet, while a quadruped is an animal which has four feet. Bi and quad refer to two and four, respectively. *Ped* in Latin or *pod* in Greek refers to foot. Earlier we saw that the root object is the topmost object in the hierarchy that controls all other objects (Figure 8.4).

A hierarchy is defined by a parent–child relationship. This means that the parent object controls the movement of the child object. It is possible for a joint to be a child of another joint and still be a parent to another joint. For a joint to be categorized as a parent, it should be at an upper level in the hierarchy than any other joint(s). Joints that are below this parent joint in the skeleton hierarchy are called child joints. The child or children joints are controlled by the movements or the transformations of their parent joints.

If you recall from the earlier chapters on modeling, actions like translation and rotation are among the transformations. When a parent joint is rotated, the child joint also gets rotated. Similarly, the child joint gets translated when its parent joint is translated. When we move the upper arm, the lower arm is automatically moved because the upper arm (parent) controls the lower arm (child). In fact, in our own skeletal system, our shoulder bones, upper arm, and lower arm will not be of much use without the palm and our fingers. When we are trying to grab a pen or a cup of coffee, even though the upper arm and the lower arm move forward to help the fingers get within the grabbing distance, actually our fingers do the action of grabbing (Figure 8.5).

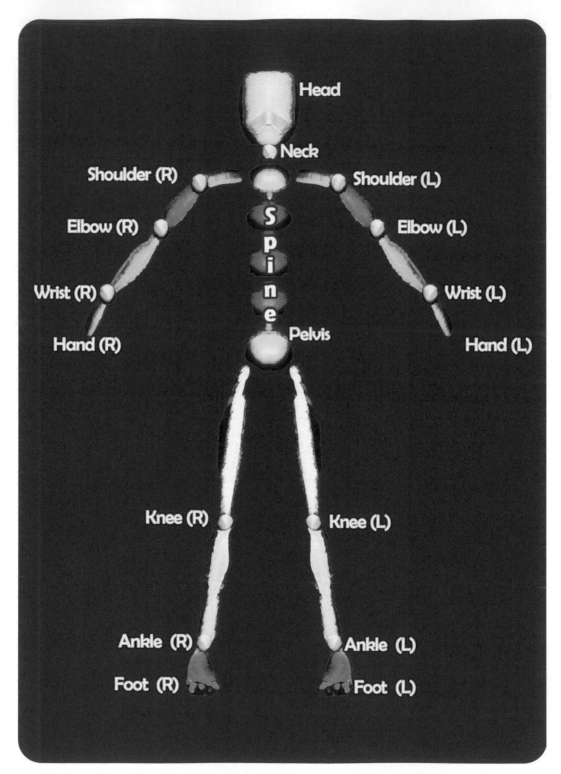

FIG 8.3 Biped system of bones and joints with root at the pelvis.

2-legged Birds & Humans

4-legged Animals

FIG 8.4 Bipeds and quadrupeds.

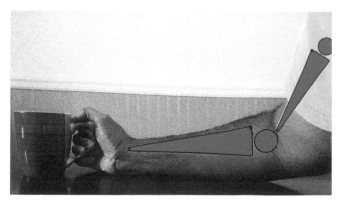

FIG 8.5 Parent–child control in hierarchy.

Essentially, end effectors are gripping tools that are used to hold or grab things. There are many categories of gripping tools such as astrictive, impactive, ingressive, and electrostatic grippers. Based on the position and orientation information (what is given and what is to be calculated), there are two key categories of kinematics, namely, forward kinematics and inverse kinematics.

In FK, the final position of an end effector is obtained from the angles at the joints. On the other hand, IK involves calculating the joint movements and angles required to obtain a specific position. In industry, robotic end effectors are used in innumerable applications such as welding, coating, painting, assembling, and dispensing. IK allows computing the joint factors such as movements and angles required to position the robotic arm (end effector) that is required for the operations such as painting, assembling, or picking up something.

This is similar to how we use our limbs to do various tasks such as:

- Drawing a picture of something
- Typing a particular key on the computer keyboard
- Picking up a pen from the table
- Hitting the soccer ball with a leg

In industrial or robotic context, these are known as "end effectors." End effectors are also known as actuators or grippers. The end effectors are the actual tools that come in contact with the objects that we use. Whether we are writing with pens, steering the wheel of a car, or throwing a ball into a hoop, we use our several parts of hands and our body, but the actual act of writing or throwing is done by the end effectors that are in direct contact with the actual object.

It will be much easier to understand the joints and skeleton hierarchy just by taking a look at our own human skeletal system. We will look at some important types of joints from our own skeletal system that are relevant in this context: ball and socket, pivot, hinge, gliding, and saddle (Figure 8.6).

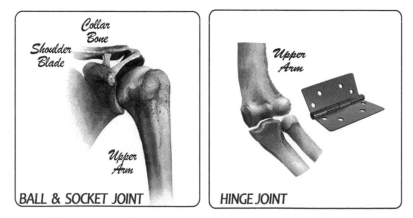

FIG 8.6 Ball and socket joint and hinge joint.

We have a ball and socket joint at our shoulder and hinge joints at our elbow. Ball and socket joints are considered to have the maximum range of motion of all the joints in the human body. They are highly mobile because they allow backward and forward motions, left to right motion, and allow 360° rotational movements. Ball and socket joints allow side-to-side, back-and-forth, and rotational 360° movements. As you can see from the figure, one bone has a smooth curve that fits comfortably into the spherical cavity of the other bone in the joint.

Hinge joints, similar to door hinges, allow rotation along a semi-circle like those joints at our elbows and knees. Hinge joints are known as uniplanar or uniaxial, as they allow rotation along one axis; the movement is restricted to a single plane.

The saddle joint is named so because it resembles the saddle used by a horse rider. The saddle joint in our body is formed by a set of bones, with one having a convex surface and another having a concave surface (Figure 8.7).

Pivot joints are called so because one bone in the joint pivots within another bone. In the pivot joint, one bone is shaped in the form of a ring around a cylindrical-shaped bone. Typically, pivot joints allow rotary movements only about a single axis. The joint between the long bone found in the forearm known as the ulna and the other bones in the forearm known as the radius is an example of pivot joint. The collection of the bones and joints is referred to as the rig. Rigging is the process of arranging and preparing your model for animation. Using the bones and joints as handles, the rig can be used to create the many different poses that the model will be eventually animated into. As rigging involves a set of bones that resemble a skeleton, it is also commonly known as skeletal animation. There are two parts involved in this overall process of skeletal animation or rigging, the surface (mesh), and the skeleton (rig).

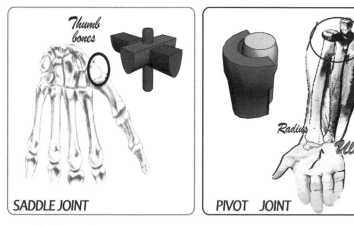

FIG 8.7 Saddle joint and pivot joint.

The *surface* or the mesh represents the skin of the character, while the *skeleton* represents the interconnected set of bones (and joints) that will be used to create the various poses required for animation. That leads us to another foundational element of animation: *poses*. Poses are indeed so powerful that even emotions can be conveyed from character poses. Even without showing or developing the facial features of a character, emotions can be demonstrated by cleverly articulated poses. By using proper posture, you can convey the character's emotions such as fatigue, happiness, frustration, or panic. Everything that you see on a digital computer graphics (CG) representation is an illusion or a simulation. In simple terms, it is make-believe. You cannot drive a car modeled in 3D just as you cannot eat an apple or an orange created in digital CG. Similarly, objects or characters that are created in your 3D scene do not carry weight. But, again with poses, you can convey various attributes such as weight, force, speed, and strength.

Forward and Inverse Kinematics

Kinematics is a branch of mechanics, which deals with studying the motion of objects, and It deals with the motion of a hierarchical skeleton structure. Once the set of bones forming the skeleton have been organized, there are two ways in which the animation can be performed, namely, Forward Kinematics (FK) and Inverse Kinematics (IK). In both FK and IK, the skeleton hierarchy is manipulated so that the character can be posed in desired ways to achieve the end animation. In FK, the bones are transformed to make them get into a specific position, while in IK, one can directly move the end effector, based on which the bones automatically adjust.

Let us try to understand FK and IK using the notion of the end effector we discussed earlier. In FK, the end effector's position is calculated from the joint parameter values. In IK, the joint parameter values are calculated from the end-effector position. If FK can be thought of as a top-down approach, IK can be thought of as a bottom-up approach. In FK, the inputs are the joint angles and the end-effector coordinates (x, y, z) are the outputs. In IK, the inputs are the coordinates of the end effectors, and the outputs are the joint angles.

As we saw in the earlier chapters, while the development of computer animation has been relatively recent, traditional animation has been in existence long before the advent of computers. Even today, digital animation is built on the fundamental concepts of traditional animation.

Depicting motion (or movement) in digital CG animation involves capturing the change of position over time to understand as well as describe the inherent topological (geometric) relationships. But animation is essentially about "timing." Hence, the variables involved in kinematics include:

- Position
- Orientation
- Time
- Distance
- Speed

The study of motion of an object or a group of objects in kinematics entails understanding the notion of end effector or manipulator. The *end effector* is the tool found at the end point of a robotic device. The end effector refers to the final link in a chain of joints of a robotic device, to which tools are attached or with which operations are performed.

Whether modeling humanoid or non-humanoid characters, factors pertaining to modeling, lighting, and rendering always need to be considered in view of the system resources and processor capabilities. We saw earlier that if the density of the polygons (resolution) becomes low, the model becomes faceted.

In the physical activities, a hierarchical chain of bones and joints are involved as shown in Figure 8.8.

When we use our hand to draw or pick up something and use our legs to kick, the final position (placement) of our palm or foot is dependent on the bones and joints. The final position of the palm depends on the chain including the shoulder, upper arm, elbow, forearm, wrist, and palm. Similarly, the chain for the leg includes the pelvis, hind leg, knee, foreleg, ankle, and foot. In our day-to-day life, our body coordinates the movements of our limbs and

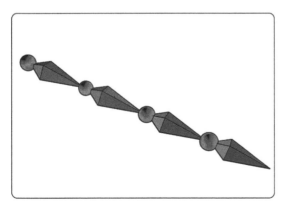

FIG 8.8 Hierarchical connection of bones and joints.

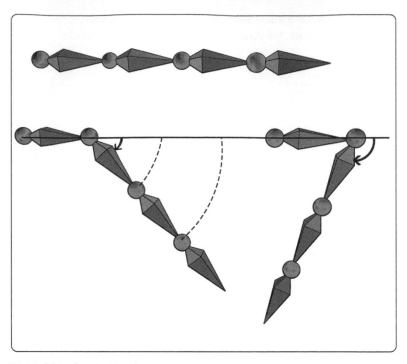

FIG 8.9 Children (bones) rotate with parent.

joints to accomplish the tasks we do. This is similar to a common approach to building characters for animation, known as the *segmented* approach. In segmented characters, the joints we discussed earlier are modeled distinctly (disjointedly) from the bones that they connect. However, this can leave inappropriate seams visible at the places where the segments are connected. Such seams can be hidden, or some new objects such as belts, shoulder ornaments, socks, or neck ties can be created over them to hide the unseemliness. Whatever the category of animation, in CG, the animator identifies the specific position for the end effector, and the joint angles required to obtain that position for the end effector are computed by the animation program or software (Figure 8.9).

As you can see in Figure 8.9, when the bone 2 is rotated, the children bones also get rotated; however, the parent bone of bone 2 is not rotated. The children follow the transformations of the parent bone. In the case of FK, as shown below, you see that movements created when the children follow the parent are arc movements. As indicated by the dotted lines, the other joints following the parent move along curved paths.

In FK, to accomplish a specific position for the end effector, the parent bone is rotated first followed by the child bone. So, with FK, the direction of flow of motion is from parent to child. Using this approach, rotational transformations can be used to achieve curvilinear or arc motion (Figure 8.10).

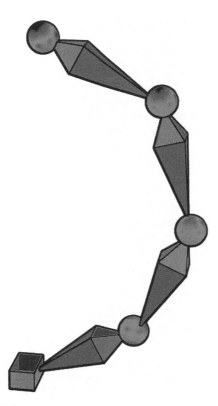

FIG 8.10 Positioning end effector.

When it is required to lift or drop the character's hand, using the FK approach, first one would start with shoulder rotation followed by the elbow and the wrist. While it may be possible to easily accomplish many movements in this manner, achieving some movements may not be practical using this approach. For instance, if the end of the chain (end effector) needs to be positioned in a specific location, FK may not be the most efficient approach. In such cases, the solution is IK.

Consider the case of the last bone in the image above that is placed inside the box. If using FK, the other parent bones have to be transformed so as to locate the tip of the last bone inside the white box. So, effectively, the end effector is positioned by transforming preceding parent bones. On the other hand, with IK, the end effector can be selected and dragged directly into the desired location. The other bones automatically adjust (transform) themselves as the joint is selected and moved.

Generally, when looking at a character, the audience is concerned mainly with the external appearance. However, in 3D modeling and animation, the internal organization or structure is also important. In fact, in 3D modeling, this internal structure is made up of a hierarchical set of bones referred to as the skeleton. The bones and joints in the skeleton control the movements of the character. One important thing that you need to consider when recording animation with the camera is the *transition* or continuity.

Elements of Character Design and Posing

A well-designed character is a great tool to narrate the story. The design of the character must show a good understanding of the plot and the script to align character's traits and the overall personality accordingly. Design is a creative process, and there is no single correct approach to design. We will look at some of the common procedures employed in the design process. Character design is an essential process in many fields including video games, animated movies, illustrated books, cartoons, and mobile/computer games. As you can see in Figure 8.8, remember that it is not about just moving the character, but about moving the audience.

One of the meanings of the word *pose* in common language is "to position something" or "to place in a location." The same holds true in CG terminology as well. Posing involves conveying the emotions through body language. Just as a spoken language is a tool for communication, posing is also a (body's) language for communicating (Figure 8.11).

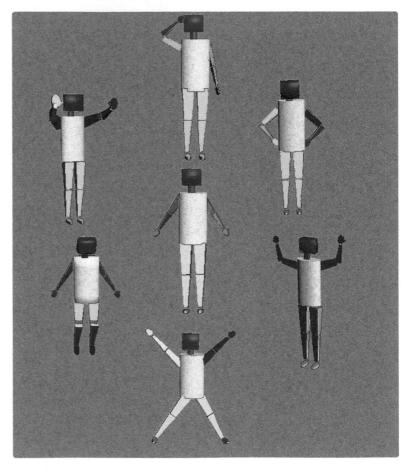

FIG 8.11 Character posing.

What kind of pose you use should be driven by what it is that you intend to convey such as:

- Is your character very happy?
- Is your character searching for something?
- Is your character presenting a nerdish appearance?
- Is your character upset or scared?
- Is your character angry?

Here we will discuss some of the noteworthy considerations involved in character design.

Kinetics is the study of poses, whole body motion, including head and hand movements, and facial expressions as a means of communication. A character's posture conveys powerful messages about the character's overall personality and the emotions involved. Posing characters in a clear, engaging manner that expresses the appropriate sentiment at one glance is a high art.

Purpose

Each character has a purpose. Good character design stems from a proper understanding of the character's true nature and the role of the character in the plot. Characters with distinctive traits and visually engaging personalities tend to resonate well with the audience. All decisions about character design should always consider the overall role of the character in the story and should result after careful deliberation of the range of actions (motions) that the character will be required to perform as the plot evolves. The main function of a character is to fulfill the role in the plot. Hence, each and every choice made with respect to designing the character must have a "reason."

Balance

One important aspect that needs to be considered when designing a character is the achievement of *equilibrium* or balance. Balance is imperative. The target is to achieve a good balance among all objectives in view of the constraints or limitations applicable to the project on hand. The first thing you need to consider is style. With your concept art, you should already have defined this to some extent, but now it is time to hone in on the precise look you want to go for in design and animation. Style is infinite in its conception. Do you want your film in its approach to be stylistically illustrative, traditional cartoon, wild and wacky? The one thing you most likely don't want to do is to have a character design style that is very dissimilar from your background or environment style. Or do you? (Perhaps your film will totally contain that kind of off-beat novelty.) Chances are, though, that you'll want a compatible style throughout. But then again animation is capable of anything, so don't entirely close off all your options at this stage. Don't forget, too, that using a rounded, curvilinear style of line approach will give you a softer, cuter style

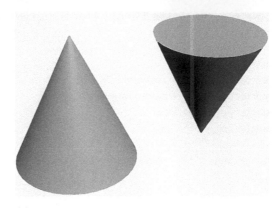

FIG 8.12 Object stability.

of character. Angular, rectilinear line and form will give a more aggressive, hard-cut style of character. Similarly, with the colors you use, generically pastel shades imply a softer, cuter style, whereas pure primary colors suggest a more "out there," wacky kind of personality.

The shape or form of a character influences the stability. From a geometric point of view, objects with wider bases tend to have greater stability. The pyramids or other huge buildings designed with wide bases bear examples of stable structures. Taking a look at Figure 8.12, you can say that obviously the cone resting on the base has greater stability than the one on its tip.

Objects with wider base area tend to have higher stability. According to the laws of physics, with more surface area in contact, there is increased friction, which makes it harder to move, thus increasing stability. This is the reason that for transporting purposes, wooden logs in cylindrical shape are preferred than those that are box-shaped (Figure 8.13).

Another important aspect that is important in this context is the center of gravity. The center of gravity represents the point of balance where the entire body's mass is concentrated. By providing support to the body at this point,

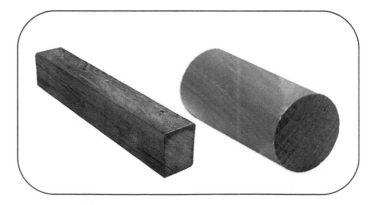

FIG 8.13 Contact area and friction.

the entire body can be supported so that it is balanced or is in equilibrium. For human beings (and characters) also, there is a center of gravity, and in order to be balanced, this center of gravity needs to be properly supported so that the weight is evenly distributed. From the character design point of view, the character should be perceived by the audience as properly balanced. Otherwise, this can be disconcerting and may interfere with the appeal of the character and also affect the staging of the plot.

In character animation, to achieve a balance, typically, the weight is either distributed evenly or unevenly among the feet. However, the weight can also be spread among other parts of the body including the knee, or elbow and hips (in a supine position). Remember that even though generally the legs carry the weight of the body, it is not always the case depending on the character's pose. At times, people lean on a table or lean against a wall or lean in other ways. In such cases, the weight distribution is done by other body parts as involved. Keeping a pose balanced is very important. The body is simply a system of joints that is trying to stay in balance. Each bone acts as a tiny lever, distributing the weight of the body through the spine to the hips and then down through the legs to the ground. If a pose is out of balance, the character will appear as if it's about to tip over. If the body is slightly out of balance, the eye will still pick it up and see the pose as wrong without an apparent reason. In the image below, it is obvious that the right pose is unbalanced (Figure 8.14).

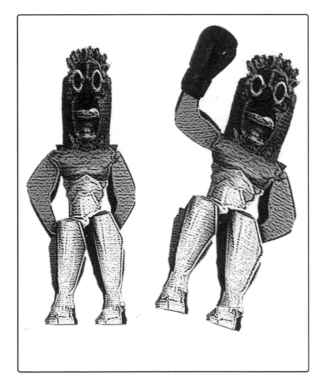

FIG 8.14 Balance and posing.

The shift in weight of a character or an object is determined by the center of gravity. Especially when a character alters its pose, then a shift in the center of gravity occurs, resulting in the weight shifting from one leg to another. You may have noticed in public places like train stations or bus stations or libraries, how people shift their weight by leaning to one side or altering their poses.

Posing

Good posing also sends clear signals about weight and *balance*. As we saw earlier, a character's rig (internal skeleton used to control the animation) is a hierarchical system of bones and joints. An audience can easily make out a pose that is out of balance. With anthropomorphic (human-like) characters, most software associate the root of the rigging control to the hip.

Action poses are an important category of poses, wherein it is important to depict the character in motion. Ultimately, animation is about movement. Characters do a wide range of movements such as running, playing, dancing, jumping, walking, pushing, and pulling. The line of action is a hypothetical or imaginary line that describes the motion of the character (Figure 8.15). Whatever the action, be it running or jumping, the line of action helps define the motion and also to fuse it well with the entire character. If most of the weight is on the left leg and some on the right, the center of gravity will be closer to the left foot. As the weight shifts over to the other foot, the torso will follow that line.

To understand balance, let us just revisit some high-school physics. *Center of gravity* is the specific point in an object that represents the average location of the weight distribution across the object. Center of gravity is also referred to as center of mass where the value of gravity remains relatively constant. If a vertical line passing through the character's center of gravity also passes through the supporting base, then the character is considered to be in balance. For human beings, the base of support is the area directly below the feet, including the region covered by the feet or the footwear. For other real-world objects, the base of support is the area on which the object stands or makes contact with the ground on which it is standing. In case of objects with legs, like chairs or tables, in addition to the area covered by the legs, the base of support also includes the area between the legs.

For these reasons, balance is imperative. While buying a car, one must consider various factors, including the mileage, desired amenities, safety features, and seating capability, and try to find the optimal deal within a cost constraint. Similarly, when designing a character, the considerations mentioned above need to be taken into account. The target is to achieve a good balance among all objectives in view of the constraints or limitations applicable to the project on hand. Two very closely related aspects when designing character poses are *balance* and *symmetry*, which are not equivalent. Let us look at symmetry.

Symmetry

Now, let us discuss symmetry. One of the very simple and important rules that animators follow to obtain a natural look from their character poses is to keep them *asymmetrical*. In the real world, we will rarely find ourselves

FIG 8.15 Symmetry and asymmetry. (Image courtesy: Stephanie, A.)

(human beings) in symmetrical poses. Hence, a character that is in perfect symmetry will look strange and unnatural. If you want a dynamic scene that is well composed, you will introduce asymmetry in your character's poses. As you can see in Figure 8.15, the character on the left is in a symmetrical pose, and on the right-hand side, you see the character in an asymmetrical pose. The pose on the right-hand side is more dynamic, while the pose on the left is neutral and boring.

In Figure 8.15, it can be seen that the character on the left exhibits almost perfect symmetry and hence is not specifically drawing the viewers' attention to any particular aspect. On the other hand, the character on the right has a light placed on the character's left side and hence adds shade to the other side of the character's face. Also, the hair of this character shows asymmetry. These asymmetrical features add more interest and intrigue to the character on the right.

Silhouette

In Figure 8.16, you can see that without the use of any materials or any advanced modeling or light or any other cues, just the outline showing the poses conveys different kinds of emotions (Figure 8.16).

FIG 8.16 Martial artists and ballerinas.

Line of Action

To establish proper continuity, you must understand the *line of action*. There is another line of action that we will see later in Chapter 10 on composition, which is a hypothetical line in the scene that links your primary scene characters. This is an imaginary line along which your subject moves or looks.

From the point of view of posing, the line of action here we are discussing is about the line of action for the character, which is a hypothetical line that indicates the character's pose. Note that good posing answers "the why" and "the what" through "the how." In the image below, for each character pose shown, there is an implied line (not an actual line) along the direction of each pose (Figure 8.17). It should be noted that in Figure 8.17, the facial expressions in all the poses are the same, as in fact there is no facial expression at all. Still, the poses communicate a wide range of indications or signals.

Line of action can be extremely powerful when combined with silhouette. Figure 8.18 just shows two cacti plants, and obviously there is no facial expression involved. However, you can see clearly how the plant on the left seems to be terrified or scared of the plant on the right just from the line of action and the outline. Various character postures such as a specific manner of walking, relaxed speaking, energetic movement, or a laissez-fair attitude all form an inherent part of the character design and development, and play a crucial role in establishing a strong emotional rapport with the audience.

Surface Characteristics: Color/Material

The surface characteristics of a character refer to colors and/or materials (texture) used on the character. Shown below are different textures and materials on the modeled snail character (Figure 8.19).

Colors are closely associated with emotion as their specific colors and color ranges are associated with particular cognitive responses. For instance, colors such as blue and green (also known as background colors) are associated with creating a soothing, assuring, or relaxing effect. Red is a hot color that is used to indicate a sense of emergency or urgency. This is the reason that the color red is used in traffic signal lights and in the stop signs. Shades of orange are used to grab attention or indicate excitement or zestfulness. Yellow is used to create a sensation of energy, cheerfulness, or healthiness. The whole range of colors used in a rendering is referred to as the color scheme, which will be discussed in detail in the chapter on lighting and rendering later. By and large, the successful and popular characters and scenes from the hit movies and animation flicks have all used a carefully thought-out color scheme. The colors in any effective character and/or scene were not just an accidental coincidence or the results of a random process. The team of personnel in charge of surface characteristics plan every color, hue, and shade in an extremely meticulous manner so as to build the character appeal and facilitate a coherent understanding of the plot.

FIG 8.17 Poses and line of action.

FIG 8.18 Line of action.

FIG 8.19 Textures on 3D-modeled characters.

Level of Detail

The amount of detail required in a character is inherently related to the following:

- Speed of motion of the character
- Range of motion of the character
- Distance of the character from the camera

Distance from the Camera

The distance of the character from the camera can also influence the detail on a character. A character that is going to be shown in close-up or extreme close-up several times throughout the animation must be modeled with greater attention to detail than a character that is going to appear only a couple of times in long shot. Once again, this goes back to the storyboard, and a properly planned storyboard will be able to foresee and include these details well in advance of the actual production process. *Off-screen space* refers to the space that is not actually seen in the shot or the frame but is still part of the model or the scene. *On-screen space* is the actual things we see in the final scene. The distance of the character from the camera is related to the actual space that the character will fill or take up on the screen. Using the same logic as discussed under the earlier sections pertaining to the range of character movement and speed of motion, the character designer and modeler need to strive to find a good balance between the detail required and the distance while considering the other factors discussed here.

Speed of Character Movement

There are several character types such as the primary character, secondary character, and background characters. Not all these characters need to be modeled with the same *level of detail* (LOD). The speed of the character is closely related to the LOD and the actual amount of refinement or subtlety involved in designing, modeling, and rendering the character. Based on this, the speed of character movement can be categorized as follows:

- Static or stationary
- Slow-moving
- Medium-paced
- Fast-paced

If the character is a primary character in the animation and is static or slow-moving, then obviously the audience has greater time to focus on the details of the character. In such a case, extreme attention to detail is a worthy investment of time on behalf of the character development team and all those involved in the character design. However, consider a character that is going to appear in the background or a character that moves very fast. In that case, the audience will not be actually seeing the character in greater detail. In such a case, discretion should be exercised into determining how much time should be invested in designing and modeling the character to meet the requirements of the plot without compromising the quality.

Appeal

This is also prominently known as the 12th principle of animation (these principles that were covered in Chapter 7 on animation). *Appeal* or character appeal deals with making the character more endearing and engaging for the audience (Figure 8.20). A poorly planned character, with poor drawing, a complicated design, or awkward shapes, which the audience cannot relate to, results in poor appeal. The pose or the gait also plays an important role in designing a good character. All traits of the character, including the color or the material, texture, gait, pose, and lighting employed, should be in tandem with the intended personality of the character being modeled. If a character is supposed to have a calm or serene personality, the design of the character should elicit the same response or emotion from the audience.

Recall the various animated CG movies that you have seen and try to decide what your favorite characters are. Ask yourself why you still remember them despite the fact that you might have seen those years ago. What are some of the remarkable features of these characters that come to your mind

FIG 8.20 Style and appeal.

when you think of them? You may be able to think of a lot of features, but, surprisingly enough, you will find the gait or pose of these characters will form an important aspect of making them so memorable.

Range of Motion: Facial Expressions and Gesticulations

The LOD in a character is also inherently related to the range of facial expressions that the character will be required to do later as well as the type of movements and gestures to be performed by the character during the character animation stage. This is the reason that extreme care is exercised during pre-production, especially storyboarding. If all the motions of a character detailed in the storyboard are predominantly in the facial area and involve the arms, and none of the movements are associated with the hips or the legs, then that particular range of motion need not be included when building the character (as it is never going to be used later). However, this is easier said than done. It is important that a 3D model is created to allow all kinds of motions that the character is intended to perform according to the plot. While there is no strict rule of thumb that can clearly state the instructions in black and white, with experience, the character modeler will be able to predict with a good probability the kind of movements an animator will perform with a specific character over time (Figure 8.21).

FIG 8.21 Modeling for animation.

The figure shows anthropomorphic characters designed in a hierarchical form. While there are several types used to classify character models based on the methods used and the purposes they will serve, one common classification is based on whether characters are humanoid or not. A *humanoid* character is defined as one having human traits or resembling humans, that is, having two feet and arms, torso, face, and so on (e.g., humanoid robot). On the other hand, characters that have a morphology (form/structure) that is significantly different from humanoid characters can be called *non-humanoid* characters.

Modeling and Character Design: Considerations and Constraints

Typically, designing the character is a collaborative effort involving personnel from pre-production, production, and sometimes even post-production stages. The director and the technical director work with the character designer, modeler, layout artist, animator, and many other people. Designing a character is a creative exercise that takes into account various factors such as:

- What is the level of detail required in the character and does this go with the requirements of the overall plot of animation?
- What kind of animation will the character be performing eventually?
- What are the factors to be considered from a *kinematics* perspective? Does the character design show cognizance of these factors?
- What are the constraints in terms of system resources?
- What are the limitations in terms of modeling capabilities?
- What are the rendering considerations?

By now, you should have understood that modeling complex real-life characters and fictional or mythological characters is quite a complex process indeed. When you are capturing your animation involving such complex models, camera animation plays a key role in properly capturing the diligently and meticulously created models. Hence, during the learning stages, one should experiment a lot with the camera positions and orientations. This involves exploring several views such as top view and side views, and trying various motions such as dolly, pan, or zoom.

Example of Scene Modeling (Effects) with Lights

We will be looking at light in detail in Chapter 9, but here we will discuss just in the context of the current chapter. Besides the actual colors on the character itself, the lighting applied to a character also plays an important role in setting the overall mood. The image below shows the same scene under four different lighting conditions, each of which brings their own flavor to the scene and can create a different ambience suited for different moods (Figure 8.22).

FIG 8.22 Lights for scene modeling.

There are three lights, known as the key light, fill light, and rim light (see three-point lighting in lighting chapter), used in a typical scene. Typically, in a digital environment (e.g., a computer-generated imagery, model, or scene), the RGB color model is employed. This is an additive model wherein the *additive primary colors* (or primaries) are red, green, and blue. The *additive secondary colors* (or complements) are cyan, magenta, and yellow. Cyan is the complement of red, magenta is the complement of green, and yellow is the complement of blue. Digital color selectors or color swatches use two prominent modes to combine these additive colors: RGB and HSV (hue, saturation, value). Besides the color, there are other qualities of light with respect to the character such as the intensity, light type (point, spot, direct, etc.), and hotspot that also play a role in influencing the character appeal.

Interview with Tom Brierton, Expert in Animation and Motion Picture Visual Effects

Bio of Tom Brierton

Tom Brierton has been involved with animation and motion picture visual effects for over 40 years. Specializing in stop-motion puppet animation, Brierton taught traditional and computer animation at Columbia College Chicago, The Illinois Institute of Art at Schaumburg, Calumet College at St. Joseph in Whiting, Indiana, The Chicago Art Institute, and Purdue University in Hammond, Indiana. An accomplished sculptor and model builder, Brierton taught computer modeling and texture mapping, and stop-motion puppetry. In addition to his animation background, Brierton is also an accomplished machinist and has machined stop-motion armatures for 30 years. He has sold puppet armatures throughout the world.

Brierton's father, John "Jack" Brierton, was a fingerstyle guitarist who taught Tom to play the guitar and read music. Graduating from high school in 1976, Brierton attended Southern Illinois University at Carbondale, and finished with undergraduate and graduate degrees in music theory and composition in 1988 and 1993, respectively.

Retiring in 2019, Brierton continues to work on his own film projects and write music. He and his wife currently reside in northwest Indiana. His website can be found at: https://tombrierton.wixsite.com/website.

Interview

1. **You have many years of experience in animation. What are your thoughts on the importance of a plot and the role of characters in the plot?**

    One might say that plot is a critical part of storytelling. Without a good story, plot, and characters, the film can easily become lifeless and dull, regardless of whether it's a live-action or animated film. In the 2007 feature-length animated film, Ratatouille, one of the supporting characters, notes that not everyone can be a great chef, but a great chef can come from anywhere. The point being is that not everyone can write a great screenplay, but a great screenplay can come from any film genre. For years, film producers (not all, but some) have made the mistake of assuming that a critically and financially successful film (say, a horror film for example) made its money by having a monster appear in it. So, they would make another movie about a terrible monster, but sacrifice the plot and story in favor of having the monster from the previous film appear again, but not flesh out interesting characters, and not making an effort to make the story's sequel just as engaging as the original film was. Not an easy thing to do. As a result, people trash it and it makes no money. The 1979 horror film Alien was financially and critically successful not necessarily because it had a terrifying monster in it, but because audiences identified with the characters and their (and our) innate desire to escape danger when necessary. But there are all kinds of monsters, and the scariest one is the one who is your everyday next door neighbor like Norman Bates or Dennis Rader: people who appear mentally well-adjusted but in reality are maladjusted killers. Alien's sequel, Aliens, was equally successful as its predecessor because its director/writer, James Cameron, understands the importance of audience empathy and identification, and the roles that the actors develop as the story unfolds.

2. **Today there are many digital tools available to model characters and perform rigging. However, a solid understanding of the principles of animation and the fundamental elements of character modeling, animation, and rigging is still highly advocated by experts in the field. What are your thoughts on this? Why is a knowledge of these basic principles and the fundamental aspects of animation so important?**

Many seasoned professionals in the field of animation feel it's necessary for animation students to get exposure to, and experience from, the basic rules of animation. The "Nine Old Men" of the Disney studio developed the 12 principles of animation, and these principles are still with us today.

Rigging has more to do with computer animation, as rigging is more practical for creating a physical skeletal system to drive the movement of the wireframe of a computer character, at least characters that are supposed to be realistic. Squash and stretch are probably the most important aspects of the 12 principles of animation, but it's mostly used for animation characters that distort their movements. These distortions must go by fairly quickly. When an action moves quickly, such as running, squashing and stretching should appear on a subconscious level, while at the same time appearing normal when played back at 24 frames per second (traditional film speed) or 30 samples per second (digital film speed).

3. **How does good pre-production (storyboarding) help with making a good animation?**

Storyboarding can help a great deal when designing a scene for an animated film, but it is labor-intensive. If you tell a live actor, "Walk from point A to point B, and take six seconds to do it", the cameraman will shoot six seconds of real-time footage, following the actor as he or she walks across the set within six seconds. If you tell an animator, "Have Scooby Doo© walk from point A to point B, and take six seconds to do it", it will take much longer to do because animation is a time-lapse process. If you're a key animator and you must draw Scooby's key poses, then pass those keys over to an in-betweener who will then need to draw the in-between poses. You will never get these drawings done in six seconds; more likely a few days. Storyboards are therefore critical with this type of filmmaking. This process does not get any easier in computer animation. You still need to create the key poses and then keyframe those poses. The computer animation software will play back the animation timeline, including the in-between poses, but the computer will interpolate these in-betweens like a robot. This will result in creating an absolutely 100% technically smooth movement, which does not occur in real life (an exception being a machine or the Atomic Clock). Hence, you must go back into the timeline and tweak Scooby's key poses so that his walking appears more natural than mechanical.

Sometimes an animation student will (in the beginning of their studies) assume that the computer can do most of the work for them, and do it quickly. I call this the "Where's the make animation cool button?" mentality. That's a lazy way to learn. The only way you're going to make a compelling or "cool" animation is to learn how to create a good story with interesting characters, lay it all out as storyboards, and practice, practice, practice on your character animation. Animators are actors, but to reiterate they act in time-lapse, which can be very labor-intensive. But the more prepared you are when going into an animated production, the better off you'll be when you're trying to meet a deadline.

Chapter 8 Quiz

PART I

True/False (Circle the Correct Choice)

1. Design is a creative process, and there is no single correct approach to design.
True False

2. The main function of a character is to fulfill the role in the plot.
True False

3. Characters with distinctive traits and visually engaging personalities tend to resonate well with the audience.
True False

4. A biped refers to an animal with three feet.
True False

5. Typically, when the audience look at a character, they see the external appearance, which is also referred to as the rig or bones.
True False

6. In a hinge joint, one bone has a smooth curve that fits comfortably into the spherical cavity of the other bone in the joint.
True False

7. The end effectors are the actual tools that do come in contact with the objects that we use.
True False

8. In a hierarchy, the parent object controls the movement of the child object.
True False

9. Bone and socket joints are highly mobile because they allow backward and forward motions, left to right motion, and allow 360° rotational movements.
True False

10. The shift in weight of a character or an object is determined by the center of focus.
True False

11. Saddle joints are known as uniplanar or uniaxial, as they allow rotation along one axis.
True False

12. In both FK and IK, the skeleton hierarchy is manipulated so that the character can be posed in desired ways to achieve the end animation.
True False

13. Typically, pivot joints allow rotary movements only about two axes.
True False

14. On-screen space refers to the space that is not actually seen in the shot or the frame but is still part of the model or the scene.
True False

15. The nature of a joint defines (or restricts) the freedom that the character has in its movement at that joint.
True False

16. The skeleton design should be done in a way to allow the range of motions that the character should eventually be able to perform.
True False

17. In both FK and IK, the skeleton hierarchy is manipulated so that the character can be posed in desired ways to achieve the end animation.
True False

18. Hinge joints are known as uniplanar or uniaxial.
True False

19. It is not possible for a joint to be a child of another joint and still be a parent to another joint.
True False

20. Character appeal, which refers to how believable and appealing your character is, is one of the 12 basic principles of animation.
True False

PART II

Multiple Choice Questions (Choose the Most Appropriate Answer)

1. The primary purpose of _____ is to create a skeleton that can be used to operate, control, and animate the character.
   a. Storyboarding
   b. Texturing
   c. Modeling
   d. Rigging
   e. Painting

2. Characters that are similar to human being in form are referred to as_____ .
   a. Anthropomorphic
   b. Mesomorphic
   c. Zygomorphic
   d. Hemimorphic
   e. Pleomorphic

3. The degrees of _____ is a measure of the number of independent movements of objects.
   a. Tendon
   b. Momentum
   c. Force
   d. Speed
   e. Freedom

4. The _____ object is the topmost object in the hierarchy that controls all other objects in a scene.
   a. Parent
   b. Branch
   c. Root
   d. Child
   e. Sibling

5. Ped in Latin or pod in Greek refers to _____ .
   a. Head
   b. Bone
   c. Ear
   d. Eye
   e. Foot

6. _____ joints allow rotation along a semi-circle like those joints at our elbows and knees.
   a. Saddle
   b. Ball and socket
   c. Ball
   d. Hinge
   e. Pivot

7. In _____ kinematics, the end effector's position is calculated from the joint parameter values.
   a. Reverse
   b. Forward
   c. Inverse
   d. Backward
   e. None of the above

8. The _____ joint in our body is formed by a set of bones, with one having a convex surface and another having a concave surface.
   a. Saddle
   b. Ball and socket
   c. Ball
   d. Hinge
   e. Pivot

9. In _____ kinematics, the joint parameter values are calculated from the end-effector position.
   a. Reverse
   b. Forward
   c. Inverse
   d. Backward
   e. None of the above

10. The _____ , a sizeable apparatus, consisted of an enclosed box in which a looped strip of film was passed between a lens and an electric light bulb.
    a. Praxinoscope
    b. Phenakistoscope
    c. Kinetoscope
    d. Kinetograph
    e. All the above

11. The joint at the shoulder is an example of a _____ joint.
    a. Saddle
    b. Ball and socket
    c. Ball
    d. Hinge
    e. Pivot

12. In _____ kinematics, to accomplish a specific position for the end effector, the parent bone is rotated first followed by the child bone.
    a. Reverse
    b. Forward
    c. Inverse
    d. Backward
    e. None of the above

13. A quadruped is an animal which has _____ feet.
    a. 4
    b. 3
    c. 2
    d. 1
    e. None of the above

14. The center of _____ represents the position through which the whole weight of the object acts.
    a. Velocity
    b. Momentum
    c. Force
    d. Gravity
    e. None of the above

15. For a joint to be categorized as a _____ , it should be at an upper level in the hierarchy than any other joint(s).
    a. Flexible
    b. Stationary
    c. Parent
    d. Child
    e. None of the above

16. For rigging purposes, the _____ is considered to take the weight of the upper body and pass it to the ground through the legs.
    a. Head
    b. Torso
    c. Neck
    d. Hinge
    e. Pivot

17. _____ screen space refers to the space that is not actually seen in the shot or the frame but is still part of the model or the scene.
    a. Reverse
    b. Off
    c. On
    d. Back
    e. None of the above

18. The surface or the mesh represents the _____ of the character.
    a. Skin
    b. Bone
    c. Skeleton
    d. Joint
    e. None of the above

19. _____ screen space is the actual thing we see in the final scene.
    a. Reverse
    b. Off
    c. On
    d. Back
    e. None of the above

20. A _____ character is defined as one having human traits or resembling humans, that is, having two feet and arms, torso, face, and so on.
    a. Hierarchical
    b. Stationary
    c. Humanoid
    d. Child
    e. None of the above

CHAPTER 9: Lighting

As the eye is the best composer, so light is the first of painters.

– Ralph Waldo Emerson

WHAT WILL YOU LEARN IN THIS CHAPTER?

- What are some basic concepts of physics applicable to lighting in computer graphics (CG)?
- What are reflection, refraction, and dispersion?
- How materials are classified based on light interaction?
- What is meant by opacity, transparency, and translucency?
- What is color?
- What are the common color theories?
- What is additive model in digital lighting?
- What is meant by HSV model?
- What are some important properties of CG lights?
- What is three-point lighting?

DOI: 10.1201/9780429186349-9

- What are the different types of CG lights?
- What are linear lights and volume lights?
- What are direct and indirect lights?
- What is meant by ambient light?

As mentioned in the earlier chapters, modeling and animation are tools you use to communicate something to the audience. *Lighting* helps you get this message across and enables the audience to better appreciate your creation. Good lighting can make or break your carefully created 3D model scene and animation. Lighting plays a critical role in presenting a 3D scene, the animation, and the overall message unmistakably across. An appreciation of art and studying the world around us help create better lighting in your scene. As we will see later in Chapter 10 on composition, lighting significantly influences what parts of your scene are highlighted and what are not. Before we get into the aspects of lighting of a 3D computer graphics (CG) scene, let us take a brief look at the basic theory of lighting.

Before we start discussing "digital" lighting, we need to take a brief look at "lighting" (in the natural world) and the art and science of color, which is inherently interrelated to lighting. The scope of this book will not allow us to get into too many technicalities of the light theory. We will discuss only some of the basic physics behind lighting, as required for you to understand and appreciate CG lighting. Even though color and light are words that we frequently use in our day-to-day life, technically, these are hard to define due to a subjective aspect involved. Many scientists and researchers consider that color and light are perceptions and hence are inevitably and intrinsically subjective in nature. Numerous attempts have been made to describe color and light. While we can define a straight line unambiguously as the shortest *distance* between two points, it may not be easy to come up with an unequivocal and objective definition for color or light. But, remember that these are not the only things that pose a quixotic problem of this nature. Color can be best categorized as a perception like many of the other things we feel or experience. The perceived color of an object, among other things, depends on the nature of the incident light and also the person observing the color. We will briefly look at various related aspects including form, composition, lights, color, color model(s), and *shadows* before we get into lighting design in the digital CG scenes.

Revisiting High School Physics

Light is a form of electromagnetic radiation. Visible light is only one small portion of a family of waves called electromagnetic (EM) radiation. The EM spectrum ranges from very long wavelengths (radio waves) to very small wavelengths which are at the other end of the spectrum. Visible light is near the middle of the spectrum. Light is part of a much larger band of waves represented by the electromagnetic spectrum, which includes other types of radiation known to you such as radio waves, micro waves, infrared, and x-rays. From Figure 9.1, you can see that the visible light is between

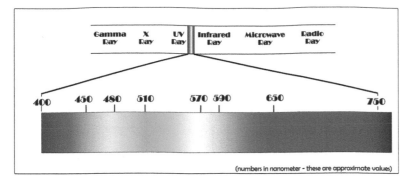

FIG 9.1 Visible spectrum.

the infrared and ultraviolet radiations. Approximately, visible light has a wavelength ranging from 400 to 750 nm. One nanometer is one-billionth of a meter (1/1,000,000,000). For the purpose of this book, let us assume that when we say light, we are referring to this visible part of the electromagnetic spectrum.

Typically, light's wavelength is expressed in nanometers. One nanometer is equal to one-billionth of a meter. In other words, one meter is equal to one billion nanometers (1 m = 10^9 nm). Our goal here is to obtain a general knowledge of light and color, so that you can better recreate or simulate them in your digital 3D worlds. Photographers, 3D artists, modelers, and cinematographers all need to know how light works so that they can understand how it is simulated digitally. Subsequently, this will facilitate the understanding of digital color representation that is inevitable in computer graphics.

Optical Properties of Lights

In the real world, light reacts differently when it is incident on different surfaces. Let us look at some optical properties of light that are often simulated within CG scenes.

Reflection

Reflection refers to the process when a light ray that is incident on an object rebounds or bounces off. Very flat smooth surfaces practically reflect the incident light completely. This is why we can see our reflection on a mirror. However, not all surfaces completely reflect the light incident on them. The law of reflection says that the angle of incidence is equal to the angle of reflection. The amount of reflected light is determined by the physical characteristics of the material. For instance, an object's reflection on a highly polished stainless steel surface is different from the reflection on an aluminum surface (Figure 9.2).

In CG terminology, there are two important types of reflection known as diffuse reflection and specular reflection depending on the direction(s)

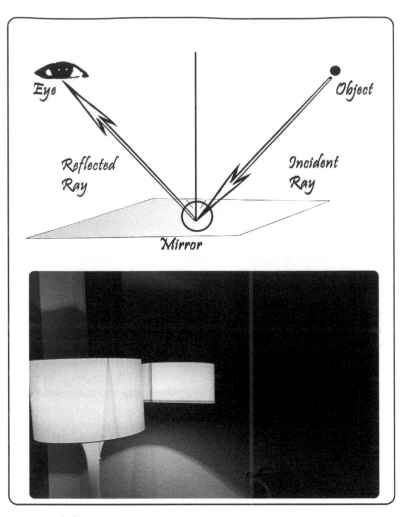

FIG 9.2 Law of reflection.

of the reflected light. When the incident light rays are reflected back at many different angles, it is referred to as **diffuse reflection**. On the other hand, when the light rays are reflected at just one angle, it is referred to as **specular reflection**. Typically, smooth surfaces produce specular reflection and rough surfaces produce diffuse reflection. Hence, you can see that the reflection from a mirror or a perfectly still body of lake is specular, while the reflection from rough surfaces such as cardboards or sidewalks produces diffuse reflection.

Refraction

Refraction refers to the process of bending of light that occurs when light travels from one medium into another. As you can see from Figure 9.3, the straight pencil appears bent. A small fun fact for you: as the speed of light in

FIG 9.3 Refraction.

water is less than its speed in air, light refracts causing the pencil to appear bent. For the same reason, if you were to hold a pencil with part of it showing behind a glass, you may see a similar effect as observed here. To be exact, there is a difference between the speed of light in air and in vacuum (travels 1.0003 times slower in air compared to vacuum). It is important to note that the refraction effect becomes more pronounced as the speed of light in a medium reduces.

Dispersion

Let us now look at another phenomenon known as dispersion. When white light enters a glass prism (from air), the constituent colors get separated. Different *light colors* have different speeds as they move through the glass prism and get separated. Hence, the white light entering the prism gets separated into the constituent colors (ROYGBIV or VIBGYOR, standing for violet, indigo, blue, green, yellow, orange, and red). In fact, it is this same principle behind the formation of rainbows. Water droplets from a rain refract the incident light into the constituent colors as above creating the rainbow (Figure 9.4).

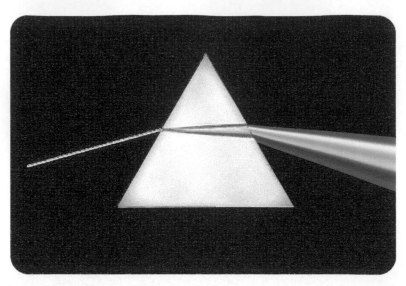

FIG 9.4 Dispersion.

Material Classification Based on Light Interaction

Materials we come across in the real world can be classified into three major categories based on their interaction with light.

Opaque: Do not allow light to pass through. All light incident on an opaque surface is absorbed.

Transparent: Transparent materials like glass allow light to pass through them completely. Hence, we are able to see what is on the other side of a transparent glass.

Translucent: Translucent materials allow light to pass through, but they diffuse the light. Hence, objects on the other side of a translucent material (translucent glass) cannot be seen clearly.

Below, we see two images shot from the inside of two rooms. In both cases, obviously you cannot see through the door because the door is made of opaque wooden material. In case of the room on the left, the glass on the door is transparent, which enables seeing what is outside the room clearly. In case of the room on the right, the glass is translucent, which means that light can still pass through, but we are not able to see through the glass (Figure 9.5).

Over the centuries, notable works were done by artists, researchers, and scientists to unravel the mystery of color. The art and science of color have fascinated inquisitive minds all over the world that led to numerous discoveries which paved the way for path-breaking inventions. Sir Isaac Newton developed the notion of a *color circle*, and various versions and variations of this have been made over the centuries. A *color wheel* is a

FIG 9.5 Opacity, transparency, and translucency.

method of organizing the various colors of the *color spectrum*, and it helps to understand the relationships among the colors.

Color and Color Theories

In simplistic terms, color refers to the light reflected by an object and is defined in terms of *hue, value,* and *intensity.* Hue refers to a specific shade of color or range; that quality of the light which is generally classified as blue or red or green. In other words, when we talk about a color being red or green, we are actually referring to its hue. Value refers to the lightness or darkness of an object or its surface. Intensity is used to describe the purity of a color. Colors high in intensity are considered to be robust and bright, while pale or dull colors are considered as low in intensity.

Over the centuries, color was (and to some extent, is) a highly debated topic of contention. Over the centuries, many scientists, mathematicians, artists, and physicists, including Rene Descartes, Isaac Newton, and Leonardo da Vinci, have tried to define color in many different ways. Even though we refer to the word color so frequently in our day-to-day lives, color is an extremely complex phenomenon. This perception depends not only on the source of light and the object but essentially on the perceiver (the observer). Without getting too deep into the science and philosophy of color, for the sake of building models and *rendering* them and to keep it simple, it is fine to say that color refers to reflected light and it works fine for the most part as required for understanding light in images and about simulating light and color in digital creations. Just understand the bottom line that rather than defining color as an inherent and unchanging property of an object, it is actually safe to say that color is a "perception."

The notion of color as we know it today and the basic principles of color that are being applied in numerous applications are based on significant contributions by a number of scientists and researchers. The scope of this book will not allow us to delve in extreme details into their experiments, hypotheses/postulations, etc., and hence, we will just briefly look at few notable contributions. Thomas Young suggested the presence of three kinds of photoreceptive cells in the eye, with each type of *photoreceptor* being receptive (sensitive) to a specific range of the visible light spectrum. This was later improved by Hermann von Helmholtz, who stated that specific photo receptors are sensitive to shorter wavelengths and others being sensitive to long wavelengths. Their efforts together led to the formulation of the trichromatic *color theory*, which is popularly also known as *Helmholtz–Young theory*. According to this theory of *trichromacy*, the retina in our eyes is composed of three types (tri) of color receptors which are also known as cone cells that are sensitive to specific color wavelengths and help us in perceiving the associated color information. Ewald Hering proposed another theory, which is popularly known as the *opponent color theory*, that postulated the existence of four basic colors (paired as opposing colors). These opponent channels (red vs. green, blue vs. yellow, black vs. white), in accordance with the opponent color theory, are not observed or perceived together.

Isaac Newton developed the notion of color circle, and various versions and variations of this have been made over the centuries. A color wheel is a method of organizing the various colors of the color spectrum, and it helps to understand the relationships among the colors. Figure 9.6 shows the primary colors, namely, red, blue, and yellow.

These are called *primary colors* since pure yellow, pure blue, and pure red cannot be obtained by combining any other colors. However, when these primary colors are mixed, they produce green, violet, and orange.

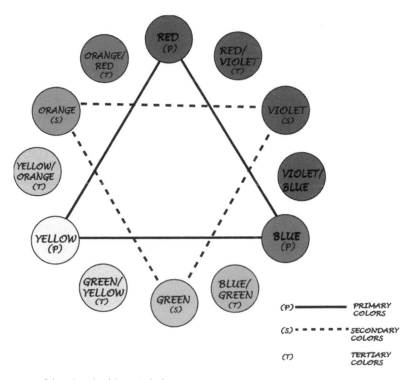

FIG 9.6 Subtractive colors (pigment colors).

FIG 9.7 Painting (subtractive colors/pigment colors).

The color we are referring to here is actually "pigment color." By this, we mean that we are referring to the colors in terms of those colors that we see in paints, inks, dyes, etc. (Figure 9.7).

During earlier centuries, the *RYB* colors (red, yellow, blue) were considered primary colors as those were the most suitable approximations that could be found and hence were used as primary colors from which other colors could be created by mixing. However, the modern combination of cyan, magenta, and yellow can produce a wider range of colors with greater precision than RYB. In fact, for purposes of clarity, many artists, painters, and designers refer to the RYB as the older or former color wheel and the *CMY* as the modern or new color wheel. If we use these new primary *pigment colors*, CMY, we will get the following secondary colors: cyan and magenta → blue; magenta and yellow → red; yellow and cyan → green.

Subtractive Model

In the subtractive color system (also known as pigment colors), red, blue, and yellow are called primary colors since pure yellow, pure blue, and pure red cannot be obtained by combining any other colors. However, when these primary colors are mixed, they produce green, violet, and orange.

As you can see, orange is almost midway between yellow and red; violet is between red and blue; and green is between blue and yellow. So, when two of the primary colors (yellow, red, blue) are mixed in equal quantities, they yield orange, violet, and green, which are known as secondary colors. Colors that are opposite to each other on the color wheel are referred to as complementary colors. Violet is the complementary of yellow, green is

FIG 9.8 Subtractive color theory.

the complementary of red, and orange is the complementary of blue. Any three colors that are balanced midway from each other on the color wheel are referred to as the triad colors. One important aspect that you need to note with respect to this discussion is that the color we are referring to here is actually "pigment color." By this, we mean that we are referring to the colors in terms of those colors that we see in paints, inks, dyes, etc.

The process that explains the color theory as we observe in case of pigments (pigment colors) and the colors resulting from the mixing of primaries is known as the subtractive process or model. According to the *subtractive model*, an object appears to be of a particular color as that is the color that the object emits after subtracting all the other colors from the incident light (which is white). Typically, subtractive color models start with white color, and each object (or material) subtracts different colors and whatever color that has not been subtracted (the color emitted) is the object's color as we see it. The important takeaway here is that in the subtractive model, the material (pigment or dye) removes or subtracts colors from the incident light and the color that is not subtracted is what we see (Figure 9.8).

In contrast to the subtractive model we discussed here that starts with white light, we will soon look at a model known as the *additive model* which starts with black (darkness). This model serves to explain the notion of light, especially as perceived in simulated or artificial systems such as a TV or a monitor.

Additive Model and Digital Lighting

The notion of light as we see in digital display devices is explained by the additive model. In the additive model, the final color is obtained by combining lights of different colors (Figure 9.9). The basic building blocks of digital displays are pixels (short for picture elements). The pixels in a digital display are made up of red, blue, and green lights. Red, blue, and green (RGB) are known as the *additive primary colors*. The idea behind the additive color system may become clearer if you consider the light projection systems used in concerts and discotheques. These light projection systems combine different colored lights that overlap and mix with each other which results in the final (additive) color. When all colors of light are combined together, the resulting light is white in color. Similar to the primary/subtractive colors in the subtractive model, the combination of the additive primary colors results in what are known as *additive secondary colors*.

While in the real world, creating lights of standard colors may not be that challenging, specific colored lights may be extremely hard to create as actual physical properties are at play. However, in a simulated digital model, it is possible to create a light of almost any color that one can imagine. We saw earlier that the (simulated) light in a CG environment is based on the additive model. Different CG software and programming languages employ various conventions to represent colors in this additive model. One common convention that is frequently used to represent the red, green, and blue (RGB) values employs a [0–1] scale. On this scale, 0 represents the complete absence of a specific color and 1 is the presence of the color in full. So, on this scale, the maximum values of RGB are represented as follows:

Red – [1, 0, 0]
Green – [0, 1, 0]
Blue – [0, 0, 1]

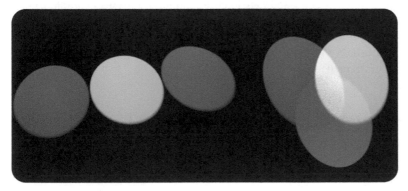

FIG 9.9 Additive primary colors.

FIG 9.10 Digital painting (additive colors). (Image courtesy: Stephanie, A.)

The presence of all the three additive primary colors to their maximum values results in white light and the absence of color is black.

White – [1, 1, 1] (maximum values of RGB on a scale of 0–1)
Black – [0, 0, 0] (absence of color)

To produce good contrast for your final rendered image, proper use of the primary colors with their complementary colors is required. Complementary colors are found opposite to each other on the color wheel. One of the very important things that needs to be understood about complementary colors is that they are not "substitute" or "opposite" colors. If x complements y, x and y are interdependent or x makes y complete (and vice versa). Hence, complementary colors go hand in hand, and they work well together when used to get a proper color contrast. The chapter on composition will cover details pertaining to the use of color with respect to composition (Figure 9.10).

Color Attributes and HSV Model

Hue is considered as a variety of color, and hence is often referred to as a shade of color (gradation). The variations in the light wavelengths are perceived as different hues or shades. In day-to-day language, when we refer to colors (and their characteristic shades), we are actually referring to what are known as *chromatic* colors. In fact, when we are referring to a chromatic color, we are actually referring to a hue. On the other hand, the family of colors including black, white, and gray are referred to as *achromatic* colors. As white, black, and gray lack hue, they are called as color neutral.

When we refer to how bright (vivid) or dull a shade (hue) is, we are talking about *saturation*. Saturation refers to the concentration or pureness of a hue. In photographic terminology, saturation denotes the intensity of a color. Let us consider painting for example. When an artist is comparing bright red color with a faded red color, the artist is referring to color saturation. So, you can think of saturated colors as *high-intensity colors* and *unsaturated* colors as *low-intensity colors*.

Value refers to the amount or proportion of black in a color. A scale of 0–1 is employed in several software programs, wherein the value 0 represents total black and the value 1 represents complete white. Value is also often referred to as *brightness*, which is why the *HSV model* is also referred to as the HSB model as we will see shortly.

We have discussed three important characteristics of color above, which together constitute the basis of one of the popular color models known as HSV (hue, saturation, value). The HSV model is also known as the HSB model, as in color terminology value is identified with the brightness of a color.

Objectives of Scene Lighting

Even though this is one of the most common analogies offered frequently to explain the importance of lighting, it is one of my most favorite. Imagine an art collector or a painter or a sculptor having a huge room full of great paintings or sculptures. Imagine if this room had no windows or had no artificial lighting. It will not be possible to appreciate the beauty of the pieces of art without light. The same thing applies to your 3D scenes. Lighting is what enables your audience to appreciate the diligently modeled 3D scenes and the carefully executed animation. However, lighting needs to be done very carefully in careful consideration of the ultimate goal. Always remember that your 3D scene and your animation are tools for "communication." It may be a movie or a game, but there is always a plot and there is narration. So, before we look into the lighting fundamental and properties of light, let us discuss the ultimate goals of lighting.

Directing the Audience

Hmm. Doesn't that sound a little overarching? Directing actors or a scene or a movie – yes. But, how can one direct the audience? That is in fact what skilled directors do. Think of a time when you were in the movie hall with friends/family and the coming attractions had finished. You may just remember the first few minutes after the actual movie started and then the next thing you know you are deeply engrossed in the plot and only after a considerable time or at the end of the movie did you realize that you were in a movie hall. I am quite sure that we all have experienced this at some point of time. A movie is so captivating that we totally lose sense of the surroundings and are absolutely immersed in the movie. We actually would be looking at where the director actually wants us to see throughout the length of the movie. Even though the director of the movie was not standing next to us telling us what to watch out for and where exactly to pay attention, we were subconsciously paying attention to the aspects that the director intended us to.

This is no easy task. We will also look at this later in composition. By the clever use of lighting cues, the director and the director of photography can draw attention to specific aspects of the scene. Some parts can be highlighted, while some can be underplayed. In a book, even though the reader may read the description of a scene, there are lots of things that are left to imagination. However, in visual storytelling, everything is presented explicitly. While there are advantages to this, there also is tremendous responsibility on the director to present in a way that is coherent and compelling and not confusing.

There is a delicate balance between keeping the audience engaged and confusing them. A well-crafted plot can be visually engaging only if it has been properly executed; on the other hand, a chaotic visual composition may leave the audience confused. Lighting plays a very important role in this.

Creating the Ambience

We call it by different names: atmosphere, mood, aura, quality, or tone. We have had these thoughts when we think of the milieu: "I like the overall atmosphere in that restaurant. The overall tone of the movie was very positive. The movie puts me in a good *mood* every time I watch it." In all these cases, we are referring to the *ambience* that can refer to the overall setting or the cumulative *emotions* elicited from a production. Lighting plays a critical role in setting the ambience for a scene. If you look at the scene in Figure 9.11, it shows a poignant moment filled with emotion showing the girl and the cat. It leaves much to wonder about the actual nature of the interaction, but it is a very poignant scene that is very moving. The entire scene has a rich yellow background with matching light intensity to augment the richness of the scene complemented by the yellow and brown texture of the girl's costume accentuating with the cat's fur.

FIG 9.11 Lighting and ambience. (Image courtesy: Stephanie, A.)

Creating the Depth Perception

Typically, all the modeling and the final animation are viewed on a "flat screen." Ultimately, what are being viewed are 2D images in succession (animation). You may have seen a 3D film wearing special viewing glasses. For getting a 3D image, images from two different points of view (perspectives) are overlaid on top of each other. This kind of approach involves programming each eye's image by employing red and cyan color filters, as these are considered to be chromatically opposed. However, the red and cyan glasses have been replaced by polarized glasses in recent times to achieve the stereoscopic effect. The special viewing glasses (anaglyphic glasses) help each eye filter out the chromatically opposite color, thus creating the 3D image. However, here we are talking about viewing the output, rendered video file, in the form of an .avi or .mp4 file. Rendering is the process of creating a 2D image from the 3D models. The video file is the result of a sequence of these images viewed in succession at a specific frame rate.

Lighting, along with shadows, plays a critical role in the stereoscopic depth perception. Generally, viewers tend to look at an image's brightest spot. When trying to portray depth using lighting, there is no one approach that works for all settings. Setting up the front of your scene to be bright against a darker backdrop works in some cases, while sometimes you can have dark front against a brighter backdrop. Soft, uniform light typically tends to smoothen out the scene, giving an overall flattened look to the scene.

One of the most fundamental differences between CG lighting and real-world lighting is that you have relatively greater control with *CG lights* than the real-world lights. In the real world, when you turn on a light, all physical laws are automatically followed. Among other things, light gets reflected and refracted as it is meant to be and shadows are formed automatically. In 3D scenes, where light "needs" to be from a specific direction in a specific intensity and shadows "need" to be in a specific part of the scene in a specific shape and intensity, it gets a bit tricky in the real world. If a *fill light* is added to reduce the intensity of a shadow, in doing so, it may cause additional shadows elsewhere. Similarly, when a new light is added to form a shadow in a specific way, this new light may affect the overall scene lighting balance. However, in CG lighting, you can turn your lights on and off as you prefer and you can also choose to turn shadows on or off for a specific light. People who have worked with real-world studio lighting will tell you how the physical lights get hot and special care and gloves need to be used to handle and turn lights. However, with CG lights you can adjust the parameters for a light with a few clicks of a button. But, remember the bottom line: CG lighting would not exist without the progress made over the centuries in lighting in various disciplines such as fine arts, theater, plays, and opera. There are different qualities of light, such as brightness/intensity, color, and angle/throw pattern.

The different types of light used in graphics modeling are as follows: point light, spot light, directional light, and area light. We will look at them shortly.

Occasionally, some storyboard artists may accompany some shots with lighting diagrams explaining the setup of the scene lights. This involves:

- The number of lights to be used in the scene
- The type of lights
- The placement of the lights
- The orientation of the lights

The above step can provide a very rudimentary idea of how the scene's lighting setup will look like. But, as lighting is more of an experiential phenomenon, it is not practical to expect the work on paper to provide a precise idea of the actual lighting in the scene. In studios and Hollywood productions, stand-ins are employed during the lighting setup process to facilitate exploration and testing before finalizing the actual lighting that will be implemented in the scene. Industry projects involve pre-lighting sessions to ensure proper lighting during the actual production process. Nevertheless, a bit of initial planning with lighting can help get an idea of the processing power required and will also facilitate avoiding drastic surprises during final rendering (especially when involving photometric lights and advanced photorealistic rendering techniques).

Earlier in the modeling chapter and subsequently in the animation chapter, it was mentioned that be it a model or a picture or an animation, you are communicating something to the audience.

The use of lights entails meticulous planning, as this is extremely crucial to successful rendering. We already looked at the properties of lights. But, let us look here specifically at some properties from the point of view of lights and their role within a CG scene. **Pictorial lighting** is used in professional photography in a highly organized setting where images of subjects can be captured so as to portray them in an appealing manner. To get the optimal effect, besides proper lighting, many other aspects such as materials (clothing), props and effects, background, and hair should be carefully planned and designed.

One of the important things that you need to pay attention with respect to modeling and animation is that you need to look at how the lighting affects the model (static) from one frame, but in an animation that lasts over multiple frames, you need to check how the lighting affects the scene and the 3D objects over the entire course of the animation.

Properties of CG Lights

Placement and Orientation

The position of a CG light refers to the location (x, y, z coordinates) of the light within the scene. Just like a modeler can move a ball or any other object in a CG scene, the light is also an object that can be selected and transformed. The light in a CG scene can be translated and rotated to achieve the desired position and orientation within the scene (Figure 9.12).

The position and orientation of a light influence the angle of incidence of the radiation on the scene objects, and this in turn influences the highlights and shadows. When positioning a light, care must be taken with respect to the distance of the light from the character or the subject being illuminated. The distance at which a light is located from an object controls the angle at which the light rays are incident on the object, and this in turn determines the position and the strength of the shadow. Hence, summarily, the placement of lights in a scene should pay due attention to all of the following:

- How far away is the light from the primary character or the subject?
- What is the function of the light (key/fill/rim)?

FIG 9.12 Depth perception.

- What are the requirements for properties such as highlights, falloff, and mid-tones?
- What kind of shadows are needed?

Types of CG Illumination

There are several different types of lights used to illuminate the models in a CG scene. Let us look at some of the most common light types here (Figure 9.13).

Omni Light

The root "omni" means all (as in omnipresent or omnipotent). An omni (or *omnidirectional* light) is called so because it radiates light in all directions equally. An omni point is also commonly known as *point light*. A star (e.g. the sun) is a good example of a point light. As can be seen in Figure 9.13 (top), an *omni light* is positioned exactly in the center of scene, and it is surrounded by plane objects on all sides (except the front, where the camera is placed) to show the light rays radiating in all directions. The spherical object is just

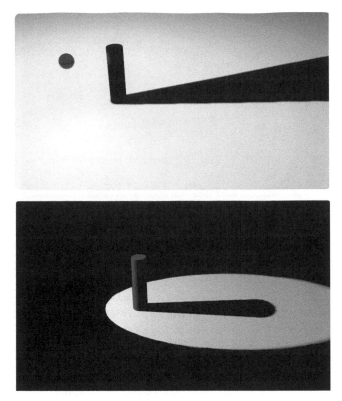

FIG 9.13 Omni light (top) and spot light (bottom).

shown to symbolically indicate the position of the light. The light object itself is not visible here, only the radiation.

Spot Light

Unlike omnidirectional lights, *spot lights* radiate light in only the specific direction that is typified by a conical shape as shown in Figure 9.13 (bottom). The image corresponding to the spot light has all the plane objects found in the omni setting earlier, but instead of omni light, a spot light has been placed in the top left corner and you can see the conical *illumination*. Lamp shades are examples of spot light. Spot lights offer better control than point lights as the angle of the cone light can be adjusted. Also, the orientation can be adjusted to create the desired illumination effect.

Directional Light

Directional lights are also known as *infinite lights*, and their intensity does not vary with distance. Also, when the rays of the directional light are incident on the scene, they are always parallel to each other. In fact, if a spot light is moved very far away, the spot light can be used to imitate a

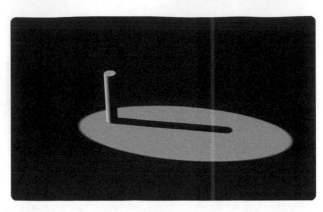

FIG 9.14 Direct light.

directional light as the light rays seem to be parallel when they shine on the scene (due to the distance). It is due to this reason of the extremely distant placement that the sun, which was earlier referred to as an example for point light, is also an example of an infinite light. The *direct light* in the illustration is once again part of the same setup we used for the omni light, but the direct light is used in place of the omni light. (The boundary lines and arrows are just used to symbolically represent the direct light and the direction of radiation, and they are not actually part of the direct light in the CG scene ; Figure 9.14.)

Linear Light

Linear is a special type of CG light which does not have any width, but only length (and hence the name). A tube light is an example of a *linear light* as the rays from it illuminate the scene in a lengthwise pattern (Figure 9.15).

Area Light

Unlike the linear light, the *area light* represents an area such as a rectangle or an ellipse (typically circles). However, area lights can be of any shape (polygon) defined on a plane or a flat surface. Also, due to the area factor, the computational demand imposed on the system by placing an area light is an important factor to be considered. Indiscriminate use of area lights can slow down the system and cause inordinate delays in computation and hence affect rendering times.

Still, if used judiciously, area lights can serve as excellent tools to simulate soft and uniform light sources (Figure 9.16).

Area lights are used in CG scenes for imitating soft lights that are also known as scattered lights. Soft lights create blurred shadows and are used for generated larger profound highlights.

FIG 9.15 Linear light.

Volume Light

Volume lights come in different primitive shapes such as sphere, cone, box, and cylinder, and their illumination is confined or restricted to the volume enclosed by the corresponding geometric shape. Unlike the CG light source we saw earlier, volume lights are not intended to simulate any real-world light source but serve to offer greater precision and control in terms of the desired illumination effect required in a scene. Due to their inherent nature, *volumetric* lights can be used to avoid the undesirable effects caused by other lights. For instance, the effect of a spot light or a directional light can be felt over the entire scene or a considerably larger area of the scene. However, if the *digital lighting* team desires to confine the effect of a light (and hence the resulting shadows) to a specific region, volume lights are a good choice.

FIG 9.16 Area light.

The light that is actually used inside the volume can be one of the earlier CG lights. When a spherical volume encloses a linear light, the objects inside the spherical volume will be illuminated in accordance with the properties of the linear light. Nevertheless, the effect of the linear light will be restricted to only the volume enclosed within the sphere.

Ambient Light

In common language, the word ambience refers to the overall quality or atmosphere of an environment. The ambient light in CG is inspired by this notion, which serves to completely and uniformly illuminate a CG scene. Ambient lights are used both in CG scene depictions of outdoor and indoor environments (Figure 9.17).

Ambient lights can be used to create foggy, smoky, or other kinds of atmospheric effects in outdoor scenes, and in indoor CG scenes, they can be used to simulate the effect of light rays that have been reflected or bounced off so many times from so many surfaces that they lose their directional property. Actually, this is indeed the basic notion behind the uniformity of the ambient light. As the light has no direction, transforming the light (translation or rotation) does not influence its effect on the scene.

FIG 9.17 Ambient light. (Image courtesy: George, H.)

Direct and Indirect Lights

Depending on how the light from a source of illumination reaches a target object, light is classified as direct or indirect. The light that reaches a target object from the source directly is known as the direct light. Consider the example shown in Figure 9.18. The light rays indicated by the solid line indicate the direct light that shines directly from the lamp to the object below. The dashed lines show the light that hits other scene objects like the floor and the wall before reaching the object (lamp shade).

FIG 9.18 Direct light and indirect light.

Three-Point Lighting

Also, from the functional points of view, lights can be classified as follows:

- Key lights
- Fill lights
- Rim lights

Three-point lighting is a very popular and commonly used lighting scheme for organizing lights in a scene (Figure 9.19).

As implied by its name, the "key" light is the primary or principal source of light in a scene. Being the most significant light source, the *key light* has the

FIG 9.19 Scene lights.

utmost effect on the rendering (image). The majority of the shadows in a scene are a result of the key light, and these are also the strongest shadows in the scene. The key light establishes the central ambience of the scene and hence greatly influences the overall mood resulting from the image. Conventionally, the key light is located at the front and to the right (can also be on the left) of the primary object or character in the scene at an angle of about 30° to 60°.

We saw that the *primary lights* in a scene are the key lights. Now, let us look at the *secondary lights*, which are known as fill lights. In the real world, in addition to the direct light from a light bulb or a source of illumination, objects in a scene also receive the indirect light that has been bounced from other surfaces. Fill lights simulate the effect of such reflected light. Besides, as you can see from Figure 9.20, the side of the character facing the key light is brightly illuminated, but there are details on the other side that are obscured by the shadow. As the name implies, the fill light serves to fill in these darker areas (created by the shadows from the key light).

Details pertaining to these can also be included in the lighting diagrams accompanying the storyboard or in the storyboard itself. The key light is the most significant light source in the scene and is typically positioned sideward and above. The fill light usually is used to fill in dark areas created by the key light and is hence placed on the other side of the key light. The *rim light* is placed behind a character's head or an animal's body, and it highlights the rim or the external surface or fur. This is used to create a halo effect.

Understandably, the fill light is positioned on the side opposite to that of the key light, as the shadows caused by the key light are found here. Thus, by varying the fill light intensity, one can control the shadow effect caused

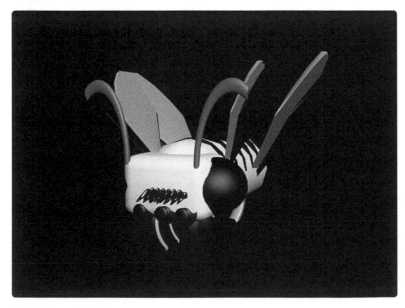

FIG 9.20 Three-point lighting.

by the key light. Fill lights can be used to fine-tune the overall tone and the contrast of the scene to achieve the desired effect. The *complementary color theory* can be used for selecting the proper combination of key light-fill light colors to better compose a scene. Rim lights can be used to make the characters stand out from the background and thus are useful in highlighting or emphasizing a specific part of the scene.

Let's Get Emotional!!!

The relation between colors and emotions is so inherent that even in our day-to-day chitchat, we use colors so frequently to express emotions. For instance: he felt *blue* when his proposal was not accepted. Here, blue means depressed/sad. In the phrases *yellow* press or *yellow* journalism, *yellow* represents journalism of exaggeration. In the sentence "Extravagant practices put the company in red," red implies *debt*.

Different colors may have different connotations in different cultures. The same color that is used during a joyous occasion in one culture may be perceived as a color for a mournful occasion.

Color	Possible Connotations/Interpretations
Yellow	Energy, hope, joy, happiness, optimism, brightness, daylight, summer, gold, etc.
Lavender	Femininity, grace, refinement, elegance, etc.
Orange	Vibrancy, passion, fervor, energy, enthusiasm, warmth, flamboyant, engaging, etc.
Green	Health, environment, healthy, rejuvenation, infancy, springtime, bounteousness, profusion, distrust, provision, naivety, greed, misfortune, vigor, etc.
Brown	Minimalism, homeliness, soil, steadiness, earth, outdoors, dependability, security, strength, etc.

As colors are very effective in eliciting emotions, they are used in flags to represent the values of a country, state, or an organization. In Chapter 10 on composition, we will discuss more about colors with further examples from the point of view of visual composition. An animation is about a story; it is about a plot. This involves emotion(s). Lighting is a very important component in modeling and animation as lights reveal the models in their full splendor and, more importantly, establish the overall ambience or mood for the scene. Lighting a 3D CG scene is as important as lighting a museum of art exhibits. Just as patrons of an exhibit of paintings or sculptures cannot see and appreciate the work of art in the absence of light, your audience will not be able to see your 3D scene without proper lighting. No matter how great the modeling effort is, no matter how engrossing your animation is, without proper lighting, the audience cannot see any of the modeling/animation.

It is not just about revealing the 3D scene, but lighting is more about revealing the scene *with a purpose* or a manner according to the purpose or motivation of the scene.

Summary and Important Considerations in Lighting

Color refers to the light reflected by an object and is defined in terms of hue, value, and intensity. Hue refers to a specific shade of color or range; that quality of the light which is generally classified as blue or red or green. In other words, when we talk about a color being red or green, we are actually referring to its hue. Value refers to the lightness or darkness of an object or its surface. Intensity is used to describe the purity of a color. Colors high in intensity are considered to be robust and bright, while pale or dull colors are considered as low in intensity.

Lighting is also an important concern from the resource/constraint perspective as lights contribute to the overall processing time during the rendering stage.

Light enables us to see the scene. When you take a photograph in the real world, without proper lighting, a 3D scene that you capture with your camera may look two-dimensional. This is because improper lighting fails to reveal the dimensionality of the objects in the scene, thus failing to create the stereo or depth perception. Lighting also influences the overall mood of the scene and hence affects the emotion. While with proper lighting, you can show your model and animation in the best possible manner, it is also absolutely possible to ruin the modeling efforts with poor lighting.

Now, if you spend some time interacting with lighters in the real world by observing what they actually do to light a scene and talk to them about some of the really challenging experiences, you will be able to truly appreciate how fortunate you are to be doing the lighting within a digital environment. First and foremost, real-world lights involve weight which is an important factor when it comes to moving, positioning, operating, and handling those lights. In a CG scene, you just need to select and translate the light within the coordinate system, while in the real world, it is a relatively cumbersome task. Care has to be taken in properly handling not only the light but also the associated fixtures and all pieces of equipment required to hold the light in the correct position and facing the exact direction.

In a real-world scene, an indoor studio, or an outdoor movie setting, there are limitations to where a light can actually be placed. If there is an actor, the lighting technician cannot position the light right in front of their face. Similarly, there are several other practical considerations as well as constraints that govern the placement of lights in the real world. However, in a CG scene, one can place lights almost anywhere and everywhere, which indeed sounds exciting. So, just because you can do anything with CG lights, you should not just do so. While CG lighting has its fair share of advantages when compared to real-world lighting, the digital lighting process needs to be done with utmost care to elicit the proper emotion that the scene demands.

In addition to the pros discussed above, another key advantage in digital lighting is the ability to exclude the scene lights from being rendered. In other words, the CG lights used to illuminate a scene, irrespective of their placement in the scene, will not show up in the final image created from the 3D model or will not appear in the animation created from the model. Different software programs provide different options with respect to the visibility of lights in a scene. Irrespective of the default options provided by programs, the property of visibility of lights can be turned on or off as desired. While CG lights that appear as icons or regular objects can be repositioned and oriented to any desired or required position, their visibility property can be manipulated to prevent them from actually appearing in the final rendering.

Key Terms Used in This Chapter

Additive Model
Additive Primary
  Colors
Additive Secondary
  Colors
Achromatic
Ambience
Area Light
Back Light
Background Colors
Brightness
CG Lights
Chromatic
CMY
Color Attributes
Color Circle
Color Compliments
Color Spectrum
Color Theory
Color Wheel
Complementary Color
  Theory
Complementary Colors
Cool Colors
Digital Lighting

Direct Light
Distance
Emotion
Fill Light
Helmholtz–Young
  Theory
High-Intensity Colors
Hot Colors
HSV Model
Hue
Illumination
Indirect Light
Infinite Light
Key Light
Lighting
Light Color
Linear Light
Location
Low-Intensity Colors
Mood
Omni Light
Omnidirectional
Opponent Color Theory
Orientation
Photoreceptor

Pigment Colors
Placement
Point Light
Position
Primary Colors
Primary Lights
Rendering
RGB Model
Rim Light
RYB
Saturation
Secondary Colors
Secondary Lights
Shadow
Simulated Systems
Spot Light
Subtractive Model
Three-Point Lighting
Triad Colors
Trichromacy
Unsaturated
Value
Volume Light
Volumetric
Warm Colors

Chapter 9 Quiz

PART I

True/False (Circle the Correct Choice)

1. Lights play a very important role in setting the ambience and hence greatly influence the emotional aspect.
True False

2. Colors that are opposite to each other on the color wheel are referred to as primary colors.
True False

3. Many artists, painters, and designers refer to the RYB as the older or former color wheel and the CMY as the modern or new color wheel.
True False

4. According to the additive model, an object appears to be of a particular color as that is the color that the object emits after deducing all the other colors from the incident light.
True False

5. The subtractive model serves to explain the notion of light, especially as perceived in simulated or artificial.
True False

6. When we are referring to a chromatic color, we are actually referring to a hue.
True False

7. You can think of saturated colors as high-intensity colors and unsaturated colors as low-intensity colors.
True False

8. Fill lights can be used to make the characters stand out from the background and thus are useful in highlighting or emphasizing a specific part of the scene.
True False

9. An omni light is also commonly known as spot light.
True False

10. Directional lights are also known as infinite lights, and their intensity does not vary with distance.

True False

11. Area lights can either only be rectangular or circular.

True False

12. Area lights come in different primitive shapes, and their illumination is confined or restricted to the enclosed geometric shape.

True False

13. Blue and green are referred to as hot colors.

True False

14. In a real-world scene, an indoor studio, or an outdoor movie setting, there are limitations to where actually a light can be placed.

True False

15. In digital lighting, one has the ability to exclude the scene lights from being rendered.

True False

Feedback: In digital lighting, one has the ability to exclude the scene lights from being rendered.

Part II

Multiple Choice Questions (Choose the Most Appropriate Answer)

1. A _____ is a method of organizing the various colors of the color spectrum, and it helps to understand the relationships among the colors.
   a. Color wheel
   b. Color scheme
   c. Color space
   d. Color white
   e. Color tableau

2. When two primary colors are mixed in equal quantities, a/an _____ color is obtained.
   a. Tertiary
   b. Infinite
   c. Secondary
   d. Pseudo
   e. Upgraded

3. _____suggested the presence of three kinds of photoreceptive cells in the eye, with each type of photoreceptor being receptive (sensitive) to a specific range of the visible light spectrum.
   a. Ivan Sutherland
   b. William Donaldson
   c. Isaac Newton
   d. Thomas Edison
   e. Thomas Young

4. When we are talking about how bright (vivid) or dull a shade (hue) is, we are talking about _____.
   a. Hue
   b. Whiteness
   c. Darkness
   d. Saturation
   e. Value

5. _____ refers to the amount or proportion of black in a color.
   a. Hue
   b. Whiteness
   c. Darkness
   d. Saturation
   e. Value

6. HSV model is also referred to as the _____ model.
   a. HSE
   b. HSB
   c. HSA
   d. RGB
   e. CMY

7. The notion of light as seen in digital display devices is explained by the _____ model.
   a. Subtractive
   b. Deductive
   c. Inclusive
   d. Additive
   e. Exclusive

8. When all colors of light are combined together, the resulting light is
_____ in color.
   a. Brown
   b. Black
   c. White
   d. Cream
   e. Yellow

9. The _____ light is the primary or principal source of light in a scene.
   a. Central
   b. Key
   c. Fill
   d. Rim
   e. Kicker

10. _____ lights simulate the effect of reflected light.
   a. Central
   b. Key
   c. Fill
   d. Rim
   e. Kicker

11. The _____ light highlights the rim (Figure 9.11) or the outline of
the object and hence is usually placed behind the object.
   a. Central
   b. Key
   c. Fill
   d. Rim
   e. Principal

12. _____ lights are a special type of CG light which do not have any
width, but only length.
   a. Linear
   b. Omni
   c. Volume
   d. Ambient
   e. Area

13. _____ lights are used in CG scenes for imitating soft lights that are also known scattered lights.
    a. Linear
    b. Omni
    c. Volume
    d. Ambient
    e. Area

14. _____ lights come in different primitive shapes such as sphere, cone, box, and cylinder, and their illumination is confined or restricted to the enclosed shape.
    a. Linear
    b. Omni
    c. Volume
    d. Ambient
    e. Area

15. Which of the following is an example of a background color?
    a. Red
    b. Orange
    c. Green
    d. Yellow
    e. White

CHAPTER 10: Form, Composition, and Rendering

When you change the way you look at things, the things you look at change.

– Max Planck

CHAPTER LEARNING OBJECTIVES

After carefully studying this chapter, you will be able to answer the following:

- What are the various important elements of composition?
- What is perspective and how does it affect composition?
- What are linear, height, overlap, and diminishing size perspectives?
- How is a low-angle shot different from a high-angle shot?
- What is the rule of thirds?
- How do lines influence composition?
- What is digital rendering?
- How are raster images different from vector images?
- What are the steps in the rendering process?

DOI: 10.1201/9780429186349-10

- What are some popular image formats?
- What is a pixel and what is pixel resolution?
- What is a bit plane and how is it related to color depth?

What Will You Learn in This Chapter?

This chapter introduces the importance of *form* and *composition* in the context of rendering, which involves transforming a three-dimensional (3D) model into two-dimensional (2D) images (renderings). The important criteria are about presenting the form using appropriate composition for the ultimate objective of rendering. Important elements of composition that enable audience to grasp the message being conveyed are discussed. The chapter then discusses the appearance of the subject from a long shot and a close-up shot, and from the point of view of positive and negative spaces. Subsequently, the discussion covers the different ways in which the stereoscopic and distance aspects can be shown in a composition. The significance of *lines* as elements of composition is covered as they tend to lead and direct the attention of the audience. Finally, the *digital rendering* process and the various different file formats are discussed.

In Chapters 2, 4, and 5 on modeling, the discussion revolved on the creation of objects to make your model. Now, we will look at two important elements, namely, form and composition, in the context of rendering. Rendering is the process of transforming a 3D model into 2D images (renderings). There are two common modes of rendering, namely, image and video. It is this final rendered version that is seen by the audience. Due consideration to form and composition is extremely important when presenting what is originally a 3D representation as a 2D representation.

Composition represents a vast subject matter that has been covered by experts in the field of arts, photography, imaging, etc. in huge volumes. We will only discuss the visual compositional aspects as applicable to the 3D models and animations created from them. In all probability, you must have used the word "composition" in multiple contexts even before you saw that in the context of computer graphics (CG) rendering. As part of language courses, students write essays and literary works which are referred to as composition. Loosely stated, any musical piece of work is known as a composition. Musical composers are the people who create or "compose" musical works. The composition discussed here in this chapter in the rendering context is not very different from the literary composition or the musical composition. What basically one does in a literary or musical setting is what you will do when doing a composition for rendering. It is the act of "laying things out or putting things together" for a purpose. The word purpose is extremely important because the same set of things can be arranged or laid out in a different manner for different purposes. In the following sections, some of the very fundamental elements of composition are covered in the context of digital rendering (Figure 10.1).

FIG 10.1 Different types of composition.

While rendering typically refers to an image, a rendering can also be a sequence of images (video). Photos (images) and videos are two common forms of rendered output. In digital CG terminology, rendering refers to the process of creating a 2D image from a 3D model.

A *photograph* is a tool for communication. A photograph communicates something. Hence, first and foremost, you need to have something to communicate. It can be:

- An advertisement to market a car
- A photo that captures the serenity of a scenic location
- A shot of an architectural marvel that captures the grandiosity
- A fashion photograph that reveals the richness of the design
- A design rendering that shows an interior design scenario to a prospective customer

In all the above examples, there is a clear purpose and motivation. The objective of the photograph influences all aspects including lighting, form, and composition. A photograph hence inevitably is driven by its purpose/function/motivation. The motivation behind composition is to engage the viewers by directing their attention. This is what successful movie directors and accomplished photographers do.

If you pick up a newspaper published in a foreign language, you may not be able to read the text written in it, but you can surely view the pictures or photographs published in it. In fact, anybody speaking any language can view the pictures. Just like music, photographs speak a universal language. A piano recital can be heard and appreciated by audience that includes people who speak different languages. A photograph of an event or a natural attraction from one corner of the world published in an international newspaper is viewed and enjoyed by people around the world. This the reason that professional photographers for newspapers and magazines need to be experts in composition. Let us consider the following examples:

- A victorious team and the captain receiving the world cup soccer trophy
- Presidents of two nations signing a peace treaty
- Record-breaking feats at the International Olympics

Capturing such epic moments involves considerations of several factors including human emotions where applicable. This is where the experience and the composition skills of professional photographers come into play. The photograph of the winners of a grand-slam tennis event that occurred in a city somewhere in the world appears on the pages of leading sports magazines or newspapers. This photo has to be well composed and needs to capture the rich emotions in their entirety. The following sections explain the subtle cues and principles used to achieve a successful composition.

Form and Composition

Earlier, we saw that rendering involves capturing a 2D image from a 3D-modeled scene. Whether rendering an image from a 3D model or capturing a real-life photograph, *without proper composition*, "what you (the creator) of the image see will not be what the audience see." Rendering presents a challenge as well as an opportunity. The "challenge" involves capturing the best possible 2D representation from a 3D model. This is a challenge because you as the creator know the 3D representation in its entirety, whereas the audience will only know the scene through the image you are rendering. Hence, recreating stereoscopic perception (depth) and showing the spatial/ topological relations among the scene objects is a challenge.

So, where is the opportunity? There is also an opportunity because you have the ability to control what the audience see. Be it a real-world scene or a rendering from a 3D model, you can show ONLY what you want to show. This gives tremendous power in the hands of the image creator as scene aspects that reinforce your message can be emphasized and those aspects in the scene that are not well formed and/or weakening can be underplayed or can even be eliminated by clever use of various compositional tricks that we will be seeing shortly. This has been successfully employed when using photography in various areas such as politics, movies, industry, and marketing to highlight and underplay aspects selectively. So, there are three aspects to this:

- What in your scene do you want to show?
- Why do you want to show them?
- How do you plan to show?

FIG **10.2** Different art forms. (Image courtesy: Lakshmi, C. and Pavithra, A.)

The various aspects of composition that we will discuss later will help you with the "how" aspect. The answers to "what and why" should be basically already with you from the pre-production/storyboard. The following sections will discuss important compositional aspects that need to be considered when you think of questions such as where to capture the 3D model from, at which angle, what color lights to use, and where to position and orient them.

We have actually discussed a lot about *form* during the modeling chapters as form represents the shape or the exterior of an object. However, here our discussion of form is in conjunction with composition, as the concern is about presenting the form using appropriate composition for the ultimate objective of rendering. Be it a painting or a bottle art or a photograph, composition is extremely important (Figure 10.2).

Elements of Composition

The elements of composition serve as cues that make the audience see what the creator of the rendering wants them to see in the rendered image or video. This is what makes an image or a video successful. If you try to recall an absolutely remarkable movie that you saw, you might realize that for the entire length of the movie, you were totally engrossed into the plot, blissfully unaware of even where you were sitting or with whom you were sitting. Such is the power of creative composition that it can totally sway the audience. Directors of hit movies and creators of memorable photographs use the various elements of composition to sway or control the audience. Various compositional elements such as perspective, color scheme, lights, and shadows composed in tandem with the edges or lines, positive and negative spaces, yield superior visual organization. These act as indirect controls that convey the message from the creator of the composition to the receiver. When the message that is being conveyed is transmitted properly via the medium (photograph/video), then the audience can feel and appreciate the original intended emotions. That is the recipe for a successful movie or a photograph-clear communication. Let us look at some of these "indirect controls" that can help better compose the final rendered image.

Perspective

Perspective refers to the viewpoint, similar to how the word is used in everyday jargon. Just as people have different perspectives on various matters and issues, a modeled 3D scene or a real-world scene can be observed from different perspectives. From the perspective of digital rendering and composition, "how the scene is shown" (to the audience) is what truly matters. In leadership and management circles, one common example to illustrate the difference attitude can make is "the half-empty or half-full glass of water." The general contention is that what an optimistic person sees as being half-full might be seen by a pessimistic person as being half-empty. While the subject being seen is the same, the perception is different. Similarly, how a scene or model is shown affects how the subject matter is perceived by the audience (Figure 10.3).

FIG 10.3 Increasing details of objects with closer view.

FIG 10.4 3D-modeled scene from varying distances/angles. (Image courtesy: Justin, H.)

Let us consider an example for a broader idea of the concept of perspective. In Figure 10.3, look at the images starting clockwise from the top left. The direction of the arrows shows how the details of the objects increase. In the image on the top left, in the very large city scape, the size of the objects is very small and they continue to become smaller as they are farther away from the point of view. Similarly, you will also note that the object tones diminish as they get farther away from the point of view. The image to the right of the top left shows a relatively smaller section of the city, the one below that shows a specific apartment complex, and the image on the bottom left shows just a couple of small houses within the community. The details of the individual scene objects are clearer in the bottom left image, while the objects are shown in the least detail in the top-left image.

Now, let us extend the same notion to a 3D-modeled scene. In order to show a diligently and meticulously modeled scene in all its glory, it is important that an optimal perspective is chosen. How close or far away the *camera* is from the subject can affect the perception. Figure 10.4 shows the modeled 3D scene from different distances. Likewise, the angle at which the camera is oriented with respect to the subject also influences composition. We will discuss this shortly under the section on *high-* and *low-angle shots*. In order for the composition to be effective, the perspective must reveal the subject and the scene using proper distance and angle (Figure 10.4).

Form and Volume

Form represents the external appearance and is considered to be an entirely visual characteristic. Form encompasses volume, which means that it is different from a shape. Shapes such as circle, rectangles, and other polygons have only area and are hence 2D. However, being 3D, form includes width, length, and height (volume=width * length * height). The 2D shapes are what we refer to as flat shapes (with zero depth), and the 3D forms are physical objects that we come across in our daily life such as soccer balls, and boxes and almost any object with depth. See 2D shape which is almost invisible from top view as it has zero depth against the other 3D objects.

Many different types of classifications of forms are available in different contexts. From the modeling and animation perspective, forms can also

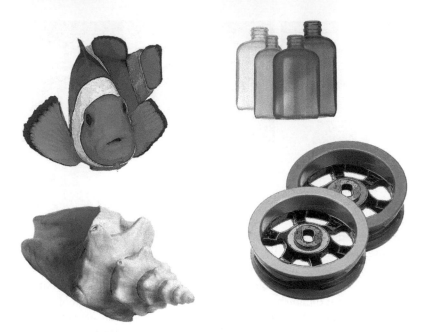

FIG 10.5 Organic (left) versus man–made forms (right).

be classified into organic forms and mathematical forms. Organic forms are those that we see in nature such as birds, animals, and plants, which are normally asymmetrical and irregular. These natural forms tend to have curved appearances which are aesthetic and soothing. On the other hand, man-made shapes including boxes and spherical objects are characterized by regularity and symmetry (Figure 10.5).

Positive Space and Negative Space

When you are capturing the image of a subject, the space in the image frame consists of the actual space occupied by the object (subject) and the remaining space. Various shots such as long shot, medium shot, close-up, or tight close-up also control how much of the subject appears on the rendered image against the backdrop of the scene. The relative proportion of positive space with respect to the negative space is an essential feature of the scene composition. Positive space is made up of the image subject or the foreground objects, and the negative space includes the space surrounding or behind the foreground objects (Figure 10.6). Successful photographers employ extremely resourceful ways to use the negative space to convey their messages in a special manner. Perspective is in fact inherently related to how much of the foreground object is seen with respect to the background (ratio of positive to negative space).

In the 3D space, positive space indicates the volume occupied by the subject or by the pieces of work of art, and the empty space surrounding these works of art refers to the negative space.

FIG 10.6 Positive (left) and negative (right) spaces.

Different Perspectives

There are different ways in which the stereoscopic and distance aspects can be shown in a composition. In the real world, we see the same scene simultaneously with two eyes, and this is processed by our brain to provide the stereo vision. However, when composing a photograph or a video, we are in essence taking a 3D world and putting it into a 2D canvas. There lies the challenge of showing depth and distance. Various different perspectives discussed below enable showing the stereo perception and distance features based on the purpose of composition.

Linear Perspective

With *linear perspective*, by properly placing the camera from the subject, one can control the depth required in a composition. How lines, edges, planes, and shapes come together, and at what angle they approach each other helps us with stereo perception (Figure 10.7). Obviously, the size (width) of the sidewalk shown in the picture is almost the same throughout, but it can be seen that the part of the sidewalk in front (nearer to the camera) seems wider than the sidewalk at the farther corner (which looks pretty narrow).

FIG 10.7 Linear perspective.

FIG 10.8 Height perspective.

Height Perspective

While linear perspective pertains to the scene depth as it applies along the ground surface, *height perspective* deals with elevation above the ground. Instead of the effect being horizontal across the ground and waning in the distance, the vanishing point in this case is along a vertical plane. When you are looking up at a tall structure or a building, it seems to converge or become smaller (Figure 10.8).

Also, the relational placement of subject against the horizon affects the perception of its height by the viewer. Using this technique, the structure or building is portrayed closer to the horizon, and this not only makes it look far away but also makes it look quite tall.

Overlap Perspective

The *overlap perspective* is another technique for conveying the depth perception, and it uses occlusion to accomplish this. When you look at Figure 10.9, you can see which buildings are in the front as those are seen completely without any occlusion. The object (trees) that is nearer to the camera is seen in full without being obscured, while those behind the front object(s) will be obscured depending on the distance between those objects and the objects in front (Figure 10.9).

FIG 10.9 Overlap perspective.

Dwindling Size Perspective/Diminishing Size Perspective

The dwindling size perspective/*diminishing size perspective* creates the illusion of objects diminishing in size (hence the name), even though all the objects are equivalent in size. Although all the lampposts are of the same size/ dimensions, the ones closer seem to be taller than the ones farther away. In other words, the sizes of the lamp posts seem to "diminish" with distance (and hence the name). The image below shows same-sized marbles arranged along a line on a table. The marbles "seem" to be getting smaller in size as they get farther away from the point of view (Figure 10.10).

How the scene is composed using these different perspectives influences the viewer's perception of the subject of the scene. Let us now see how angle affects the composition of a scene.

FIG 10.10 Diminishing size perspective.

What's Your Angle?

Just as perspective and positive/negative space influence the scene's perception by the audience, the angle in which the subject is shown can tell different things about the subject. Figure 10.11 shows low-angle shots. The shot on the left shows an object, and you can see that the size of the object seems highly magnified or imposing due to the camera position below and looking up at it. Similarly, if you look at the character on the right-hand side, the camera is positioned below the character and looking up to the character. Typically, low-angle shots can be used to show traits such as size/enormity, nobility, and power and typically to exaggerate attributes. If you recall a shot from a movie involving a monster or a giant, typically, the very first shot introducing such a character would be a low-angle one in order to emphasize the massiveness and the sheer size of the character upon the audience (Figure 10.11).

On the other hand, high-angle shots are intended to show a character as timid, submissive, meek, insignificant, chaotic, etc. These kinds of shots are also used to underplay a character. In a high-angle shot, the camera is positioned above the character or the subject and aimed so as to point down on the subject. High-angle shots are employed in situations wherein the subject or object is underplayed or portrayed as smaller in size, susceptible, puny, powerless, vulnerable, or weak (Figure 10.12).

FIG 10.11 Low-angle shots.

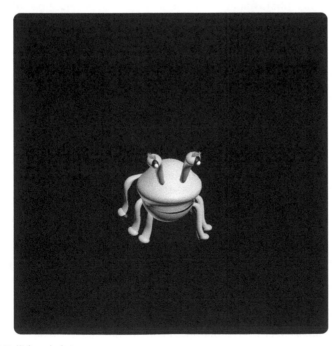

FIG 10.12 High-angle shots.

FIG 10.13 Rule of thirds. (Image courtesy: Dhruva, M.)

The Rule of Thirds

Imagine that you are vacationing and are in a renowned tourist attraction. Say, the Eiffel Tower, the Leaning Tower of Pisa, the Taj Mahal, or the Statue of Liberty. You see the monument that you have been wanting to see for a long time and now that you are seeing it, you immediately reach for your camera. You position your camera and adjust it so that the monument is in the "dead-center" of your photo frame. You are about to click. STOP! Placing a subject of interest in the "dead-center" of a photographic composition is a big mistake. To make your composition more meaningful and vibrant, it is a good idea to follow the famous *rule of thirds*.

According to this rule, to better compose a picture, put the frame into three equal parts horizontally and three equal parts vertically (Figure 10.13). Placing your subject along one of these lines (horizontal or vertical depending on the nature of your subject) will create a good composition. Or you can also position the subject at the points of intersection created by these lines. Anyway, remember never to keep your subject in the exact center of your frame of composition. Move it off-center for achieving better results.

Lines

Lines are extremely significant elements of composition as they tend to lead and direct the attention of the audience. Broadly, we can classify lines into straight and curved lines. A straight line is the shortest distance between two points.

It is of utmost importance to recognize and use lines to achieve the desired compositional effect. Even subtle lines in photos or rendered images can greatly influence the overall mood resulting from the image. If unnoticed or used improperly, lines can even create the exact opposite effect to that of what was originally intended by the composition. Lines in a photograph can bifurcate or divide the frame, thus splitting the attention of the audience. On the other hand, ingenious compositions used lines to unify, thus creating a coherent composition. Lines can be used to highlight specific elements in a composition and to underplay some elements.

The rule of thirds covered the importance of placing subject along one of the lines that divide the frame into three (horizontally or vertically). One of the commonly perceived impacts of lines is that they tend to "lead to something." Upon seeing lines in a photograph or a rendering (of a 3D model), the viewer's eyes tend to follow those lines, and objects situated along those lines attract attention. Lines also convey a wide range of feelings. The following are different types of lines that can be found in a rendered output:

- Horizontal lines
- Vertical lines
- Diagonal lines
- Straight lines (linear)
- Curved lines (curvilinear)
- Jagged lines (serrated)

Horizontal lines run across (parallel to) the frame of composition and can indicate vastness, enormity, or limitlessness. In Figure 10.14, the horizontal line depicted by the horizon shows the vast expanse of the region. Horizontal lines are typically used to symbolize a state of *equilibrium*. You can also think of a horizontal line as indicating a relaxed state as we are in when we are lying down or sleeping, which is in contrast to the mood denoted by a vertical/standing up position.

FIG 10.14 Horizontal lines in composition.

This idea of rest or relaxedness manifests itself in various forms, and horizontal lines are used to convey various signs of equilibrium such as:

- Balance
- Restfulness
- Peace
- Serenity
- Poise

In Figure 10.14, you can see the horizontal line of the horizon at the far end and you can also see the horizontal lines formed by the waves, the horizontal line formed by the railing, etc. The horizontal lines corresponding to the horizon and the waves create sense of peace, leisure, and restfulness.

Vertical lines can evoke emotional states pertaining to stateliness, power, loftiness, sturdiness, stability, etc. Consider a tall building or tree standing on the ground and their firm placement on the ground instantaneously creates a sense of stability. From another perspective, just as horizontal lines can be linked with a state of rest/relaxation/balance, extending the same logic vertical lines (symbolizing standing up or working) can be used to insinuate energy and power. Figure 10.15 shows structures that are tall and imposing. These represent vertical elements in the scene.

FIG 10.15 Vertical lines in composition.

FIG 10.16 Diagonal lines in composition.

Diagonal lines are, by and large, considered to be more dynamic and vibrant than horizontal and vertical lines (Figure 10.16). For this reason, if your composition is solely composed of horizontal and vertical lines, it is viewed as boring, monotonous, or dull. Diagonal can make a composition lively, by generating a vibrant and energetic sensation. Straight lines denote steadiness or stability.

In the above image, you can see that the bungee jumper in action represents a dynamic process and the line representing the jumper's posture is neither horizontal nor vertical, but diagonal. Similarly, with amusement ride, you can see that the diagonal lines make the picture more vibrant and dynamic.

Jagged or serrated lines are used in a composition to add a zesty feeling or a sense of excitement to your composition. As these lines are characterized by sharp angular elements, they create feelings of tension and fear in the viewer's mind. These can also evoke emotions such as discomfort, confusion, and chaos.

A scene predominantly consisting of man-made objects (e.g., buildings) tends to be populated with straight lines.

Typically, organic (natural) scenes tend to contain *curved lines* such as those occurring in many living organisms, insects, birds, human body parts, rivers, streams, and natural paths (Figure 10.17).

Two prominent curves that are used in composition named after alphabets are the *C-curve* and the *S-curve*. These are also used in architecture to create an organic look and feel. Figure.10.18 demonstrates the C-curve in architecture (similar to alphabet C rotated 90 degrees clockwise) on the left and a bird with an S-curve on the right.

The S-curve (a curved shaped in the form of the alphabet "S") is a popular element used in photographic composition to indicate elegance and a

FIG 10.17 Curved lines.

FIG 10.18 C-curve (left) and S-curve (right).

smoothing effect. C-curves can be used to border and surround the elements of interest in a composition.

Digital Rendering

Now that we have covered several aspects of composition, let us get into the actual details of the digital rendering process, whereby we can obtain the 2D image from the 3D model. First and foremost, digital rendering is lot more economical and convenient. In the real world, professional photography is a relatively expensive process that involves significant costs in terms of a professional camera, film, lights, and various other materials in the off-screen space. Even using the actual lights (*key lights*, *fill lights*, *rim lights*) and timing them has to be done very carefully and precisely. If not, this will lead to wastage of resources and will cost a lot. But, with digital rendering, you create virtual camera and virtual lights, and apply virtual materials to your objects. If you are not satisfied with the image you composed, just use another camera position, adjust your lights, and take another shot using your virtual camera. However, you need to make sure that you are following the rules of the composition and you are using the various elements such as lines, colors, lights, and shapes to create a proper composition that helps you communicate your message through the rendered image.

Steps in Rendering

Whether it is real-world photography or an effort to render an image from a digital 3D model, you need a model. In real-world photography for the cover pages of magazines and ad campaigns, human models are employed (and they get paid a lot too, right!!!). In digital modeling, your rendered output can be a single frame (image) or a sequence of frames (video). But, you inevitably need a "model." This can be a model of just one object or a whole scene involving many objects. Different modeling platforms and software use different set of steps to create the final rendered output. However, the general rendering process in the CG involves the following basic steps:

1. Create the 3D model
2. Set up the camera and lights
3. Apply proper materials on your models
4. Determine the *shading* technique
5. Render animation

Formats of Rendered Images

There are two common types of graphics image formats, namely, raster and vector. *Raster images* are image files made up of a *grid* of cells (*pixels*). Raster *resolution* becomes pixelated when they are scaled up (when you zoom in). One of the most popular image formats that we frequently used in our day-to-day lives and on the web, the .jpg image, is a raster image. If you open a .jpg image on your computer and keep zooming in, you will soon start seeing the small squares known as pixels. You no longer will see the face of a person or a tree or a monument (or whatever the subject of the photograph is), but you will see differently colored pixels. Below you see the raster image (pixelated when zoomed in) of a flower and the corresponding vector (crisp even when zoomed in) representation (Figure 10.19).

Unlike raster images, vector graphics can be scaled without losing quality. No matter how much you zoom in to a *vector image*, you will not get the blurry appearance that you get from a zoomed in raster image. This is because vector images are created using primitive geometric shapes such as points, lines, and polygons, which are drawn using mathematical formulae. Hence, however much you zoom in, these mathematical equations are used to redraw the points, lines, and polygons constituting the vector images at that level of scaling.

Examples of well-known raster file types (formats) are psd (Photoshop document), jpg/jpeg, bmp, tiff, and png. Examples of popular vector image formats include eps (encapsulated post script) and ai (Adobe illustrator©). Both raster and vector images have their pros and cons. One of the biggest

FIG 10.19 Raster image (top) and vector image (bottom).

advantages with raster graphics is the abundance of detail that can be generated. Innumerable hues and shades can be represented with raster images. The more the bit planes in an image, richer the details and shades it can represent. When using raster images, the level of sophistication that can be achieved with respect to image editing is very high. Software tools are also available to take a raw or captured image and modify to meet custom requirements. The cons of raster images include loss of quality with enlargement and large file sizes as they are based on pixels.

On the other hand, vector images can be scaled indefinitely and do not occupy that much space on disc due to their use of simple geometric shapes. However, owing the same reason that they depend on simple geometric primitives, vectors are not good at handling and/or creating various advanced effects that can be created using raster images and the alpha channels. While the ability to add *color depth* to raster images using *bit planes* paves the way for rich *chromatic resolution*, there is no such equivalent capability in vector images that can match the color sophistication (of raster images).

Pixels, Resolution, and Bit Planes

We will look at raster images in greater detail in this book. Pixels are the basic building blocks of raster images. (Pixel stands for picture element.) Just as living organisms are made of cells, images are made of pixels. If you keep zooming in on any .jpg image that you have stored on your laptop, sooner or later you will see the pixelated version (that shows the pixels making up the image). A raster image is actually a grid of pixels that together make up the final object that you see in the image, for example, a flower, a building, and a ball. Resolution tells us about the actual amount of detail contained in an image. Normally, when referring to an image containing a particular number of pixels, we are actually referring to its *pixel resolution*. Pixel resolution is measured in ppi (pixels per inch). So, an image that is 6″×4″ (6″ wide and 4″ tall) with a 72 ppi pixel resolution contains a total of 1728 pixels.

Chromatic resolution is a term that is used to indicate the total number of colors that an image can contain and display. Chromatic resolution, also known as *color resolution*, depends on the number of bit planes. Bit plane is a term that is used in several fields including signal transmission and raster imaging. A digital signal can be represented using bit planes, and the bit planes in a raster image help store the color information of the image. Just as a raster image itself is a grid of pixels, a bit plane is a grid of cells. Each cell in the bit plane can contain a number (a single digit number). The term bit refers to *binary* digit, which means that the value contained in it can be a binary value (either a zero 0 or a one 1). Each grid cell on the bit plane is linked to a corresponding pixel on the actual image.

If an image needs to contain a wide range of colors, then the image must contain more bit planes. A single bit plane can show either black or white; 0 being black or the absence of color and 1 being white. With two bit planes, four different color values can be shown as (00,01,10,11). The numerical system that we are most acquainted to is the *decimal* system. When we are talking about binary digits, we are using what is known as the binary system. We can understand binary calculation using a direct vis-à-vis comparison to our knowledge of decimal computation. Numbers in the decimal system use a base of the number 10, and numbers in the binary system are represented using a base of number 2. Table 10.1 shows the bit value and the number of colors that it can represent.

TABLE 10.1 Bit Value and Number of Colors

n-Bit Color	Number of Colors
1 bit	2
2 bit	4
3 bit	8
8 bit	256
16 bit	65,536

File Formats

Rendered images are used for different applications such as desktop publishing, graphics design, print media, web design, and prepress applications. As the saying goes, necessity is the mother of invention. Many of the file formats were invented or improved from the existing versions based on a specific need. When we choose to buy a vehicle, we choose the model based on our requirements, priority, and how much we can afford. Based on our budget, we all may have different preferences with respect to safety features, mileage, seating capacity, audiovisual amenities, etc. Similarly, there are many different file formats that are available, and each file format has its own unique characteristics. Table 10.2 discusses some of the popular image formats, both raster and vector.

When selecting a file format for the final rendered image, one must consider the ultimate purpose for which the image must be used. If an image will be used for high-quality printing, then it must use CMYK color mode and should be saved in tiff or eps format (Table 10.2). If the client needs an image that needs to maintain its quality upon scaling, then vector format should be resorted to. For an image entailing rich color combinations and lots of color manipulation functionalities, raster will be a prudent choice. When selecting a format for an image, the following must be given due consideration:

- Image size (actual memory space occupied)
- Image resolution
- Color depth (chromatic resolution)
- Color mode
- Channels
- Format (raster/vector)
- Application for which the image is generated

Saving an image in a high-resolution format when not required will waste storage and result in transmission issues. On the other hand, using a format that cannot handle the level of detail, color depth, and resolution demanded by the application will result in poor-quality rendering. Hence, utmost care should be exercised and the decision for the image format should be made with due consideration to all the aforementioned factors. Also, when working on modifying or enhancing an image, it is a recommended practice to keep saving intermittently at various steps. Even though different photoediting software allow you to undo several changes that you have done, some changes such as unifying or combining some elements or converting a vector element to raster or vice versa can do permanent changes to the image that cannot be undone. So, it is a good practice to maintain multiple versions, which you can at least retain till you are satisfied with the final product that you want. If you are not satisfied with your work, instead of having to start back, you can go with one of these versions and continue from there, which is quite time-saving.

Having looked at some of the technical aspects of rendering, let us look at the emotional aspects associated to colors and few common color classifications.

TABLE 10.2 Common Image File Formats

Image File Format	Extension	Details and Description
JPEG (*Joint Photographic Experts Group*)	.jpeg/.jpg	One of the most popular image formats used extensively on the web and digital cameras. The lossy compression used results in loss of quality of the original file when saved in .jpg format. Convenient for storage and transmission. Uses 8 bit per color (8 bit for red, green, and blue each).
SVG (*Scalable Vector Graphics*)	.svg	Vector format developed by several organizations especially for the World Wide Web. Used for interactive web applications.
TIFF (*Tagged Image File Format*)	.tiff/.tif	Uses LZW (Lempel-Ziv-Welsh) compression and used predominantly in prepress/publishing applications. Allows using both 8 bit and 16 bit per channel of color.
GIF (*Graphics Interchange Format*)	.gif	Popular for web-based applications and for creating image-based animations. Uses LZW compression like the .tiff format. Allows storing color information from 1 bit to 8 bit but is limited to only 8 bit maximum for all three channels combined.
EPS (Encapsulated PostScript)	.epsf/.eps	A device-independent format that consumes significantly high storage space. Employed when high-quality wireframe representations need to be reproduced in press/print applications. Excellent quality for print, but large file sizes pose storage and transmission problems.
PS (*PostScript*)	.ps	Vector graphics format developed by Adobe systems and is actually a programming language used in publishing. Also used extensively for straight-forwardly laying out pages electronically and eventually for printing.
BMP (*bitmap*)	.bmp	Popular in Windows© environments and is device-independent with respect to the display devices. Allows multiple color resolutions including 4/8/16/32 bits per pixel.
PNG (*Portable Network Graphics*)	.png	Uses lossless compression and is an open source format used widely on the internet. Supports the use of alpha channels for transparency and interlacing.

Hot Colors/Warm Colors

Just as blue and green bring forth feelings of relaxedness, calmness, or coolness, colors such as red and orange can elicit a sense of emergency, urgency, or importance. Color red is a highly visible and distinguishable color in the spectrum owing to its long wavelength. Hence, red color is capable of instantly grasping out attention instantaneously. This has been exploited for situations that demand warning about a dangerous situation or when immediate attention is required. Think: stop signs, sirens, fire engines, and red traffic lights. It is for this reason that stop signs and signals use red to bring a vehicle to stop (Figure 10.20).

This attention-grabbing nature of red light is the reason that it is used in traffic lights for "stop." Red, the color of blood, besides conveying a state of emergency or urgency, is also used to implicate patriotism, courage, gallantry, resoluteness, kinship, etc. While extremely saturated shades of orange and red are considered as hot colors, mild orange and yellow are also used to represent energy, excitement, and overall healthful ambience.

While artists tend to associate red with feelings of affection and immense passion, red is also used to portray rage and anger. In Figure 10.21, you can see how the emotion of anger gets accentuated by the red light shining on the character's face.

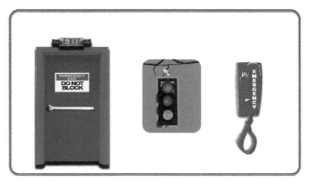

FIG 10.20 Red color to grab attention.

FIG 10.21 Red light to accentuate anger.

FIG 10.22 Blue and green: cool/background colors.

Cool Colors/Background Colors

When outdoors, the two most common colors that we might see are blue (of the sky) and green (of the vegetation). Often times, the blue sky and green pastures create a sense of calmness and relaxedness, which is a reason they are also known as cool colors (Figure 10.22). Dark blue and majestic blue are associated with attributes such as power, truthfulness, knowledge, and seriousness. This association with trustworthiness is also the reason why we often see blue or majestic blue in the logos of banks and credit card companies as a symbolic message to the customers that they can be trusted to handle their finances. In other words, when using blue, the financial institutions want to convey that "your money is in safe hands."

Generally, people tend to feel placid and tranquil when surrounded by the sight of green pastures and the blue sky. These are aptly named background colors as we see them often in outdoor environments. Also, blue and green are referred to as cool colors as they remind us of the cool, joyful free-spirited sensation of Mother Nature. Blue is used to convey various connotations such as relaxation, grandiosity/magnificence, and stability. On the other hand, blue can also be used to represent a gloomy setting or to elicit a melancholic response.

Color Connotations

Yellow

Yellow is generally considered as a bright and happy color, which evokes positive emotions. Yellow is also related to hope. Based on the shade, yellow can be used to attract attention without causing a sense of panic or alarm. Varying kinds of yellow such as bright yellow, soft yellow, and dark yellow

FIG 10.23 Scene with yellow lights. (Image courtesy: Justin, H.)

can create different kinds of emotions. While lighter yellow can create a calm and placid feeling, bright yellow can create cheerfulness and exuberance. However, yellow can also have negative connotations such as those related to anxiety, timidity, and deception. In colloquial language, yellow-bellied is used to refer to cowardly behavior.

Yellow is the color of the sun, the provider of energy to the earth. Yellow color is also used in interior design to add brightness and energy to living spaces. Figure 10.23 shows two different colored lights added to a 3D-modeled scene. You may see how the yellow light enhances the calmness and placidity to the setting, while also adding little energy to the scene. Also, the yellow color to the metal objects like the stand of the candle brings the scene together.

Orange

Orange represents the venturing spirit, youthfulness, spiciness, enthusiasm, and excitement. We already looked at color meanings of yellow and red, and orange results from the mixture of yellow and red. Hence, this obviously makes it a color to express warmth, energy, zest, and enthusiasm. Orange is also used to represent fast-paced nature and excitement exuding happiness and joy, releasing inhibitions.

In our daily lives, we come across the color orange in a wide range of things such as traffic signs indicating road work, traffic cones, fall leaves, in addition to orange being used in fashion design, clothing, and for other objects where it attracts attention without being overpowering (like red). Nevertheless, despite orange's reputation as an inspiring and hopeful color, the negative connotations of orange also refer to untruthfulness, dependence, cynicism, stinginess, aloofness, etc.

Orange is also associated with health and renewal due to the positive connotation stemming from its association to orange-colored fruits such as nectarines, oranges, and tangerines. In oriental cultures, such as Chinese and Japanese cultures, orange implies joy and love. In India, saffron, an orange-colored spice, is considered to be a sacred color. In the United States, orange is the color of the popular Jack-o'-lantern used in Halloween.

In Figure 10.24, you can see a real-world scene with orange lights and a 3D-modeled scene with the carved pumpkins. You can see how orange adds more zest and vigor to the compositions.

FIG 10.24 Orange lights in real world (top) and 3D-modeled scene (bottom). (Image courtesy: George, H.)

Neutral Colors

Let us wrap up our discussion of colors by discussing what are known as neutral colors or neutrals. Common neutral colors include white, black, brown, and gray. The word "neutral" itself is used to refer to impartiality, nonalignment, indifference, etc. Unlike some of the colors such as red and blue we discussed earlier, neutrals are used to highlight the foreground colors. Neutral colors are not only used to emphasize other colors but can also be used to underplay or tone down those colors, which may tend to have a highly overpowering trait.

Black

Black is a common and strong neutral color. You may recall from our earlier discussion on the color spectrum and subtractive color model that black is the resulting color when all incident visible light has been absorbed. Hence, it is also used to indicate darkness or the absence of light. You can see how black adds more elegance to this kitchen design (Figure 10.25).

In several western countries, black is the customary color used in sad occasions such as mourning. In oriental cultures, for example, Japanese, black is associated with mystery, imperceptibility, etc. Other connotations of black include mystery, evil, and death.

Black is also associated with masculinity in Latin cultures and is a desired color for gents' clothing. The positive connotations for black include formality, power, elegance, class, and intricacy. Black can also indicate power, authority, submission, etc. This is the reason that priests wear black robes (to indicate submission to God) and those in the legal professional such as judges and advocates use black outfit.

FIG 10.25 Black color in interior design.

White

Neutrals are an important element in the design process. The color white is typically associated with cleanliness, virtue, purity, innocence, etc. It is also considered to represent *balance*, totality, and completion. It is considered to represent fresh beginnings and as creation. Hence, it is also associated with innovative and creative attributes.

When clear white light is passed through a prism, the constituent colors are revealed, namely, VIBGYOR or RPYGBIV (red, orange, yellow, green, blue, and violet). Composition wise, white color can be thought to contain an equal balance of the visible colors in the spectrum. This also lends itself to its association with the attributes such as impartiality, objectivity, open-mindedness, independence, and neutrality.

Due to the color white's association with peace and purity, a white flag is considered to be a universal symbol of truce or peace offering. White also indicates purification, both externally and internally, of one's inner self. White is frequently associated with weddings in the western cultures and is the color of the bride's dress. Being considered as an uncontaminated, pure color, it is used to indicate holiness and also sanitary facilities such as hospitals and nursing homes. However, in some cultures, white is also associated with sad occasions such as funerals. Excessive white can also indicate lack of vigor and stimulation.

We looked in detail about the various colors and their connotations in design. Closely related to colors is "contrast" which is an important design principle. Excellent compositions can be created by proper use of color contrast. Color is a powerful tool to direct the audience's attention. In Figure 10.26, you can see how we tend to immediately look at the one object with the different color. The contrast makes it stand out of the rest of the objects and grabs our attention (Figure 10.26).

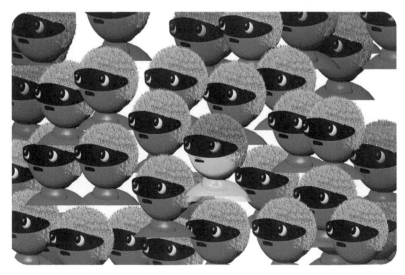

FIG 10.26 Color contrast to attract attention.

In a Nutshell

In this chapter, we covered the importance of a clear purpose in your image and how this motivation impacts the overall quality of image composition. One important rule of thumb that needs to be understood is "what you (the creator) of the rendering see is not what the audience see." The chapter discussed the three aspects, namely, "what, why, and how" with respect to creating a composition. Various elements of composition including perspective, lines, and angle were covered. Subsequently, the importance of the "rule of thirds" was covered. The process of digital rendering where virtual cameras are used to capture the 3D digital models was discussed. The difference between two major graphics categories, namely, raster graphics and vector graphics, was explained. Important vocabulary in the context of rendering such as pixels, resolution, bit planes, and color depth was discussed in the context of digital rendering. Different image file formats that are used in diverse applications including desktop publishing, World Wide Web, prepress, layout, and print applications were discussed.

The elements of composition serve as cues that make the audience see what the creator of the rendering wants them to see in the rendered image or video. Various compositional elements such as perspective, color scheme, lights, and shadows composed in tandem with the edges or lines, positive and negative spaces, and yield superior visual organization. These act as indirect controls that convey the message from the creator of the composition to the receiver. Different perspectives such as linear perspective, height perspective, overlap perspective, and dwindling size perspective can be used to create depth perceptions and other kinds of depictions to communicate the visual message appropriately. Just as perspective and positive/negative space influence the scene's perception by the audience, the angle in which the subject is shown can tell different things about the subject. Typically, low-angle shots can be used to show traits such as size/enormity, nobility, and power and typically to exaggerate attributes. On the other hand, high-angle shots are intended to show a character as timid, submissive, meek, insignificant, chaotic, etc.

To make your composition more meaningful and vibrant, it is a good idea to follow the famous rule of thirds. According to this rule, to better compose a picture, put the frame into three equal parts horizontally and three equal parts vertically. Lines are extremely significant elements of composition as they tend to lead and direct the attention of the audience. Different types of lines such as horizontal, vertical, diagonal, curved, and jagged lines elicit different kinds of emotions from the audience. Two prominent curves that are used in composition named after alphabets are the C-curve and the S-curve. These are also used in architecture to create an organic look and feel.

The chapter also discussed important technical aspects of rendering and covered the emotional aspects associated to colors and few common color classifications.

Key Terms Used in This Chapter

Balance
Binary
Bit Plane
Bitmap
C-Curve
Camera
Chromatic Resolution
Color Depth
Color Resolution
Composition
Compositional Elements
Curved Lines
Decimal
Diagonal Lines
Digital Rendering
Diminishing Size
  Perspective

Equilibrium
Fill Lights
Form
Graphics Interchange
  Format
Grid
Height Perspective
High-Angle Shot
Horizontal Lines
Jagged Lines
JPEG
Key Lights
Linear Perspective
Linear Lines
Lines
Low-Angle Shot
Overlap Perspective

Perspective
Photograph
Portable Network
  Graphics
PostScript
Pixel
Pixel Resolution
Raster Image
Resolution
Rim Lights
Rule of Thirds
S-Curve
Scalable Vector Graphics
Shading
Tagged Image
Vector Image
Vertical Lines

Chapter 10 Quiz

PART I

True/False (Circle the Correct Choice)

1. The elements of composition serve as cues that make the audience see what the creator of the rendering wants them to see in the rendered image or video.
True False

2. Perspective refers to the viewpoint.
True False

3. Negative space is made up of the image subject or the foreground objects, and the negative space includes the space surrounding or behind the foreground objects.
True False

4. Long shot, medium shot, close-up, or tight close-up does not control how much of the subject appears on the rendered image against the backdrop of the scene.
True False

5. With linear perspective, by properly placing the camera from the subject, one can control the depth required in a composition.
True False

6. The overlap perspective uses occlusion to illustrate depth perspective.
True False

7. The linear perspective creates the illusion of objects diminishing in size (hence the name), even though all the objects are equivalent in size.
True False

8. Typically, high-angle shots can be used to show traits such as nobility, power, and enormity.
True False

9. High-angle shots are used to underplay a character.
True False

10. Keeping your subject in the exact center of your frame is an example of good composition.
True False

11. Diagonal lines are considered to be more dynamic and vibrant than horizontal and vertical lines.
True False

12. Raster images can be scaled indefinitely.
True False

13. Two bit planes can be used to show two colors.
True False

14. Mathematical equations are used to redraw the points, lines, and polygons in a raster image.
True False

15. JPEG is a vector format developed by several organizations especially for the World Wide Web.
True False

16. The color white is typically associated with cleanliness, virtue, purity, innocence, etc.
True False

17. Red and orange are considered as cool or background colors.
True False

18. Vector images are made of pixels.
True False

19. Jagged or serrated lines are used in a composition to add a zesty feeling or a sense of excitement to your composition.
True False

20. Typically, organic (natural) scenes tend to contain curved lines such as those occurring in many living organisms, insects, birds, human body parts, rivers, streams, natural paths, etc.
True False

PART II

Multiple Choice Questions (Choose the Most Appropriate Answer)

1. _____ resolution is a term that is used to indicate the total number of colors that an image can contain and display.
   a. Image
   b. Chromatic
   c. Digital
   d. Temporal
   e. Remote

2. With _____ perspective, by properly placing the camera from the subject, one can control the depth required in a composition.
   a. Linear
   b. Height
   c. Close-up
   d. Diminishing size
   e. Overlap

3. The relational placement of subject against the horizon affects the perception of its _____ by the viewer.
   a. Linearity
   b. Height
   c. Close-up
   d. Size
   e. Overlap

4. The _____ perspective is a technique for conveying the depth perception, and it uses occlusion to accomplish this.
   a. Linearity
   b. Height
   c. Close-up
   d. Size
   e. Overlap

5. As_____ lines are characterized by sharp angular elements, they create feelings of tension and fear in the viewer's mind.
   a. Horizontal lines
   b. Vertical lines
   c. Diagonal lines
   d. Straight lines (linear)
   e. Jagged lines (serrated)

6. The _____ perspective creates the illusion of objects diminishing in size (hence the name), even though all the objects are equivalent in size.
   a. Linear
   b. Height
   c. Close-up
   d. Diminishing size
   e. Overlap

7. Horizontal lines are used to convey various emotions such as:
   a. Balance
   b. Restfulness
   c. Peace
   d. Serenity
   e. All the above

8. Which of the following is a vector format developed by several organizations especially for the World Wide Web and is used for interactive web applications.
   a. JPEG
   b. SVG
   c. TIFF
   d. BMP
   e. EPS

9. Which of the following is employed when high-quality wireframe representations need to be reproduced in press/print applications?
   a. JPEG
   b. SVG
   c. TIFF
   d. BMP
   e. EPS

10. Which of the following formats uses LZW (Lempel-Ziv-Welsh) compression and is used predominantly in prepress/publishing applications?
    a. JPEG
    b. SVG
    c. TIFF
    d. BMP
    e. PNG

11. Which of the following formats allows storing color information from 1 bit to 8 bit but is limited to only 8-bit maximum for all three channels combined?
    a. GIF
    b. SVG
    c. PNG
    d. BMP
    e. EPS

12. Which of the following open source formats uses lossless compression and supports the use of alpha channels for transparency and interlacing?
    a. PNG
    b. SVG
    c. PNG
    d. BMP
    e. EPS

13. What is the maximum number of colors that can be represented with 3-bit planes?
    a. 1
    b. 0
    c. 8
    d. 16
    e. 4

14. What is the maximum number of colors that can be represented with 2-bit planes?
    a. 1
    b. 0
    c. 8
    d. 16
    e. 4

15. Chromatic resolution is also known as _____ resolution.
    a. Image
    b. Color
    c. Digital
    d. Temporal
    e. Remote

16. _____ represents the venturing spirit, youthfulness, spiciness, enthusiasm, and excitement.
    a. Gray
    b. Blue
    c. Orange
    d. Yellow
    e. Black

17. _____ is an example of a neutral color.
    a. Red
    b. Blue
    c. Orange
    d. Yellow
    e. Black

18. _____ is associated with masculinity in Latin cultures and is a desired color for gents' clothing.
    a. Red
    b. Blue
    c. Orange
    d. Yellow
    e. Black

19. When clear_____ light is passed through a prism, the constituent colors are revealed, namely, VIBGYOR or RPYGBIV.
    a. White
    b. Blue
    c. Orange
    d. Yellow
    e. Black

20. _____ color lends itself to its associate with the attributes such as impartiality, objectivity, open-mindedness, independence, and neutrality.
    a. Red
    b. Blue
    c. Orange
    d. White
    e. Black

Index

Note: **Bold** page numbers refer to tables and *italic* page numbers refer to figures.

Milton Keynes UK
Ingram Content Group UK Ltd.
UKHW052138200923
429085UK00003B/5

9 781032 137735